SAN
FRANCISCO
TENDERLOIN

Other Titles by Dr. Larry Wonderling

SEDUCTIVE ILLUSIONS, How to Resist the Lure of Society's Smoke & Mirrors
ISBN: 0-9659415-0-7

THE ULTIMATE EVIL
A San Francisco Mystery Novel
ISBN: 0-9659415-5-8
ISBN 13: 97809659415-5-6

MINDING YOUR MATTER, A Breakthrough Health and Fitness Model Without Formal Diets and Exercises
ISBN: 0-9659415-7-4
ISBN 13: 97809659415-7-0

SAN FRANCISCO TENDERLOIN

True Stories of Heroes, Demons, Angels, Outcasts and a Psychotherapist

Lawrence Wonderling, Ph.D.

Expanded Second Edition

CAPE FOUNDATION PUBLICATIONS
Bullhead City, Arizona

CAPE FOUNDATION PUBLICATIONS
Bullhead City, Arizona
E-mail: capfound@aol.com
Carol Eversole, Editor

First Printing, © 2001
Second Printing, © 2002
Third Printing, © 2004
Expanded Second Edition, © 2008

Library of Congress Catalog Card Number: 99-076752
ISBN: 0-9659415-6-6
ISBN 13: 978-0-9659415-6-3

Cover by: Norman Cyr, Kristin Miller and
                 Aeonix Publishing Group

Photographs by: San Francisco History Center
                 San Francisco Public Library
                 Carol Eversole

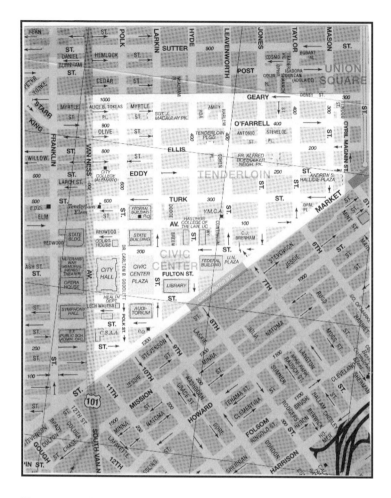

For over 100 years The Tenderloin has waxed and waned within the shadow of the Geary, Van Ness, Market and Mason Street outer perimeters. Its epicenter is somewhere around Ellis and Jones.

Contents

★ New Stories

This book is dedicated to the people of the Tenderloin who taught me about loyalty, courage and tolerance.

ACKNOWLEDGMENTS

One of the toughest parts of writing a book or updating its second edition is knowing when it's finished. After numerous re-reads, I am still unable to spot those extra words, typos, convoluted sentences and faulty grammar. Again I deeply appreciate the suggestions of Dick Bender, Jan Elster and Leona Villa, all of whom helped transform this book into a more readable, shorter finished project. The kind encouragement and support of Don Dutil, Lorene Leon and Phil Papadopoulos were also invaluable to the completion and promotion of this book. I'm grateful to all of you.

Special thanks to the California State Automobile Association for permission to reprint a portion of their San Francisco map; Shelby Collins of the San Francisco History Center, San Francisco Public Library for his assistance in utilizing historical pictures; Danny Gibble and Linda Padavono for permitting the use of the original Chez Paree marquee photograph on the cover of this second edition book and Carol Eversole for her indispensable editorial efforts.

Prologue

For many, the Tenderloin is considered an ugly blemish, an unsightly smudge on the beauty of San Francisco. So why not erase it rather than write about it? That's because no one's been able to erase it in over a hundred years.

This may be justification enough to nominate the Tenderloin an integral part of San Francisco history. It didn't just happen by chance. The Tenderloin was etched into the San Francisco infrastructure long before San Francisco recognized the word. It fulfilled some basic urban needs then, and it still does.

The Tenderloin, however, is not what the legends, fables and distortions are all about. It's really about people. The Tenderloin simply serves as a historical landmark representing those people who have shaped, reshaped and defined it for over a century. Without the people, there would be no stories, no legends and certainly no book about the Tenderloin.

Everyone has a story, and some stand alone, prominent and forever memorable. Most stories, however, have little public prominence, and if not told, such tiny stories are just forgotten. Like a single piece of thread, these single stories tend to be absorbed into a larger prominence when combined with other pieces of thread. Then we have a tapestry of interwoven stories that becomes a unique place—the San Francisco Tenderloin. Regrettably, when the entire tapestry unfolds, those dynamic pieces of thread are obscured and the individual stories are lost.

We all love a good story, and most important are

each of our "tiny" personal stories. There's simply nothing more significant to each of us than *each of us*. Perhaps then, the Tenderloin legacy is a collection of those single threads, not the whole tapestry. Even so, the significance of our lives and the wonders of our stories aren't remembered unless told. This may be the simplest reason for this book—*to tell true stories about real people, while demystifying their Tenderloin*.

There are prey and predators, saints and sinners, the bright and dull, the young and old. All of those represent the Tenderloin, a dynamic assortment of stories, never simply a static location. Again, using a metaphor, this book unravels some of the Tenderloin tapestry to reveal its people and their tiny stories, those strands of thread.

This may be why the Tenderloin is such an enigma. It has a fixed singular reputation as bad, yet it's all about its many people, who are neither fixed, singular nor all bad. The Tenderloin constantly changes, depending on how it's viewed, who is telling the story and, most important, the people you meet there.

Specifically, this book is about very special people who, in some way, were part of the Tenderloin. All the stories are true, all the characters are real and all their memories have vitally impacted my life. The Tenderloin is also real, and as the set and setting for these stories, understanding the Tenderloin as a whole may help understand its people as individuals. This is why the first chapter provides a historical review of the Tenderloin's persistent "uptown" presence in the heart of "downtown" San Francisco.

Chapter 1 explores the Tenderloin's remarkable resilience in surviving, despite its chronically negative reputation. In fact, it continues to survive into the twenty-first century; and there still seems to be no known force in San Francisco that can make it go away.

Eliminating Tenderloin buildings has always been easy, but eliminating most of its people is not really an option. They simply have nowhere else to go. So, each of the remaining chapters is about one of those persons who, at least for a while, also had no place else to go. Some were friends, one was a relative and the majority were my clients.

As a clinical psychologist, with a predominately Tenderloin practice for over twenty years, I acquired an unusual case load of resident drug substance abusers, transvestites, robbers, murderers, schizophrenics, street winos and, of course, victims.

Most of the stories are of their unique struggles, which required unorthodox treatment procedures to help them. Although many of the dates and names have been altered to preserve confidentiality, all of the stories and second edition updates are accurately based on clinical records, letters or more recent interviews and walks through the Tenderloin that helped focus my drifting memory.

The essence of this book is its three interrelated topics:

➤ The enigmatic Tenderloin as a stubborn presence in San Francisco.

➤ The people whose unique stories unfolded within the Tenderloin.

➤ The Tenderloin practice of a clinical psychologist who learned about that wide chasm between the theoretical treatment of diagnosed patients and the realistic treatment of troubled individuals.

1

THE SAN FRANCISCO TENDERLOIN

A Chronicle of Myth and Reality

As the second millennium continues to slip well beneath the western horizon, San Francisco is still a soaring, world-class celebrity of undisputed charm. It remains a tourist Mecca of dazzling sights and unforgettable pleasures—well, most of it. Even in San Francisco, there are a few places city officials would prefer to be off-limits to tourists and avoided by residents. One such place is called the Tenderloin, a name of debatable origins.

Although its faded remnants are of a glistening past, it's hard to argue about the worn-out look of today's Tenderloin. Ironically, it's even more difficult to agree about its reputation. While its dilapidated appearance still shows traces of the golden days, time has tarnished those days with distortions fashioned from rumors and exaggerations. For those who actually knew its colorful past, the Tenderloin is still an unforgettable area of fond memories, deep in the heart of San Francisco's history. Towering hotels, like the Hilton, luxurious apartments and fine restaurants—all bordering the Tenderloin's deteriorating buildings—have helped obscure this area, but not enough to ignore its crusty legacy, etched in myth and reality.

The Tenderloin is older than either bridge, smaller than most shopping malls, as well known as the cable cars and as amorphous and dynamic as the beautiful, but treacherous San Francisco Bay. It's neither an official district with well-defined boundaries nor a well-defined name on a San Francisco map. It has just been in the heart of San Francisco for practically ever, or at least as long as San Francisco has been a liberal city of incredibly diverse people, many of whom need a Tenderloin.

Mention this area to old-timers raised in San Francisco and they'll smile longingly, while rasping endless yarns about the good old days. On the other hand, those newer San Francisco residents probably know little to nothing about the Tenderloin, other than to avoid it and its unsavory reputation. Then there are the visitors who read the tourist guide books and hear the warnings from hotel clerks and taxi drivers—"Enter the Tenderloin and you risk life, limb and wallet."

These are views from the outside in, whereas there is another, more accurate, view from the inside out. Recently, in Tenderloin history, there has been an influx of poor immigrants living there, especially Asians from Cambodia and Vietnam. Many of them felt economically or culturally estranged in most of the conventional San Francisco districts or neighborhoods. Yet ironically, their minimal English and survival training under those relatively unbearable conditions in other countries have provided them with a comparative sense of safety in this area. Their presence may even contribute a stable, neighborly climate to the Tenderloin. They are no longer displaced persons. They are residents with families who seem to live securely in this reputedly risky location, along with the muggers, parolees, retirees and others who also haven't found a hospitable fit elsewhere in San Francisco.

From the outside in, it may seem remarkable that such a diverse assortment of people can live together—they do. It might seem equally remarkable that, like anywhere else in the city, people can walk through the Tenderloin without being harmed—they certainly can. In fact, since the first edition of this book, the Tenderloin has morphed into a more blatant contradiction.

Although it hasn't lost the "notorious" in its reputation, its many immigrant residents plus the ubiquitous police presence suggest it's becoming a San Francisco "safe zone." Either way, the argument is probably academic. Calculating the Tenderloin's crime rate may be a meaningless exercise. Accurately counting any event within the Tenderloin depends on its boundaries, which remain unclear.

Then there are those differences in each individual's personal view of the same situation. The Tenderloin of San Francisco is considered by many, one of the most notorious and by many others, the most notoriously misunderstood area in the city.

Depending on one's background, perspective or imagination, there are those who timidly sneak or slink through the Tenderloin and some who boldly walk or stroll with an air of indifference to stories they've often heard and don't believe. There are also those who earnestly avoid the Tenderloin, convinced they would never make it out alive. All of them are probably right. Any debate would be a stalemate and the differences irrelevant.

If the Tenderloin were defined by all of those individuals, a consensus couldn't possibly work. That's because the Tenderloin, as a whole, will always be different from the sum of those individual opinions. So, whether you tend to swagger, skip, slither or walk through the Tenderloin, your gait may have more to do with your personal fantasies or biases than historical facts.

📖   📖   📖

This book is primarily stories about some of those unique struggles of people in the Tenderloin. In telling these stories, it was essential that the Tenderloin I've known since the late 40's be a real place—not just a rumor.

In each story, the Tenderloin serves as a foundation or stage with backgrounds to clearly frame those special people within their stories. In striving to provide this more balanced, historical perspective, I reviewed all of the old books on San Francisco, especially those that mentioned the Tenderloin. I also talked to many old-timers and San Francisco historians.

This has resulted in the following brief, comprehensive history of early San Francisco and one of its impish offspring—the Tenderloin. This historical data may offer you a less biased, clearer view of the Tenderloin—maybe not. Once again, in my search for objective clarity, the compiled information glaringly suggests that what is known about the Tenderloin is a mixture of facts, fiction, exaggerations and endless personal anecdotes. The Tenderloin represents whatever we need or expect it to represent. Yet, there's certainly no argument about its endurance. The Tenderloin has been around longer than most of us and it still persists as it continues to redefine its history within the Third Millennium.

History

As farmlands are buried under asphalt, small towns grow into large cities and survival needs are typically transformed into social needs. Such change invariably invites an accelerated growth of social problems. Cities create ugly contrasts of the rich and poor, the socially adaptable and the undesirables. This last category includes the mentally fragile, the drug abusers, ex-cons, the too-old, the too-enfeebled, the too-poor and an assortment of predators. None of them blend well in societies preoccupied with conforming to a life in the big city.

San Francisco was the perfect example of that early accelerated growth at its worst. It was a small town that exploded into a huge metropolis before it could even acknowledge its growing pains. The explosive was gold, which in a developmental instant changed the leisurely, unobtrusive little hamlet into a seething smorgasbord of people from all over the world.

In pre-gold rush 1845, San Francisco, then called Yerba Buena, had a population of about 150. Seven years later, Yerba Buena, now called San Francisco, was trying to accommodate over 34,000 restless people who no doubt became even more restless and unsettled by 1862 when the population hit 50,000.

Cities typically don't develop well overnight, and San Francisco was no exception. During the gold rush years, San Francisco was more an encampment or a port of embarkation than a city. Imagine trying to adapt to a city teeming with gold-crazed, driven individuals who couldn't care less about adapting to the city. Those people were culturally, linguistically, spiritually and morally estranged from one another. They were simply an overwhelming assortment of transients. They weren't interested in establishing a positive reputation, enhancing the infrastructure or becoming a resident. They wanted gold, and there wasn't any to be mined in San Francisco. That one shared preoccupation, a singular purpose, was the one thing that brought them together and would ironically set many of them apart. They were in one sense competitors, and the sooner they left San Francisco, the sooner they could claim their fortune.

It was Gold Rush San Francisco. An amassing of people, mainly men, obsessed with an avarice pursuit that would end in frustration, desperation and disappointment for most, violence and tragedy for some and fortune for a few—very few. Many ended up back in San Francisco too-broke or too-ashamed to return to their homes. Others found their fortunes by hustling the more or the less fortunate, and still others, recognizing the potential the city offered, became its leaders, developers, businessmen and racketeers.

That mid-19th-century portrait of San Francisco contained all the prerequisites for top honors as one of the most openly wicked cities in the world. The only obstacles to such a distinction were laws, law enforcement and law-abiding citizens. Unfortunately, none of the three were prominent enough to qualify as opponents.

Perhaps Voltaire, the 18th-century French philosopher, was right in proclaiming, "Man is by nature a beast of prey, and civilized society means a chaining of this beast." In 1847, the San Francisco society wasn't very civilized. Six unsalaried town councilmen were the only organized law and order. That was apparently a valiant start that didn't go very far.

By 1851, a variety of criminals ran arrogantly amuck in defiance of a thirty-man police force. That was the year of the first of several "San Francisco Vigilance Committees" that finally evolved into a one-hundred-fifty man police force by 1856. Still, there was reportedly much less order than law, and the "beast of prey" remained essentially unchained in a city that was growing too rapidly and haphazardly to be easily civilized.

It seems too obvious that San Francisco was more interested in the economic principle of "supply and demand" than taking Voltaire seriously. Those restless, frustrated, lustful men were demanding outlets for the beast in them, and the supply was quickly provided along the waterfront, Chinatown, and a little later, the Tenderloin, the central setting for these people stories.

Pre-Earthquake Tenderloin

Why San Francisco spawned the Tenderloin is historically obvious. When and how it got its name, boundaries and reputation, and why it has survived for more than a century, is historically arguable and arbitrary. This has invited an abundance of speculations that need unraveling.

Beginning at the beginning is the first difficulty. The Tenderloin was never a recorded district or a designated neighborhood. Dates typically accompany groundbreaking ceremonies, official pronouncements, christenings, quit claims, property sales or deeds of trust. There weren't any of those documented events for the Tenderloin. In fact, it's unlikely that there were ever any intentions to create a Tenderloin. It certainly wasn't planned or even considered. It just haphazardly happened in response to a combination of circumstances. Those included a near endless new population teeming with initial impatience followed by prurient demands, boredom and loneliness. The more respectable San Francisco neighborhoods were unwilling to openly serve such demands, and the Barbary Coast, for many reasons, unwittingly promoted the Tenderloin as some sort of a compromise.

The earlier success of the infamous Barbary Coast was a geographic certainty. It serviced the lonely, weary men within minutes of their landings on the San Francisco waterfront, after months at sea. The failure of the Barbary Coast was a political certainty. It was ultra high profile, in your face, anything goes, with a brazen disregard for even a semblance of morality, law or order.

The Tenderloin on the other hand, emerged gradually as somewhat of a Barbary Coast annex. Initially it served the less-daring, more responsible San Francisco residents, who were not part of the rigid, righteously moral. They were just more prudently amoral than openly immoral. This area in the late 19th-century served as a relatively safe play-haven for such a group. The Tenderloin was "uptown," away from the drunken violence, shanghais, drugs, murders, muggings and raw, sadistic sex. It became an exciting area of entertainment, some of which was illegal, but less dangerous than the Barbary Coast or Chinatown's opium dens.

Uptown

History further suggests that the uptown entertainment district developed around the magnificent late 19th-

Original Loew's Warfield Theater - Built in 1922

Original Orpheum Theater - Built in 1926

century theaters, such as the Junior Orpheum, the Tivoli and later, into the 20th-century, the Golden Gate and Warfield. These theaters reigned as supreme entrees into the Tenderloin for the wealthy and well-established. They could enjoy the most famous of live vaudeville entertainment, exquisite meals in surrounding restaurants and "much more" north of the Market Street perimeter.

Those respectable theaters and restaurants were an invitation to the less respectable Tenderloin that was not yet called the Tenderloin. Perhaps it was just uptown, a place to serve and service those after-theater patrons, who were ready for more or less socially acceptable excitement. As for the actual name Tenderloin, a more scabrous reputation was to be established long before its name.

In 1879, the Tivoli Theater opened in the heart of today's Tenderloin. The Tivoli was a magnificent opera house, situated in a short alley called Anna Lane Street, between Eddy and Ellis Streets. The Junior Orpheum Theater opened on June 30th, 1887 on O'Farrell, off Stockton Street. Those are the well-documented San Francisco events that helped spawn the development of the Tenderloin. Both of those theaters offered international, cultured entertainment and exciting vaudeville acts, hosting such stars of music and the stage as Lillian Western and The Frederick's Troupe.

Later, as the 1920's roared along into the 40's, Amos 'n Andy, Burns and Allen, Fannie Brice, Duke Ellington, Roy Rogers, Danny Kaye, Ella Fitzgerald, Sally Rand and even Ronald Reagan were appearing in other luxurious theaters that openly neighbored the Tenderloin.

Both the Tivoli and Orpheum were rebuilt after the 1906 earthquake and fire, then flourished along with the evolving Tenderloin, for several decades.

By the beginning of the 20's, the demand for more quality entertainment was supplied by the completion of three new theaters within a few years. They were conveniently located a short walk to the Tenderloin, by then known as Uptown. The Orpheum Circuit's Golden Gate Theater on Golden Gate Avenue and Taylor Street was built in 1922. During the same year the Loew's Warfield, on Market at Taylor was also built, presenting its first world class vaudeville show. The Pantages Theater, on Market off Hyde, was completed in 1926.

During the Depression 30's, however, the vaudeville business must have experienced its own grim slump, along with the prosperity of entertainment's burgeoning new industry. Motion pictures were rapidly fascinating audiences and bludgeoning live stage performances out of business. The Pantages dynasty of palatial theaters was losing its vaudeville fans, despite the talents of artists like Sophie Tucker and George Burns. Finally, in 1929, the Market Street Pantages Theater became the new motion picture Orpheum Theater, when sold to RKO.

The Golden Gate Theater managed to tenaciously resist movies for several decades. This may have had something to do with World War II, the USO and a demand for popular stage talents. The Andrews Sisters, Tommy Dorsey's band, and their vocalist, Frank Sinatra, were some of the popular entertainers featured at the Golden Gate during the war years. Sinatra even returned in 1946 to star alone.

The audience was charged 36 cents for a matinee seat, considered excessive in the early 40's. This seemingly successful Golden Gate Theater surprisingly switched to movies in 1948. Then about a year later, the once prosperous Tivoli Theater underwent a more terminal change.

On October 29, 1949, Herb Caen's column in the *Chronicle* stated tersely, "Vanishing Sanfranciscana," which was about the Tivoli Theater becoming a parking garage.

Seven months later, in June 1950, the *Examiner*'s Will Stevens confirmed the theater's fate. The Tivoli had been "beaten into rubble by a wrecking ball."

However, as television began challenging movies, and the multi-screen, shopping mall theaters took on the TV challenge, live stage productions returned to the Golden Gate Theater—for a short while. What happened next, in 1973, suggests that the Tenderloin's presence and reputation had clearly emerged. According to the *Chronicle*, the general manager of the Golden Gate Theater, Sam Pearlman, closed the theater with the statement, "people are afraid to come here at night." Although the accuracy of Mr. Pearlman's opinion may be academic, its implications were obvious. The Tenderloin was really to blame, not the theater. Curiously, since its live stage reopening in 1979, the Golden Gate Theater has apparently been thriving and its audiences surviving, even at night, despite the Tenderloin's reputation.

Thanks to those legitimate theaters, Uptown Tenderloin had many post-earthquake clubs to accommodate after-hours uptowners looking for more entertainment. Coffee Dan, across the street from the Orpheum on O'Farrell, was one of the popular clubs with piano player, Johnny Perkins, who introduced a San Francisco favorite entitled "That Old Gang of Mine."

Around 1896, the Baldwin Stables was also flourishing Uptown as one of many clubs with lavish pool halls that cushioned lucrative bookie operations. Other forms of gambling, especially poker, were well-established in the Tenderloin for decades. Oldtimers still remember such gambling icons as Bones Remmer, Dutch White and the Kyne brothers.

There were fine hotels, like the Olympia on the corner of O'Farrell and Taylor Streets. In 1919, the weekly rate for permanent guests was a whopping $4, with the more exorbitant rate of $1 per night for transients.

There were also great restaurants and of course, bordellos that were equally great, yet much less obtrusive. One of those popular restaurants that catered to the socially well-established and their families was the Techau Tavern; while next door, Newman's College Inn was a real bargain for most anyone. Free lunches, including an enchilada, were offered with a 10-cent beer. All of that was going on within a few blocks of plush theaters and Tessie Wall's parlor, where other vital appetites were being skillfully indulged.

That was the Uptown Tenderloin, which flourished during the last few decades of the 19th-century and much of the 20th-century. It was a provocative haven for the less adventurous, the cultural snobs, the curious or the more conservative—all of whom needed to play a safe distance from the Barbary Coast. Although the north of Market Uptown boundaries have shifted with time, amazingly all the streets, except one, have retained their original names for well over a century.

Ellis Street – 1909

Ellis Street – 2000

O'Farrell Street – 1919

O'Farrell Street - 2000

Tenderloin Area

Old San Francisco maps indicate that all the streets associated with the Tenderloin remarkably existed in 1853, with the exception of Tyler Street that became Golden Gate Avenue in the twentieth century. These facts clearly document the Tenderloin area, but not its boundaries. Structures have boundaries, like buildings and shopping malls. City planners can even map out a specific area of city blocks and call it a neighborhood. But it seems to be a consensus that no one was willing to acknowledge the Tenderloin as a clearly delineated part of San Francisco.

No wonder everything about the Tenderloin, including its name, has been so elusive and debatable. How can an area be clearly boundried when it is unclearly defined by a cloudy reputation and shady activities? Those who have worked in the Tenderloin believe it can't, except for police officers assigned to patrol the area within their officially—albeit arbitrary—designated boundaries.

A good friend of mine, a retired hooker of the 1970's, explained the Tenderloin undulations most convincingly.

"I used to work the streets around Larkin, Polk and Geary," she said. "Then I'd take my tricks back to my truck on Powell."

As far as she was concerned, all of that was part of her Tenderloin. Perhaps the Tenderloin will always be as fluid as those who roam her streets as predator, prey or just good time seekers.

One geographic certainty, perhaps the only one, is that the Tenderloin has always done its smiling, sneering, panting or screaming north of Market Street. Otherwise, beyond that great divide, for those who have roamed the area, specific Tenderloin borders don't matter.

Most demographically-oriented San Francisco historians, however, are likely to agree that, into the 21st-century, the Tenderloin was fluidly bordered by Turk Street to the south, Larkin to the west, O'Farrell to the north and Mason to the east. Within those boundaries were restaurants, theaters, hotels, and apartments that sheltered low-lifes, high-lifes, racketeers, restaurateurs, prostitutes, actors and convicts—all of whom were somehow associated with controversial entertainment.

There's also some sort of consensus from a broad spectrum of authorities that, beyond those boundaries, activities quickly became more respectable. That may oddly be the central difference in their agreement. It's doubtful that respectability meant the same to everyone, especially in such a culturally and socially diverse early San Francisco. Even now, defining respectability has a great deal to do with the "respectability" of the person defining it. This may be another reason why entering the Tenderloin is similar to falling asleep. You never really know when it happens.

As historically recent as August 18, 1998, the San Francisco Board of Supervisors unanimously approved a ban on any new massage parlors in the Tenderloin, while expanding its perimeter. The ordinance "defined" the Tenderloin as "bordered roughly by Van Ness Avenue on the west, Post Street on the north, Powell to the east, and Market to the South."

It could be convincingly speculated that these new ordinance boundaries had nothing to do with expanding the Tenderloin. More likely, the ordinance was intended to eliminate more massage parlors by arbitrarily expanding the restricted area. There are several guarded conclusions that can be gleaned from the above. The

Tenderloin, as an area of risqué entertainment, began in the fourth quarter of the 19th-century. By the early 20th-century it became sufficiently wicked and dangerous to earn the title Tenderloin, and that its boundaries have fluidly ebbed and flowed north of Market, within or around the Mason, Turk, Larkin, O'Farrell perimeter and more recently beyond.

Naming the Tenderloin

Nothing seems clear cut and verifiable about the Tenderloin, not even its name. Early in its history, the Tenderloin was associated with such titles as "Uptown," "Pan Pacific," "Santa Ana Valley," "Polk Gulch," "the blighted district" and on San Francisco Police rosters as "Plot 176." Today historians and old-timers agree to its real name, the Tenderloin, but not to why, how or when it was named.

One very engaging police officer, with a seemingly endless fund of Tenderloin knowledge, retreated into an awkward reticence when asked about the name. Once he regained his composure, he explained, with a tentative mumble, "It's shaped like a tenderloin steak on San Francisco street maps."

Since triangular tenderloin steaks are hard to find, this may be the weakest of many opinions. If the Tenderloin area had been named for its triangular shape, it seems more logical that "jib" or "headsail" would have been more accurate. After all, throughout its history, the Tenderloin has been host to sailors and merchant seamen from around the world.

A more viable possibility, offered by several of the old timers, has more to do with the female anatomy than the steak or sailing ships. According to them, the Tenderloin got its name from the many brothel customers in pursuit of those sensuous "tender loins." In fact, anyone who saw the old Chez Paree marquee on Mason Street would agree the artistic appeal of the term "tender loins" is a no-brainer. In the late 1980's, *The Tenderloin Times* dropped the word "tender" and simply called the area *"The Loin."*

Perhaps those more recent working girls weren't considered quite as sensuous, or "tender." In any event, of all those anecdotes and opinions, the "extra perks" police explanation seems to rank highest in historical significance. Many retired San Francisco cops remember that working in the Tenderloin meant payoffs, which allowed them to buy a better cut of meat, i.e. the tenderloin cut.

During an interview with Kevin Mullen, a retired deputy chief of the San Francisco Police Department, he agreed that the police were responsible for the actual naming of the Tenderloin, but originally in New York, not San Francisco. Mr. Mullen provided information that, in the late 19th-century, New York had its own dangerously depraved area called "Satan's Circus."

In a book by Herbert Ashbury, he confirms that Satan's Circus was the original Tenderloin, a name coined by Captain Alexander Williams of the New York Police Department. In 1876, Williams was reportedly transferred to the 29th Precinct that had jurisdiction over Satan's Circus. When a friend later asked why he seemed so pleased, Williams acknowledged his transfer explaining, "I've had nothing but chuck steak for a long time, and now I'm going to get a little of the tenderloin."

An article in the *New York Times*, dated May 30, 1999, entitled *"The fortress that was at the head of the Tenderloin,"* offers additional support regarding the accuracy of those earlier events. *"When it was built in*

1908, it was the heart of the Tenderloin, where the police were reputed to make small fortunes off New York's heaviest concentration of gambling and prostitution. Now home of the New York City Traffic Control Division, the old 23rd Precinct station house, at 138 West 30th Street, is a spectacular mid-block surprise...."

Just how and when the name arrived in San Francisco seems to smoothly blend with the above stories, especially for those who know law enforcement officers. Both then and now, once they join the police force, they're no longer civilians. They are an elite club that shares their loyalty, experiences and knowledge wherever they are. So, later in the 19th-century, when the word gained police significance and north of Market Street gained an unsavory reputation, the term Tenderloin was the natural choice.

By the turn of the century, the word Tenderloin was famous enough that it was included in the very popular 1909 New York song entitled *"The Ace In The Hole."* The sheet music, first copyrighted in 1909, offers the repeated chorus, *"Others have friends in the old tenderloin that is their ace in the hole . . ."*

Post Earthquake Tenderloin

The Tenderloin is one of those 20th-century phenomenon that has resisted obscurity for over a hundred years, despite those righteous civic efforts to ignore it. Ironically, unlike the more publicized Barbery Coast, the well-entrenched Chinese opium dens or the once popular black Fillmore, the Tenderloin has managed to survive the 1906 and 1989 earthquakes, redevelopment, politicians, police sweeps and public indignation. It has been structurally destroyed, publicly intimidated, blasphemed and socially quarantined, all of which may have served to alter, but never eliminate, the Tenderloin.

Many of the San Francisco districts or neighborhoods that were spared annihilation were in for radical change. Some of those areas have become gentrified residential neighborhoods with their own expensive embellishments that typically include several coffee shops. Others have succumbed to parking lots, shopping malls, or worse yet—stadiums.

The Tenderloin, on the other hand, has clung to its basic 19th-century character, reputation and its name, despite a relentless city campaign to neutralize, disguise or destroy it. Anyway, structures don't usually provide districts with character or reputation. People do, and maybe this is the key to the Tenderloin's resiliency and stamina.

Early 20th Century

It's well-documented that the Tenderloin flourished its way into the 20th-century and then physically collapsed during the 1906 quake, like most of San Francisco. The next ten years were devoted to rebuilding the City, including its crime and entertainment areas. By about 1909, the Tenderloin and Barbery Coast were back in business, with new buildings and the old hustlers, customers, predators and victims. Tolerated by the police and either scorned or enjoyed by others, both the Tenderloin and Barbery Coast were in for another quake, more devastating than the earlier one.

The initial tremor was pressure from the outraged "morals reformers" who, between 1912 and 1917, successfully pressured the closing of many prominent bordellos. The major shock wave, however, occurred in

1917 in the form of "The Red Light Abatement Act," which crumbled virtually all prostitution and other illegal activities. Reportedly, the Barbery Coast was hit the hardest with a "blockade" and never recovered, despite one last and very fatal attempt in 1921.

Remember, the Barbery Coast was always a blatantly open, down your throat, no apologies embarrassment to many of the established City residents. It was realized too late that, when you brazenly thumb your nose at City Hall, you're eventually doomed.

But the resilient Tenderloin was a far more elusive and clever target. Surrounded by an area of respectable entertainment, the Tenderloin could lay low for awhile in the shadows of those magnificent theaters and restaurants that continued to host San Francisco's "respectable" regulars. History also strongly hints that the Tenderloin neither defied nor openly challenged the City, it simply lowered its profile in wait of another opportunity.

Such an opportunity gradually emerged from the rubble left by the sanctimonious activists. That renewed tolerance for Tenderloin activities was under the aegis of the very popular, vice-friendly Mayor Jim Rolph. "Sonny Jim," as he was endearingly called, later became Governor of California. Yet his principle legacy included his intolerance for prohibition, and his open acceptance of the famous Madam Tessie Wall, and her successor, Sally Stanford. Those madams were also skillful entrepreneurs who obviously helped promote their trade and along with it, the Tenderloin. Sally Stanford was later elected mayor of Sausalito, another tribute to her popularity.

It was the roaring 20's, and the Tenderloin was almost a welcomed part of the roar, at least to that significant few and their following. However, the debauchery of the earlier gold rush days was a bit more subdued. That was an area where fine foods and entertainment complimented the illegal, fine brothels, speakeasies and gambling houses. Police, however, had no tolerance for showboating crime, and during this period in the 20's, into the 30's, the Tenderloin streets were reportedly quite safe, at least from violence and other unsolicited crimes.

The 30's may be remembered as another period of glaring contrasts that no doubt exaggerated the character traits of most of the nation. It was a decade teeming with desperation, rage, suppression, greed and compassion. The conclusion of Prohibition was being celebrated, and the beginning of the Depression was being mourned by virtually all, but in different ways. There were suicides, bread lines and a selfless sacrificing for others, as well as self-indulgence despite the misfortunes of others.

Interestingly, the Tenderloin continued to flourish through those bad times, hosting anyone wanting to buy or sell unbridled pleasures. There's no documented evidence that the Tenderloin was significantly changed by that period of national transformation, and it's easy to speculate as to why.

Tenderloin people and patrons have never seemed to reflect the values, attitudes or morality of the nation. Building a stable community was not a neighborhood goal, especially since the Tenderloin wasn't a neighborhood. Basically, the Tenderloin existed for the purpose of forgetting one's problems, having fun and making money, not necessarily in that order.

As the 30's slipped beneath the 40's, a new drama would unfold to again spare the Tenderloin any drastic changes. World War II was an era of intense patriotism for those defending our country. It was a time to express basic savagery along with basic hedonistic pleasures and a time to sacrifice prudish intolerance of the basics. Our servicemen and women were risking life and limb for us, and everyone wanted to make them happy, including the Tenderloin.

As a major seaport, San Francisco was swarming with servicemen, merchant marines, shipyard workers and longshoremen. The Tenderloin quickly became one of their favorite hangouts where they were treated like lecherous heroes, as long as they had money. Using the jargon of the time, there were door-to-door whorehouses, bars, B-girls, strip joints and more bars. Everyone could find brief thrills spending or making money. In those days, as Charlie Mew, other old-timers and even I recall, there was enough booze in the Tenderloin to supply several cities, yet street drugs were rarely even mentioned.

Also during the 40's, prostitutes, although in abundance, were typically seen indoors instead of on street corners. Gays, labeled "fruits" and "queers," were still essentially in the closet, except for those brazen pioneers who hung out in such bars as the Black Cat, in the North Beach on Montgomery Street.

📖 📖 📖

The 40's seemed to linger well into the 50's in the Tenderloin, even though the supply of business had dwindled with the dwindling demand by customers. That may have had something to do with the City's dwindling tolerance for illegal fun. By 1950, the uniformed heroes of World War II had returned home to their humdrum civilian lives that didn't include return pleasure trips to the Tenderloin. Yet, the dwindling didn't last long. There were enough leftover customers and residents to keep many of the Tenderloin suppliers in business.

In any event, by 1953, there was a new crop of warriors wandering the Tenderloin before wandering Korea. San Francisco was still a port of embarkation, and the Tenderloin was a gracious host. Since our country seemed bent on consecutive wars, this hosting was to last for quite some time. Vietnam was next.

The Tenderloin's controversial prominence was still the business of selling alcohol, women, camaraderie and those exciting games of chance. Its location also remained an undeniable advantage. The Tenderloin was cozy close to the more conventionally desirable fine restaurants, motion picture theaters and live entertainment. In short, the colorful, roguish flavor of the early Tenderloin persisted, albeit a bit less vigorously, into the 50's. The glitter, however, was beginning to tarnish, along with other less conspicuous signs of murky changes.

During the first half of the 20th-century, the Tenderloin seemed more concerned with promoting its outside customers than its inside residents. They were a relatively small, poor, politically unimportant group, which no doubt added to their obscurity. The onset of the 50's, however, provided substantial clues that the Tenderloin's poor residential population was both growing and deteriorating along with its buildings.

Father Alfred Boeddeker, a Franciscan friar, recognized the plight of the Tenderloin's increasing residential population by founding St. Anthony's Dining Room on Jones Street in 1950. The response to this free dining room sadly confirmed that the Tenderloin's more pathetic transformation was no longer subtle.

Fifteen hundred meals were served per day at the Tenderloin St. Anthony's Dining Room during 1950. Two years later, the *Monitor*, the newspaper of the Archdiocese of San Francisco, reported seventeen hundred free meals per day.

Some will argue that St. Anthony's attracted poverty to the Tenderloin. More poverty perhaps, but not poverty—it was already there. Many Tenderloin residents were hungry and St. Anthony's Dining Room was simply trying to feed them. Then, in the middle 60's, Glide Memorial Church recognized the escalating survival struggle of the Tenderloin residents. It became St. Anthony's reinforcements.

St. Anthony's Dining Room

Glide Memorial Church
In the shadow of the Hilton Hotel

Glide Memorial started with a Monday night dinner, which expanded to approximately three thousand five hundred meals per day by September 1999. During that period, St. Anthony's nearby dining room was feeding two thousand people per day. According to the book, *Reclaiming San Francisco*, in 1993 the Tenderloin had a population of about twenty-five thousand, with an average annual income of $8,000, the lowest of anywhere else in the City. Those figures too clearly underscored the Tenderloin's grim transformation during the declining decades of the twentieth century.

Late 20th Century - The New Era

By the late 60's and 70's, the once flamboyant entertainment area was struggling to become a neighborhood.

The Tenderloin was undergoing the most striking characterological transition of its mischievous existence. Some called it a period of deterioration, others, the end of an era.

Regardless of what it was called, all tend to agree the changes were fading the florid fun and gaudy glamour of its earlier life into dreary grays. The Tenderloin was taking on a new, drab persona; while, during the same period, a once obscure area of San Francisco was destined to be called the Haight Ashbury.

The Tenderloin was losing its intriguing reputation and impish charm as a well-managed, professional entertainment area of exciting, albeit illicit in-house activities. As if a closet had begun to open, hustlers were taking to the streets. Bordellos were being replaced by amateur corner prostitutes and their nearby pimps. As always, bars were in abundance, but the once shadowy use of drugs was being boldly introduced to the Tenderloin streets.

Homosexuals were emerging outdoors as gays, and the gradual residential growth of the Tenderloin through the decades was culminating in a permanent neighborhood of rejects, immigrants, misfits and indigents. The reasons for these striking changes in the character of the Tenderloin through the 70's and 80's are unarguably multifaceted. Just about every historian and old-timer interviewed offered a different reason for the demise of the Tenderloin's flamboyant, need-fulfilling reign for over 100 years. Again, they're probably all right.

The 60's could easily be described as the threshold of change, triggered by rebellion against the establishment, against conformity, even against the self for not rebelling against something. This was the decade of the civil rights movement against government bigotry, the Vietnam War movement against government treachery, the Hippie movement against anything government, and a national movement of distrust in the government. Organizations were forming all over the country to challenge or monitor the government, and people were openly realizing that the government wasn't that wonderful role model after all.

Locally, San Francisco was feeling the ripples of this nationwide opposition to the establishment. The Police Department and other agencies were no longer able to operate with impunity. That meant more accountability and less bribery. Those corrupt, self-serving citadels of local government were losing their impervious resistance to public scrutiny. Consequently, illegal in-house activities were very vulnerable.

It also became increasingly obvious during those times that people were not powerless against government juggernauts. *You can actually fight City Hall and get away with it, sometimes.* Minority groups and groups with minority ideas were being heard, and no one was being hanged by their thumbs. To some, however, this eruption of socially acceptable expressions of personal rights and liberties was translated into freedom to do pretty much what you wanted.

In San Francisco, the "flower children" were dancing around, through, and over anyone in authority who resembled their oppressive parents. The "Timothy Learys" were spearheading the drug renaissance, and blacks were "testing the limits" by challenging anything with the scent of prejudice or restriction.

All of those 60's events and circumstances may well represent some of the brush strokes resulting in a darker, more dreary portrait of the Tenderloin that lingered into the 80's and 90's. As the late Herb Caen wrote in his column on June 2, 1963, *"It was a world we'll never see again. Godliness and purity now reign - don't they? And the final long shadow is being cast over the Tenderloin by the rising Hilton. The section is to become infinitely more respectable. And infinitely duller. "*

📖 📖 📖

Herb Caen probably knew 20th-century San Francisco better than any other writer, yet his view of the Tenderloin appears to have had rather meager support. One of those meager supporters was Stan Sinberg. In the September 10, 1999 *Chronicle*, he offered an article that provided a more realistic view of the Tenderloin, as he told about finding his lost car in, what he called, "San Francisco's Adventure Neighborhood." He wrote about wandering around the Tenderloin, searching for his car well into the night.

"At 2:00 a.m., in the Tenderloin, everyone talks to you. Women ask, 'Got a date?' Men say things like, 'Looking for something?' And panhandlers explain why they're not like everyone else asking for change...."

I obviously considered Mr. Sinberg's article far more representative of today's Tenderloin than those who portray it as some sort of a deadly black abyss. Incidentally, Stan Sinberg found his car and both apparently survived the night unscathed.

Unfortunately, too many writers, especially of tourist books, seem to have the dubious talent of excessively dramatizing a few bits and pieces of information into gross distortions of what is really going on.

"...do not venture into the Tenderloin District, bordered roughly by the 'triangle' of Jones, O'Farrell and Market Streets either during the day or night unless you are escorted in a vehicle (preferably a buddy in a

squad car)." or *"...there are blocks of Tenderloin downtown where it is dangerous by day and suicide by night to walk around unprotected."*

Those are near comic strip exaggerations that tend to transform a bawdy, poverty-laden area into a cruel, evil place of sinister creatures, crouching menacingly in every doorway.

Those negative caveats have a frustrating way of distorting reality into eventual fact. Such pseudo truths are also exemplified in a 1999 *San Francisco Bay Guardian* article, titled *"Best Civic Guessing Game."* The article stated, with an air of authority, *"...Which of the City's two final frontiers of gentrification - the Tenderloin or Hunters Point - will be overrun by loft-living yuppies first? Hunters Point faces a few barriers: nagging gang activity, rampant poverty, a run down infrastructure, and a distant location—but the northeast Mission can claim three of those, and, as a haven for the poor, artists, fliering* (sic) *anarchists, its days are numbered. So our money is on the Tenderloin as the final holdout; despite its downtown location, just blocks away from Union Square and Nob Hill, it's as rough now (despite reports to the contrary) as it was in the last century, when it earned its name because merchants offered SFPD officers steaks to patrol it."*

Because of that article, many readers no doubt assumed the Tenderloin was more dangerous than Hunters Point—nonsense, and that the Tenderloin's name was the result of earlier "law-abiding" merchants paying cops for protection from local criminals—more nonsense.

The Hilton Corporation certainly researched the area before building a multi-million dollar hotel that virtually embraces the Tenderloin. Hilton was obviously aware that, as guests stepped out of the hotel, they were stepping into the Tenderloin. Yet there is no evidence that any of the thousands of Hilton guests, as well as those from the other nearby first class hotels, have been terrorized into retreating from the City.

Those hotels still flourish, as do their fine restaurants, within the shadow of the unlocked, open and very accessible Tenderloin. As for the high crime rate in the Tenderloin, especially homicides, I doubt if they're killing the tourists or law abiding San Francisco residents. If they are, the news media that loves to sensationalize, is sure keeping it quiet. It seems safe to assume that, if the homicide rate is high, Tenderloin people are most likely killing each other, not San Francisco's gentry.

The Future

As the Tenderloin continues its uncertain odyssey into the 21st-century, it still has its enduring persona indelibly imprinted into the history of San Francisco. And that's despite all of those contrasting opinions by today's self-proclaimed authorities. The old Tenderloin survives, within the 21st-century, with its bulldog tenacity and volatile reputation that troubles some and thrills others. Like the Rorschach Projective Test, the Tenderloin has been and perhaps still is whatever you need or want it to be. The late Herb Caen obviously appreciated it, while others continue to catastrophize it.

Unfortunately, all of those written opinions and their exaggerated warnings are the ingredients of which phobias are made. It is especially frustrating for someone like me, who has lived and worked in the area, to recognize that catastrophizing about the Tenderloin perpetuates its dangerous reputation. Such rumors can create sheer terror in many who will make certain to avoid experiencing any part of the Tenderloin.

In 1971, the Reverend Don Seaton just may have provided the most accurate view of the Tenderloin's future, in expressing his opinion of the Tenderloin's past. As he was leaving his post as the director of the Central City Hospitality House, a neighborhood service agency, he stated, "It's not a community and never will be. It's impossible to organize the Tenderloin. It has no social structure of its own."

Such apparent indifference to organized social conformity may be the central reason for the Tenderloin's lasting charm, mystique and controversial reputation. It seems ironic that once an area is tamed or shamed into submission, it invariably becomes predictable and uninteresting. The Tenderloin is neither, possibly because it keeps recreating itself from within on an as-needed basis.

Like it, hate it or fear it, the Tenderloin is one of those rare archaeological digs that keeps rising from the rubble, probably because it has a more solid history than its muddied reputation can ever recognize—or understand. Also, for its hapless or untamed residents, there's still nowhere else to go.

A walk through the Tenderloin always offers a kaleidoscope of exciting chapters in the history of San Francisco—only if one is willing to walk slowly and look carefully beyond the poverty. There are remnants of earlier, turn-of-the-century clubs, brothels, speakeasies and hotels. Only the people have disappeared or are just too old to be recognized. Then again, maybe not.

The Tenderloin continues to harbor the poor, the immigrants, the predators, the prey, pensioners, junkies, winos, transvestites, parolees, gays, hustlers, the pimps and their prostitutes—not unlike their historical predecessors. They may dress differently, but their similarities to the past are striking. They feel they belong there because the Tenderloin accepts them without demanding they conform to the rest of the city. Since they don't uneasily stand out alone, they tend to safely blend in together. After all, the Tenderloin is all about a refuge for people who continue to weave a tapestry of unique stories.

In the seven years since the first edition of this book, both the Tenderloin and I have changed. I'm looking a bit older, while the Tenderloin seems to be looking a lot safer—perhaps too safe. The older-looking me was expected, while the Tenderloin's abrupt changes are historically surprising and curious.

No doubt, law enforcement has had a lot to do with these Tenderloin changes. The San Francisco police officers that patrol the Tenderloin in cruisers, bikes and on foot seem much more visible these days. Their new station has been flourishing on Jones and Eddy since late in 2000, right after my first Tenderloin book was published.

Still, according to Larry Vales, one of the station's cops, they have the usual three watches, with no more officers than any other station. The new station house, however, conspicuously resides in the heart of the Tenderloin; and its adjacent rooms—provided to community groups at no charge—are a wry welcome to suspicious residents.

Officer Vales added that the Tenderloin boundaries are about the same: Market Street to the south, Van Ness to the west, Geary to the north and Mason to the

east. There are still plenty of homeless people within those boundaries and according to Vales, narcotics represents the biggest crime problem. Homicides are "much lower," he said.

As another third millennium update, Officer Vales said he still wouldn't recommend walking around the Tenderloin alone at night. Neighborhood community service groups, however, maintain that only about five percent of Tenderloin residents are criminal types.

In any event, for old times, I still walk around the Tenderloin alone, day or night, feeling more protected than ever in a seedy, safe zone of rich memories and flagging charisma. Yet, each time I return to the Tenderloin I become increasingly convinced that its historic pendulum may have had an Orwellian swing toward "big brother's" over-protective parents.

Here's an example. In 2005, a lady friend and I were returning to our car after a fine dinner at Original Joes on Taylor Street, when a frail, disheveled-looking little black man approached us with a broad, toothless smile. Probably in his fifties or sixties—it's hard to tell with street people who tend to look older faster—he stepped to one side with a gallant bow, followed by a cheerful, articulate greeting.

"Good afternoon, I hope you enjoy your evening."

I smiled back with a "hi," which was the invitation he was no doubt looking for to engage us further.

"Gee you're lucky to have such a pretty lady with you."

As his smile enlarged into an open-mouth grin, we noticed a single tooth hanging from his upper gum. We both found the tooth funny yet sad, as if he just couldn't afford dentures or letting go of the last vestige of his youthful days with teeth.

Knowing what was coming next, I gave him a dollar before he could ask. *Why not*, I thought. He was pleasant, complimentary of my lady friend, and he only had one tooth.

As the old man stuffed the dollar into a frayed pocket he bowed again with a "God bless you both."

That's when a hefty cop scurried across the street. "Hey, stop bothering these people."

"He's not bothering us," I said.

Ignoring me, the cop glared at the little guy. "Get out of here," he ordered.

The tooth and gums slipped beneath the old guy's lips as he disappeared around the corner, followed by the cop.

I still remember feeling sorry for the little man with one tooth and a big smile. Of all the panhandlers I had encountered in San Francisco during my life, it was the first time a cop ever came to my unsolicited rescue, and in the Tenderloin of all places.

There's also a second edition view of the Chez Paree and its garish symbol of the more flamboyant Tenderloin days. In 2003, the Mason Street Chez Paree succumbed to a parking lot. I've been told that at least its marquee wasn't destroyed. It's been apparently resting somewhere in an obscure warehouse awaiting another *reign*.

Then in 2004, the Chez Paree was reopened at 220 Jones Street, its third or fourth Tenderloin location. Revisiting the Chez Paree in 2006 was oddly sad and regretful. Although still deep in the Tenderloin, it seemed to have strayed much too far from its colorful past.

There was no longer a hint of those openly naughty years when the Chez Paree's landmark sign was a Tenderloin beacon to anyone seeking bawdy pleasures. The building looked very tired, dull and plainly seedy as if no longer interested in even pretending to entertain. Not even the Chez Paree marquee was there to cheer it up. Sadly, its *reign* may be over.

2

RALPH

Parasites

Throughout its long history, the Tenderloin has hosted people seeking a place to live, to work or play. As a historically notorious location, it has also hosted a dangerous, menacing, treacherous and unsavory reputation. Although the evidence remains debatable, the truth doesn't really matter anymore. The Tenderloin's reputation has become its identity—its people are guilty by association. Its reputation implies that the people who exist there are equally dangerous, menacing, treacherous and unsavory. That's when we tend to forget that each person there has a unique story, which may not be remotely related to the Tenderloin reputation.

Such flawed reasoning has always been the essential ingredient of prejudice and bigotry. Create a reputation with a few facts, lots of rumors and plenty of gossip. Add a dash of ignorance, intolerance and a naive belief in hearsay; mix well and then avoid the dangerous

Tenderloin at all cost—even though you've never been there.

There is the old, decrepit man struggling to survive just a while longer; the single mother desperately trying to raise her young kids. There's the transvestite who roams the streets at night, reconfirming her identity, and the corner drug pusher with full-blown AIDS. There's the grocery store clerk who attends college at night, and the small apartment owner who is constantly concerned with filling vacancies.

Those people are no different from people living in other areas in San Francisco. There are just more of them in the Tenderloin, where they are much less uneasy about revealing their identities. In any event, overcoming the Tenderloin's reputation has never been easy—especially for a newcomer. It would require spending some time there; which is characteristically impossible for the bigot.

As a native San Franciscan, I should have known better than to accept gossip. I didn't and probably couldn't at such a young age. I wasn't aware that understanding the Tenderloin required knowing the people who live and work there. I didn't even know anyone acquainted with the Tenderloin. As a kid, I was told to stay away by many so-called well-informed adults. Those grownups had either never been there, hurriedly walked through once or were simply influenced by years of hearsay. My youthful resistance to bigotry was precariously low.

📖 📖 📖

Toward the end of the 40's, I was a Polytechnic High School senior who was about to get a priceless education that had nothing to do with academics. Family problems encouraged me to leave home earlier than I had ever imagined. Being on my own before I was ready meant part-time work and inexpensive housing if I were to remain in school. I had been raised in the Richmond and Sunset districts of San Francisco. Those neighborhoods were considered safe, respectable and relatively expensive. Still in my teens and approaching poverty, expense was a genuine concern for me and expensive hardly an option. Since "safe and respectable" were associated with "expensive," those respectable San Francisco districts also ceased to be options.

My dire need for inexpensive housing introduced me to the Tenderloin and my budding bigotry to a queasy sense of uneasiness. All those adult gossips and rumors convinced me that I probably wouldn't last a semester in the Tenderloin. The possibilities were endless. I could be mugged, raped, kidnapped, robbed, murdered or, the most heinous of all possibilities, actually become one those Tenderloin people. Looking back, my only real danger was failing to learn from a Tenderloin that had so much to teach.

I easily found a small, studio apartment on the ground floor of an old brick building in, of all places, the very heart of the Tenderloin. That was the perfect building for a young, impressionable newcomer like me. The building was very old and weary, yet adorned with remnants of her youthful elegance and charm. She was a virtual catalog of Tenderloin history.

There were decades of peeling paint, color coding her past face-lifts; worn down, beautifully patterned marble stairs; richly inlaid hardwood floors with preserved gilding swirls and traces of crimson carpet— perhaps of the open brothel era.

Sagging, weathered and looking pitifully wounded, her regal days seemed over. Then, looking more closely,

I had to reconsider. Reminders of her more flamboyant past still lingered throughout the building.

Outside, huge eaves with decorative gingerbread majestically offset the darkened, eroding bricks that were losing their grip on crumbling mortar. Such contrasts were everywhere, including the inside of my studio apartment.

The lighting and plumbing fixtures were old, out-dated, irreplaceably fancy and remarkably preserved as if still celebrating the old building's earlier splendor.

I didn't understand the historical significance of those Tenderloin relics then. I just enjoyed knowing the old building had a past. Also, I thoroughly appreciated the low rent of $50 per month, furniture included. It was by far the cheapest place I could find, and since I only had my clothes, toiletries and a few books, the stark furnishings were a genuine gift. A kitchenette that included a few cooking and eating utensils, a bathroom with an enormous four-clawed bathtub, a nightstand and an old stuffed chair were most of the basic furnishings, but not everything.

The grand prize was the elusive Murphy bed that stood on its head in the closet. Attached to a large revolving door, this tubular metal bed lurched its way from closet to outer room. Just pushing on the door would pivot the whole bed on the door's center post. In a matter of seconds, my large, barren living room was filled with bed, as I pulled the foot of the bed down to the floor. I often wondered how many times this sturdy old bed had swung into action, transforming a large living room into a small, cozy bedroom.

There was also an interesting addition to my little apartment that I hadn't noticed the first week. Beneath my two windows were flower boxes crammed with colorful flowers I couldn't identify by name. The reds, blues and yellows were wilting with neglect, yet it was apparent that whoever lived there before me expressed a tender love of flowers. Someone had taken excellent care of them. I was so impressed, I decided to continue caring for those flowers. My only concern was their precarious location. The boxes were perched low over Turk Street and all those Tenderloin dangers.

In general, I was pleased with my new home, job as busboy and my schoolwork. However, my fears and concerns about the Tenderloin neighborhood oddly prevented me from learning about the Tenderloin, as a neighborhood. I was afraid to wander out after dark. Even during the day, I hurried along as if minding my own business. In that way, I avoided any contact with those contaminated drunks, bums, junkies and thugs.

It wasn't my neighborhood; in fact, at that time it wasn't much of a neighborhood. Besides, I didn't need to be neighborly. I just needed to occupy a studio apartment in the Tenderloin. I was also convinced that, as long as I didn't hang around outside, I'd remain reasonably safe from exposure to those parasites wandering the streets.

I was surprised to discover, however, that during the first few weeks I was not only left alone, I was hardly noticed. I was even ignored as I walked to and from streetcars. The routine nods of acknowledgment from the apartment manager and an occasional smile from an old man who lived next door, were becoming almost welcomed responses to my presence.

The indifference didn't last long. By the third week, like it or not, people were beginning to recognize me as their neighbor, at least the winos. There was a typical opener. "Hey partner, can you spare some money?"

It usually seemed more like a greeting than a request. Some of the winos even laughingly asked if I wanted a drink. At the time, I didn't think that was funny or friendly. Smelly and dirty, with wrinkled clothing that didn't fit, those were skid row bums—winos. They were *parasites* that in no way resembled me. So once my uneasiness shifted to indignation, I just ignored them. Well, most of them.

There was one scrawny, typical skid row looking old man whom I just couldn't ignore. Equally hard to ignore was his big dog. He never seemed to be more than a few feet from the old skid row bum. At least a couple of times a week they would appear, virtually out of nowhere.

The scrawny wino always gave me an enthusiastic wave and smile, while big dog stood lazily nearby with a big panting grin. Still wary of Tenderloin strangers, I would walk across the street as if I didn't notice them. Regardless of when or where I walked in the Tenderloin, however, there was the old wino smiling and waving, with big dog grinning at his side.

After several weeks of his waving and smiling, along with big dog's panting grins, I finally broke down and nodded an acknowledgment of their greetings. That was the first of many encounters. If drunk, he would stagger or stumble by; and when sober, he would walk up to me with a pleasant, straightforward request.

"I need a quarter to buy some wine."

Even though he never asked twice, he didn't give up on me. As we continued to meet on the street, he simply abbreviated the request, "Just a quarter?" and finally, as if more amused than annoyed with my refusals, he would walk by with a disarming smile, "A dime?"

Always near the old wino was big dog, with a steady tail wag and big wet tongue dangling from his panting mouth.

I still hadn't said anything to the wino, other than a

few negative grunts and occasionally patting big dog. I wasn't aware yet that a relationship was emerging from those frequent encounters.

Although he stopped jokingly taunting me for a dime, he kept greeting me on the street with a warm charming smile and bulging olive-drab eyes. His face was engraved with deeply carved, happy wrinkles and pleasant natural curves. Even his mouth was cheerfully turned up at the ends, exposing what was left of his broken brown teeth. That was the face of a kind, openly friendly man. There wasn't a trace of despair or anger.

Then one day as I left my apartment building, it dawned on me. I was actually looking for them. Maybe because the old wino's mannerisms were genuinely charming and friendly, or maybe they were so delightfully easy to spot as far as a block away. He had a funny little half-hopping, half-limping walk, a unique signature that couldn't possibly be duplicated by anyone else. Another near comically peculiar trademark was his clothing that he never seemed to change. He wore a faded old red stocking cap, tattered checkered sport coat about three sizes too big, baggy denim pants tied to his waist with rope and a pair of Keds (tennis shoes) without laces. And, of course, big grinning dog was always near him. Maybe I just gave up trying to avoid them.

When down wind, I was frequently aware of the old wino before I could see him. His breath was a pungent, yet not unpleasant smell of stale wine. What really distinguished his aroma from other winos, however, was his special blend of body odor and breath. His body exuded a powerful scent of onions and garlic; which, combined with the stale wine, transformed his concoction of smells into a salad dressing—like a vinaigrette vapor trail. The wafting scent sometimes reminded me

of some of my mother's too-spicy Italian cooking—
fragrant only at a distance.

At any rate, I seemed to feel a bit more comfortable,
more relaxed in the Tenderloin when I knew he was
around. Although sadly frail and wizened, he was
sprightly, warm and happy-looking. By that time, when
he went hippity-hopping by with his broad grin and big
dog, I started smiling back. My friendly gesture seemed
to slow his pace, until he finally stopped in front of me
with a gracious bow, as if he were approaching royalty.

Oh no, I thought, my smiles were his invitation to hit
me up again. But to my astonishment, he didn't ask for
money!

"Do you ever water your flowers?" He was pointing
up the street to the flower boxes under my windows. I
was even surprised he knew they were my windows.
"They're dying," he said with a more subdued smile.

I had mixed feelings about what seemed to be a mild
scolding or maybe a hustle. It didn't matter I conceded
to myself, he was right. "No, I guess I don't, I keep
forgetting."

His smile broadened. "There aren't many flowers
around here. Can I water them and keep them alive for
you? It won't cost you nothing." His smile was subdued
again as if awaiting an answer to a critical business
offer.

When I told him I didn't mind, his whole wrinkled
face ignited into a glowing, unrestrained smile that said
it all. He was happy, nearby big dog was grinning and I
was relieved. We shook hands and exchanged names.
That was the day I got myself a gardener named Ralph
and his sidekick Mug, two lovable characters.

Mug was a great name for big dog. In those days, the word "mug" was commonly-used slang for someone's face, and big dog's head had an undeniably unusual mug. His huge head was about the size of a soccer ball, shaped into near comic-strip features. A wide, crooked mouth, big sagging jowls and huge constantly twitching nostrils created a variety of panting grins and smiles. Above his comical expressions were big brown eyes that happily followed your movements. Despite his huge chest, rippling muscles and long sharp teeth, his "mug" said it all. He had the temperament of a gentle loving dove, with the physical power of a grizzly bear.

Mug had been Ralph's best friend for over five years. He had found Mug in a dumpster where someone had thrown him when he was about three weeks old.

"Even then he had a big head," Ralph recalled, adding that although his frail little body looked dead, there had been a faint panting coming from his huge mouth. Ralph cared for Mug as a mother might care for her sick infant. He even spent some of his welfare money on injections and advice from a veterinary clinic.

Mug grew into a huge, devoted companion. They were inseparable. Never on a leash, Mug would follow Ralph anywhere, and just watching this sweet gentle giant of a dog was enough to understand that sweet gentle compassionate man.

📖　📖　📖

During his first week on the job, Ralph seemed to spend more time under, around and over the flower boxes than at his home, wherever that was. Every morning as I left my apartment, Ralph was already draped over the flower boxes, humming and watering. Even when it rained he happily hummed and watered.

"Good morning. Learn a lot and stay tall," was his usual morning greeting between hums.

When I returned, Ralph was still cheerfully tending the flower boxes and Mug was playing with a 2 x 4. I often wondered if they ever left during the day. I never asked, and seeing him and Mug there when I came home was always a pleasant event.

While Mug chewed on some enormous piece of wood, Ralph would be puttering around the pots, picking dead leaves off the scrawny flowers, removing cigarette butts and other debris and, of course, humming through his big crinkly smile.

"Hiya boss. Hope ya learned a lot today. Stay tall and have a good evening," was his typical afternoon welcome home.

Sometimes while busily fussing around the pots, he would erupt into a bellowing song that sounded suspiciously like bits of an operatic aria. When asked what he was singing, he'd just laugh and sing louder with a voice that was remarkably clear and in tune. I liked having them around, comic clothes, peculiar smells, waging tail and all.

Ralph didn't just love the flowers; he seemed to cherish the responsibility of caring for something. He took his job very seriously, with an open, unabashed sense of pride. Once, I heard him tell one of his wino friends that I had "hired" him to "save the plants in the flower boxes." As far as he was concerned, he had a real, necessary job. He was an employee, a genuine contribution to the Tenderloin community—not just a bum.

Occasionally I thought Ralph might end up drowning the flowers with his love and determination. Everyone in the neighborhood probably knew where I lived by the windows with the dripping flower boxes and wet pavement. Yet, despite my reservations about Ralph's gardening skills, the flowers began to flourish with rich green leaves and a rainbow display of colors. Even the flower boxes were freshly painted and in surprisingly tasteful, brilliant colors. I never knew where he got the paint. All I knew was he accomplished all of it on his own, no doubt with encouragement from Mug.

I was so satisfied with Ralph's work; I decided to pay him a couple of dollars a week. But, the instant I offered him money, I knew I had wounded him. That was an insensitive blunder and I'll never forget the look on the face of that sensitive man.

Ralph's usual crinkly smile quickly faded into an old wrinkled frown. He looked twenty years older, at least about eighty. He stood silent for a moment, as if in shock. Perhaps he was trying to salvage his pride and dignity. Mug looked up at him as if sensing Ralph was upset.

"Mercy me, I thought we were *real* friends. I get my pension, so I don't need money; I just like flowers and helping you."

I must have spent the next ten minutes apologizing and reassuring Ralph that we were friends, *real* friends. "Because of you, Ralph, I feel comfortable in the Tenderloin now. You've been so good to my plants and me. I thought I could be your friend and also give you a little money. I'm sorry."

Ralph stared at me intently and when I stopped talking, his deep jagged furrows softened into one of his welcomed smiles. "If I need some extra money, I'll borrow it from you and I'll always pay you back because we're friends." He looked down at Mug and scratched the big dog's head. "OK?" he asked.

I smiled at both of them. "Sure Ralph, anytime."

Of course, it didn't matter if he ever repaid me, but it certainly mattered to him. A few days before he received his welfare check (or pension check as he called it), Ralph routinely and with a curious air of pride, came to see me for his loan.

I imagined that having a good credit rating heightened his status with his friends. There was probably one other benefit. He enjoyed visiting before what he considered his "business transaction." So did Mug, who would sit grinning nearby.

Ralph never asked me for more than five dollars at a time, and he always paid me back as soon as he cashed his check. Repaying the loan was probably more important than receiving the money. Like the night he knocked on my door after cashing his check earlier that day. As I opened the door, there was Ralph trying desperately to stay on his feet, with Mug standing behind him. Ralph was drunker than any person I had ever seen before. How he found my door and why he was still standing, remain mysteries.

He hugged the doorjamb with one arm to keep his wobbly little legs from buckling. In his free hand was a wad of money that he unsteadily waved back and forth. It was a sheer wonder he could still see through his eyes. They were thin, reddish slits, beneath helplessly drooping eyelids. Even his aroma had deteriorated to a mild scent of onions and garlic, together with an overpowering scent of wine and urine.

Ralph had lost his red cap, and for the first time I could see his matted, graying hair pointing in all directions. As he made one valiant effort to enter my apartment, only his upper body moved forward. He arched to the floor, flat on his face, like an old fallen tree. When I turned him over, he was still grinning as blood spurted from his nose.

"Tas moonye I's owe ya. I sorral you bother... Mercy, I peed. I sorry."

I could barely understand him. Yet as usual, he got his message across. He just wanted to pay me before his money was all gone. By that time, Mug was licking the blood off Ralph's face.

During the next year, Ralph was always available. Rain or shine, drunk or sober, he happily watered, grinned, borrowed and paid back. I remember thinking that, because of him, the Tenderloin hadn't been a bad experience after all. I also recall envying his patience, positive outlook and cheerful disposition— all qualities I'm still working on.

He never seemed to blame or use anyone, and the only time he ever asked me for help beyond the flower boxes, was in filling out some welfare forms or consulting me if Mug didn't feel well. He was a predictably cheerful little guy, even though there were hints of another life. He sometimes spoke pensively of a wife, a child, a regular job—long ago.

At least he has Mug, I thought.

    📖   📖   📖

Then one morning, I discovered what grieving with a friend was all about. Ralph was sitting on the sidewalk under our flower boxes. He was looking up, beyond the Tenderloin rooftops as he tried to smile away a flood of tears. Mug wasn't nearby and instantly I knew what I really didn't want to know.

It took Ralph several minutes of sobbing before he could tell me what had happened. Mug had romped into the street to fetch a big stick. He was hit by a truck and killed instantly. Ralph had seen it all.

As I sat on the sidewalk next to Ralph, I remember

the taste of my own salty tears trickling into my mouth. I not only learned how easily I could cry, I learned that each person grieves in his own way.

For the next few weeks, Ralph continued to water the flowers with a faint pensive smile. There were no more happy hums or songs, and I became very worried when Ralph didn't show up for two days.

During the second evening, there was a soft knock on my door. Standing stoop-shouldered in the doorway was a red-nosed, shriveled old man who resembled so many other Tenderloin winos. He wore the usual frayed, wrinkled clothing and the smell of wine was heavy and familiar. Ralph had sometimes referred friends of his to me for help in filling out welfare papers or other documents. Not this time. I knew why the old man had come.

As the man talked, his eyes moistened into a river of tears that flooded his wrinkles and dripped from his chin.

"I thought I should tell ya, Ralph was found dead in his room. He said you were his friend."

"I was."

The old man stood silently looking down, when he added with a muffled sob, "He was my friend too."

After that comment, the dialog became awkward and superficial—probably because of my naïve, middle-class questions. "What did he die of?"

"I don't know, he's just dead."

"When is the funeral and where do I send flowers?"

"There's no funeral, he's in the morgue."

"No cemetery?"

"No, no cemetery."

When the old man finally left, I sat down feeling painfully sad, helpless and very stupid. I had a lot to learn about humanity, the Tenderloin and the expression of honest caring, no matter where you are. I was angry with myself for never having invited Ralph to dinner, and never knowing his last name. I didn't even know where Ralph had lived or the name of his grieving friend. I'll never know what caused his death, but I have a hunch grief had something to do with it.

When I left my apartment the next morning, after a night of restless reflections, I felt strangely less vulnerable and naive, more resilient, maybe even more adult. I walked slowly down the Tenderloin streets that day, looking carefully, more purposefully at the people. For the first time since moving into the Tenderloin, I began to smile and wave at all my neighbors. Their appearance didn't matter anymore.

Returning to my apartment that evening, the sidewalk under the boxes of pretty flowers was woefully dry. As my eyes again welled with tears, I realized I wasn't crying for the death of a Tenderloin wino, I was mourning the loss of a friend.

Several months later I moved to another place that favored new opportunities. Although I have often returned to my old Tenderloin neighborhood, the beautiful flowers gradually disappeared, leaving the two old rotting boxes filled with dirt, cigarette butts and other debris. Even the old brick building on Turk, so preciously steeped in Tenderloin history, is gone now.

I can't remember anything about my part-time job or the high school senior courses taken during that year. Yet, as some sort of personal memorial, I'll never forget my Tenderloin education. I learned beneath the shabby clothes, panhandling, distasteful smells, alcoholic mumblings, are people who love flowers, have loyalties, smile warmly and cry. I often think of Ralph and his big lovable dog, Mug. Then, with a deep sigh, I remember how I once considered winos parasites.

Like a kid's first love, Ralph was my first wino. He
helped me grow up in so many positive ways. I learned
about those ugly myths of wino stereotypes; and now
when I see a drunk I wonder, *what's he really like?*

Turk Street in the 40's when I met Ralph

Turk Street – 2000

3

RUDY

Everything Down the Hatch
But Meters & Coics

Similar to most of nature's creatures, we humans have an ingrained need to be with others of our species. Another need, especially peculiar to humans, is friendship—a simple term for a complex human phenomenon. Friendship is not a biological need like air, food or water; but psychologically, it may be far more essential to our humanity. Satisfying our basic biological drives nourishes our bodies and even strengthens our minds; yet satisfying our psychological need for friendship nourishes our memories and enriches our spirit. Our need for friends is hardly arguable. Defining what friends are made of is much more debatable.

There's an inexhaustible array of words in human history that chronicle our efforts to identify friendship. Acquaintance, companion, intimate, comrade, confidant, pal and even "homey" provide hints of what may define a friendship. Then there's the Mexican "amigo" suggesting we're all friends. Each of these historical ingredients offers a unique view of friendship—as something clearly personal. Like beauty, in order to understand friendship, we may have to peer through "the eye of the beholder."

My own view of friendship can't be defined intellectually. Friendship is an experience that takes years to recognize—longer to appreciate. That is why, for me, it's easier to describe friendship in a story.

Real friendships have been rare in my life, perhaps because I consider them so precious. Nevertheless, I'm grateful the first of those rare friendships began when I was a teenager, long before I recognized its beauty.

$$\square \quad \square \quad \square$$

"Everything down the hatch but meters and coics." Those impassive words echoed clearly down through the big mail chutes from the mezzanine floor above. It was my first day as a temporary Christmas helper at the Rincon Annex, San Francisco's main post office. It was within walking distance of the Tenderloin where, earlier in my brief life, I had spent some precious months growing up. Yet, at 18, I was inexperienced at just about everything worldly, including postal work. I probably didn't know the cost of a first class stamp. It's doubtful I had written any letters at that point in my brief life. That was my first year of college, and an athletic scholarship wasn't enough to cover all of my expenses. I really needed that job.

"Everything down the hatch but meters and coics."

I heard it again and I still hadn't the slightest idea what those words meant. One of the supervisors had taken me on a tour of the massive, noisy and dusty building that received and sorted hundreds of thousands of letters a week. Our last stop was the mezzanine floor, where I had been assigned to work. As the supervisor escorted me up the stairway, I began to identify the sounds of shuffling mail sacks and mail splashing into huge bins for sorting.

"Everything down the hatch but meters and coics."

At the top of the stairs were three men bent over an enormous metal tray filled with all kinds of mail. The supervisor pointed to the man with the postal badge.

"Rudy is in charge of this bin. He'll show you what to do. The other guys are temps like you. Good luck."

Before I could reply, the supervisor disappeared down the staircase. By that time Rudy, the one with the postal badge, looked up with a broad grin. He gave me a beckoning nod before he sorted a few more pieces of mail.

"I'm Larry, your new temporary employee," I said tentatively as though not sure what I was.

Rudy countered with a hardy laugh and firm hand-shake. He showed a searching, friendly stare. It was different from the usual casual glance when strangers first meet.

"Most of the time I don't know what's going on in here either. It's pretty hectic, especially during Christmas, but we'll take care of it together."

I found those few opening words reassuring.

Rudy sorted a few more pieces of mail then grabbed a big lever on the side of the bin. "Everything down the hatch but meters and coics."

"What does that mean?" I asked.

Rudy pulled the big lever when the other two temporary employees stepped back. That's when the whole table of mail slid down a metal chute. Then the table tilted back up into position as Rudy released the lever.

Rudy again smiled at me thoughtfully and sat on the edge of the mail bin. "I guess those words summarize the whole gig up here. We get mail from those conveyor belts, dump the bags on this table, sort out all the circulars and meter mail, which we throw down these little chutes."

As he talked, Rudy pointed carefully to all the chutes, belts and levers, acknowledging how simple and boring the job really was. "When all the circulars and metered mail have been removed, I say I'm going to drop all the other mail down the hatch. When the other guys and now you are finished sorting, you all step back, that's my signal to pull the lever."

At 18, I had a lot more questions, such as how to identify meter and circular mail, where do the chutes and belts go and where are the restrooms. I was also still a bit reluctant to ask about breaks and lunch.

Rudy answered all of my questions in clear detail, including those I didn't ask. "We get two morning and two afternoon ten minute breaks and a forty-five minute lunch break at 12:30. That's if you're interested." He laughed.

"Everything down the hatch but meters and coics. Now you know as much as I do." He laughed again and I felt good about my Christmas job and my new boss.

◻ ◻ ◻

That was my first contact with Rudy, one of the closest and most cherished friends in my life. The recipe for that friendship remains a bit puzzling. However, the irrelevant ingredients are much clearer.

Curiously, what initially attracts us to another person

probably has nothing to do with length or depth of friendship. In fact, such ingredients as physical appearance, mutual interests and intelligence may be irrelevant to friendship.

During our first mezzanine encounter, Rudy, in his mid-twenties, was unremarkable-looking. Moderately short and wiry, with a slightly concave chest, he would have been easily forgotten in a small crowd. His swarthy complexion was slightly acne-scarred and already creasing into wrinkles. His kinky black hair was also prematurely receding and his puffy cheeks and eyes blunted any possibility of striking features.

Rudy certainly wasn't handsome, or ugly. He was just a so-so-looking guy, who could have been mistaken for a light black or dark Latin. I never knew anything about his ancestry and it didn't seem to matter to either of us.

Rudy was also a high school dropout, with one child. He married his pregnant girlfriend, Doris, when they were both in the tenth grade. Aside from a brief career as a drummer, he had been working for the post office for almost eight years when I met him. Rudy and I had nothing in common to start with and physically we couldn't have been more different. Compared to Rudy, I was very tall and fair complexioned. Even our age disparity and marital status should have discouraged a positive alliance.

Despite our many differences, a genuine friendship had its improbable beginnings on that mezzanine floor. Reflecting back over those seven weeks as a Christmas temporary, probably the only thing Rudy and I did have in common was the mezzanine floor. There was also that stirring message, "Everything down the hatch but meters and coics."

Now, almost sixty years later, it seems the obvious

was truly obscure and the obscure is finally obvious. Rudy's physical appearance and mannerisms grew less apparent as our friendship grew more important. The building of our friendship was clearly related to Rudy's selfless human interests.

At lunchtime that first day on the job, Rudy wanted to know everything about me. I soon discovered that wasn't a patronizing gesture; he was really interested and eager to learn about all aspects of people and life. Never an athlete, and not much of a sports spectator, Rudy had endless, well-thought-out questions about my athletic scholarship, my skill as a football player and even the making of an athlete. Rudy, wide-eyed and attentive, made me feel very important, even though at 18, I wasn't important at all.

As a first semester college student, I knew little about academia. Other than football, I had no reason to be enrolled. Thanks to Rudy's probing questions, I began to grasp the importance of a college education. Rudy had a way of asking, "Why" that could expand a simple question into a search for the meaning of life.

"Why did you choose football?" "Why do we both prefer the Democratic Party?" "Why are teachers paid such low salaries?"

Rudy seemed to unwittingly encourage me to think, which in those days had been one of my least practiced activities. I must have learned more about myself and life from that high school dropout than from any of my undergraduate professors. Rudy was genuinely interested in everything except impressing others with his interests. If friendship has anything to do with listening to or learning from each other, Rudy and I were off to a great start, on that mezzanine floor.

I was always treated as a respected adult by Rudy, even when I was a teenager. Such humility may have been another building block toward our friendship. Unless I asked, Rudy rarely volunteered information about his personal experiences or accomplishments.

"There's not much you can learn from me, Larry, other than my blunders."

When pressed, however, he did tell me about his life as a musician, with its many pitfalls and about how the best of musicians succumb to drugs with the excuse it improved their music.

"Those cats were fools," Rudy added. "They just ruined their careers or their lives. That's one reason I got out. I didn't dig the drug scene." But Rudy did love drums and music.

I had always enjoyed rhythm, and once aware of that, Rudy playfully taught me about the art of drumming. When the big metal tray was empty, it became a huge drum. Together, we would tap out different drumbeats, while humming. I've never forgotten those rhythms. All it takes is big band music. Then my tables, cans and bottles become drums. But, they're still no match for the big metal tray.

📖 📖 📖

Several weeks on the job and I didn't know the names of the two other temporary workers. They frequently came in late, lengthened their lunch period and rarely talked to Rudy or me. They were both big, mean-looking guys in their thirties. They only talked in whispers and sometimes laughed privately with each other, as if mocking one or both of us.

"What's with those guys?" I asked during a break.

Rudy carefully scanned the mezzanine before answering. "They're friends of my boss, a supervisor who's worked for the post office forever. They work okay when they work, which, as you know, is pretty seldom. I've been told to give them some slack." He looked around again. "Only problem, I think they've been slitting some mail."

"You mean deliberately opening the mail?" I asked.

Rudy moved closer and softened his voice to a whisper. "I'm not positive, they're real slick. The scam is to slit open, generally with a razor blade, any letter that might have valuables, especially money. That's all I can say. It's just none of our concern. OK?"

I sipped my coffee and quietly nodded. I learned too soon, however, that Rudy's suspicions were about to ensnare me in a conspiracy that did become my concern.

Mail handlers had discovered some opened mail that postal inspectors traced back to the mezzanine. Aware of the investigation, Rudy's supervisor warned his friends, who coolly diverted attention from themselves, by reporting me. They informed inspectors that twice they saw me slit letters, but hesitated to become involved. As the prime suspect, I was last to know—I could be fired or worse, jailed.

Rudy was also unaware of the accusations against me and when interviewed by the inspectors, he denied knowing anything.

When finally questioned by the inspectors, I received my first terrifying revelation about life's injustices. They not only didn't believe my honest denials, they seemed to believe the real bad guys' lies. The inspectors did, however, arrange a second interview with Rudy, me and my accusers.

"Let me tell you again, I've never tampered with the mail, I'm not a thief," I protested. I was being glared at by those two thugs and at that point I didn't even care. All I could think about was going to jail for doing nothing wrong.

One of the accusers flicked a sour glance at me as he began growling, "He's a lying son-of-a-bitch. We saw him slit some mail."

That was too much for Rudy, who had been calmly listening. "Those are the only assholes in here," pointing to my accusers. "This kid's only been here three weeks, and now I'm sure I saw these guys tamper with the mail over two months ago."

Rudy was aware his eight years with the post office could be in jeopardy. He also knew he might be seriously beaten by those two bullies. They were mean, vindictive men and Rudy knew it.

Fortunately, I learned two other lessons that terrible day. The first was that justice could be unnervingly slow in coming. The mail handlers had reported letter slicing two months ago, following the hiring of my two accusers. I was off the hook, and Rudy and I were relieved. The second lesson for me was even more memorable. I learned from Rudy that loyalty is the very nucleus of a lasting friendship.

At the end of seven weeks, I received a pink slip announcing my termination as a post office temporary employee. The bad guys had vanished, never to bother us again, Rudy got a new supervisor and I had success-fully overcome my first glancing blow with the law.

I should have gotten a diploma instead of a pink slip, considering the rich education I received in such a brief period. I had learned about honesty, loyalty, courage, conspiracy and the onset of a friendship.

📖   📖   📖

Rudy lived in a pleasant two-bedroom apartment with his pretty, fair-complexioned, blond wife, Doris, and his cute, dark-haired, bright ten-year-old daughter, April.

Their apartment house was on Golden Gate, off Larkin, which qualified them as Tenderloin residents.

After the post office mezzanine, I enjoyed many evenings and weekends walking with Rudy and his little family. He knew the Tenderloin well as a neighborhood, and he often assured me during our walks, that the Tenderloin was probably as safe as and definitely more interesting than other San Francisco neighborhoods.

"If you want to get in trouble here, it's easy; but it's just as easy to stay out of trouble." Rudy seemed to know practically everyone in the Tenderloin, yet he wasn't involved with anyone. He even introduced me to some of the drug dealers, hustlers and prostitutes as we walked. "They're like everyone else in San Francisco. Their jobs are just different. We have a great relationship, Larry; they mind their business and we mind ours."

I always felt warmly relaxed walking the Tenderloin streets with Rudy. Maybe it had something to do with how he walked the streets with his family. I was deeply touched by the way Rudy held their hands as we strolled. He had been married to Doris over ten years, which hadn't dampened their show of affection. They still acted like childhood sweethearts, and April was always included in their hugs.

They were a strong, loving family of which I gradually became a member. I was "uncle" to April, "Larry" to Rudy and "Lawrence" to Doris. She remembered a comment I had made years earlier that no one had ever taken my desire to be called Lawrence seriously. She did.

As we all grew older, we saw each other less and oddly seemed to grow closer. April moved away after her marriage to an airline pilot; and I was drafted into the Korean War. That was when I discovered another criterion of friendship. When you're truly friends, absence does make the heart grow fonder.

Following my discharge from the service, I spent the next ten years primarily out of San Francisco in graduate school or overseas jobs. Our only correspondence was informational type letters about changes of address and health status. Otherwise, I would call Rudy when I returned to San Francisco, sometimes after several years. Rudy and Doris were never less than thrilled. As if their only son had returned from combat.

It didn't matter if I returned from Afghanistan in four years, or Sacramento in four months, the scenario was the same. A wonderful dinner with Rudy and Doris, their almost childlike excitement with my small gifts, an exhaustive summary of my trip at their insistence, coffee, doughnuts and steady conversation all evening. Then Doris would fall asleep on the sofa, as Rudy and I rambled until morning.

Unexpectedly, that return scenario changed dramatically in the winter of 1974. I had just returned from Washington, D.C. to some tragic news from Rudy. Physicians had discovered a malignant lump on one of Doris' breasts. At that time, double mastectomies were the medical trend and Doris was in the hospital waiting her turn.

Rudy was devastated, which devastated me. He rarely left the hospital and I canceled another trip to be nearby. Doris was calmly philosophical about her condition and the treatment. She and Rudy had over 40 years together, which is more than an average lifetime of romance.

"Besides," she grinned, "I sure don't need them for milk anymore."

During her long operation, Rudy and I sat in the hospital waiting room. He reminisced about his high school romance with Doris, the birth of April, their grandchild, Rudy Jr. and our long, endearing relationship. We even had a few laughs, lots of tears and waves of goose bumps.

In Doris' room, there were flowers everywhere and their friends and relatives seemed to be all over the hospital halls and waiting room.

"I never realized so many people cared about us." He slowly looked at me with a weak, red-eyed smile. "It's a lousy way to find out."

I put an arm around his shoulder and we quietly cried to ourselves.

What seemed like a lifetime of hours later, Doris was wheeled into her flowery room. The surgeon assured Rudy there was no malignancy left. Everyone wept happy tears. While I talked to some of their relatives and friends, Rudy sat silently by the bed watching his wife in deep sleep for the next three hours.

When she awakened, Rudy gently held her hand. He kissed her forehead and they shared smiling whispers for the next half hour, then he motioned me to enter the room. I was followed by a long procession of well-wishers. Gradually all, except Rudy, went home, relieved that Doris would recover.

The next morning I received one of the most shocking calls of my life. It was the frail, trembling voice of Doris. Rudy had gone home to shower and retrieve some of her personal belongings. A neighbor heard a loud crash. Rudy had fallen dead, holding Doris' overnight bag in his hand. My friend died of a cerebral hemorrhage, and Doris, shattered for months, was still in remission well into the nineties.

Rudy was my first and most valued friend. He taught me everything about friendship, without trying to teach me anything. Curiously, even now, when I think of my friend, the most vivid memory of us is on the mezzanine floor.

"Everything down the hatch but meters and coics."

I've sadly lost contact with Doris. Hopefully someday she'll come across this book, perhaps at some second-hand bookstore. Then I hope she finds this chapter and reads all about my gratitude for two friends I'll never forget.

4

BURT

Heroes

In our equal opportunity society, there's one certainty, opportunities are never equal. Both heredity's bounty and our parents' powerful influence tend to define the boundaries of our potential in pursuing our ultimate destiny. Born into a bright, rich, successful family with a robust gene pool and you will no doubt end up bright, rich and successful.

The opposite equally applies, and there's not much you can do about it. There's just nothing particularly heroic about obeying a prescribed destiny that inexorably opens or slams the doors of opportunity in one's face. Becoming an outstanding athlete when born with great abilities is certainly no more heroic than becoming an obscure bum when born with no abilities.

My heroes are generally mavericks of some sort who ignore destiny by getting up every time they're knocked flat into life's muck. Those are the unique individuals who positively change their lives or help others, not because they have orchestrated the opportunity, but because they have made the personal choice. They simply don't succumb to what is expected of them, which means they struggle to maintain control of themselves and their destinies. I've had the privilege of knowing a few of those individuals in my life. Burt was one of them.

📖 📖 📖

After I left my family and earlier Tenderloin memories behind, I continued to work on shaping my own future. There was more graduate schooling, some civil service positions and an exciting Peace Corps job that unveiled worldwide travel. That ten year odyssey provided me with all the experiences I thought I needed to launch a solid professional career.

Once back in San Francisco, I quickly discovered, to my delight, that all kinds of psychology positions were readily available. There were university teaching opportunities, secure civil service jobs and prestigious partnership options.

Harnessing that inner source of pride and accomplishment that follows a rich harvest, I merrily wandered the steep San Francisco streets. Bundled against the cold piercing winds, I was warmly emblazoned with fanciful images of $150-an-hour clients, standing-room-only lectures and professional awards galore. The Tenderloin was probably less than a fleeting thought at that time. I was on my way to fame and glory; at least that's what my imagination kept assuring me.

Then I got a call from a friend and colleague that innocently derailed my dreams of a richly distinguished professional career. It was one of those pleasant, yet forgettable phone conversations that I will never forget.

"Hey, Lar, whatcha been up to?"

That opening phrase, clear falsetto voice and impish chuckle left little doubt. It was Mike Diger. We had become good pals during graduate school, and even though we had repeatedly lost contact with each other over the years, all it ever took was one phone call to reawaken our solid friendship.

Mike was exceptionally young-looking, muscular and straightforward with plenty of street savvy. Yet employment as a civil servant in San Francisco never jaded him. His family and sports were his major interests and activities in life. As he used to say, he just needed a job to pay the bills.

We reminisced about grad school days, talked about my travels, his marriage, children and basketball games. He even dropped a few quick comments about his present job as director of Harriet Street Center, a drop-in clinic for alcoholics and other drug abusers. We had a good chat and then Mike mentioned the other reason for his call.

"Hey, Lar, I hear you're looking for a psyche job in San Francisco." Seemingly unimpressed by my comments about great job offers, he told me about Burt, an ex-wino and heroin addict.

Burt was director of Project Title XVI, a brand new drug substance abuse monitoring and treatment agency funded by the Federal and State governments. He needed a psychologist to facilitate and implement the clinical aspects of his program. However, Burt didn't just want a clinical psychologist. He wanted someone who knew the San Francisco streets and didn't mind breaking rules and regulations established by professional bureaucrats in Washington. Those were the authorities that knew nothing about drug abusers, street people or the Tenderloin where most of Burt's clients lived. Born into a dysfunctional, uneducated and un-inspiring alcoholic family, Burt's childhood training seemed to guide him relentlessly toward his early career as an uneducated, uninspired drug addict. Burt stumbled into his earliest Tenderloin career when he rolled up his sleeves to receive his first intravenous taste of heroin.

Like most hard-core addicts, it wasn't long before he was rolling up his pant legs in search of alternative veins. Burt quickly rose in Tenderloin status to a $300-a-day habit. That meant he was irrevocably hooked and in need of a second career.

At that time, his options were limited to stealing or dealing. He chose dealing heroin and other drugs. It was a supplemental career that lasted for many years. Burt prospered, with plenty of money to support his habit.

Then, like other mainline junkies, he had to face another problem money couldn't fix. He had run out of undamaged veins.

That must have been a turning point in Burt's life and a time to weigh other options. He did, by simply and remarkably kicking heroin and unremarkably shifting to a career of alcoholism.

Burt succeeded in epitomizing the disoriented, hard-core wino. He had transformed himself into a foul-smelling, thoroughly disheveled, glassy-eyed skid row bum. His home was the Tenderloin streets where he slept on the pavement. Burt's life was a disoriented blur. He was usually either out cold or helplessly struggling to maintain his balance. When conscious, he would stagger along the streets looking for other winos who might be willing to share a bottle. He never cared what he drank as long as it contained some kind of alcohol.

He belonged there and would never get out alive. Those were the sneering comments of many tourists he had offended with his crude attempts to hustle them for booze money. Ironically, there was a lot of truth in those tourists' observations. Somehow, Burt stayed in the Tenderloin, more often drunk than sober—for nearly forty years.

I had learned long before my phone conversation with Mike that kicking the chemical habit and lifestyle of a heroin user is rare. The body virtually refuses to give up heroin that has insidiously replaced many physiological protective mechanisms.

Burt must have known full well he would succumb to excruciating pain and discomfort if he gave up heroin. He did it anyway. Kicking the psychosocial habits associated with long-term drug use was less physiologically painful, but no less difficult. It's tough to trade old friends, acquaintances and routines for new ones. Besides, even if you keep your junkie friends, they won't let you change. Burt knew he had to change and he did.

Many critics would have mocked Burt as just another junkie who replaced one chemical with another. They'll even argue that it was an easy change to a similar lifestyle in his familiar Tenderloin. Any hardcore junkie would scoff at such criticism. In the Tenderloin drug community, any changes are incredibly rare. Besides, subsequently kicking alcohol and a skid row life doubles the incredible aspects of Burt's history.

I had no intention of working for an ex-bum and recovering addict, in the Tenderloin of all places. Nevertheless, I was genuinely impressed and intrigued by Mike's tale of a man who beat overwhelming odds and a hopeless destiny.

Mike had known Burt for years, and they were obviously close friends. Those were all good reasons to at least meet the man. Mike would set up a meeting.

He added with an audible snicker, "Lar, you won't
be disappointed."

He was right. During the fifteen years I worked with
Burt, I was never disappointed.

$$\square \quad \square \quad \square$$

Burt was in his early 60's when I first met him. I must
admit I was surprised the meeting was to take place in a
tavern, yet when I got to know him, I would have been
surprised if it hadn't. Burt didn't defy all odds and rise
from terminal junkie and wino to director of a federally
funded program because he was predictably ordinary.
Burt was anything but ordinary or predictable. That was
one of the major ingredients of Burt's charm. His un-
conventional surprises were never disappointing.

I was supposed to meet Burt at the Clement Street
Bar and Grill around twelve noon. When I arrived, I
found the place mobbed with an overflowing lunch
crowd. Even the entrance was bulging with a crush of
people, and I dreaded trying to find a man I didn't
know. Patrons were shouting, chuckling and arguing as
they hunched over drinks or milled about impatiently,
glancing at their watches while awaiting their tables in
the dining room.

Amazingly, Mike's brief description was all I
needed. Burt would have been easy to spot in any
crowd, and I had no trouble locating him. Seated at one
of the barroom tables was a well-dressed, casually
animated middle-aged man with black flecked, silver
gray curly hair, afro style of the 60's. He seemed to attract attention without even trying, especially from
nearby women, young and old. Burt transmitted such a
kaleidoscopic aura; he could have clearly been mistaken
for an elder statesman, a recycled hippie leader, a circus

ringmaster or James Cagney.

It was Burt all right. He shot a penetrating laser glance in my direction along with a silent, well-mouthed, "Larry?"

I found myself excitedly scurrying toward his table, as if granted an audience.

Nearing his table, I suddenly noticed everything about Burt seemed immense and overpowering, except his physical size. If he were to stand motionless, he would probably be described as a thin, well-wrinkled old man of about five feet four. However, since Burt personified perpetual motion and vitality, he was always a fascinating, craggy-faced, six foot eight—to me.

Burt beamed me a total-faced iridescent grin that instantly displayed his natural charm and open passion for people. There was nothing pretentious about his greeting, he just spontaneously seemed eager to see me.

I felt at ease already, even though I still hadn't reached Burt's table. In fact, when I finally neared his table through the swarm of people, I was again impressed with his energy and genuine humanity. I certainly hadn't expected Burt to so graciously leap from his seat and shake my hand with both of his. There was a profoundly warm message in his greeting that I have unconsciously tried to emulate. Even now, I use both of my hands to seal an otherwise indifferent handshake.

As we stood there by his table, Burt continued to shake my hand with a gentle firmness. He was staring searchingly into my eyes. Then, as if awakened from a hypnotic trance, he broke his concentration with another very warm welcoming smile.

"I finally get to meet you, Dr. Wonderling. Sit here, next to me."

It became apparent that Burt could effortlessly put

me at ease and still look me over as a perspective associate. He must have also sensed my curiosity about our meeting place. He dramatically looked around, leaned forward as if sharing a confidence and began to softly whisper in my ear.

"I've always liked a barroom atmosphere even though I haven't had a drink in years. Funny," he loudly added leaning back with a laugh, "when I did drink, I couldn't afford bars."

It didn't take long before I was unusually relaxed with this man, even though he was interviewing me for a job. I was also fascinated by his keen, laid back involvement with everything around him. He never seemed to miss the most subtle nuance of a comment or nearby conversation. Yet, there was nothing overbearing, suspicious or intense about Burt. He merely had a plain, unabashed interest in others.

At least half the bar crowd and, of course, all of the employees appeared to know Burt. He was easily able to non-verbally communicate with everyone while maintaining a close dialog with me. His clear blue eyes darted and danced all over the place in rhythm with his endless array of facial expressions and hand signals. All of his energetic gesturing was his way of acknowledging the smiles and waves from distance acquaintances. It didn't take long for me to figure out that Burt was indeed a ringmaster. During our long friendship, where ever Burt went, he could inadvertently generate his own circus of fans and performers.

There were also those residual behaviors of Burt's earlier days. He was a chain-smoker, probably using one match to start the day's chain. He said disgustedly, he had a five-pack-a-day habit.

His foul language was unrivaled, even by the worst tempered convict; yet, despite his drug career, he had never been arrested. He also had an explosive temper that was fortunately rare and quickly defused. Oddly, none of his worst traits diluted his charisma. Burt either charmed, inspired, frightened or frustrated those he knew. He even angered some, but I doubt he ever bored anyone.

"What are you going to have? Do you want something to eat?" Burt asked as he pulled on his cigarette, sipped his Calistoga mineral water and seemingly communicated with two cocktail waitresses and a bartender simultaneously. Before I could answer, one of the waitresses was looking down at Burt with a warmly adoring smile and a hand on his shoulder.

I finally managed a reply, "I'll just have coffee, please."

"One coffee coming up," she quickly said while still intently looking at Burt. Then she gently patted his shoulder, winked a good-bye and disappeared into the crowd.

I felt a little invisible in the shadow of Burt's charm. Yet, he was so likable, it didn't matter. I had no intention of ever competing with him, especially since he would no doubt always win.

When I meet someone, there's nothing more souring to me than a self-absorbed show of disinterest in what I have to say—the "me, me, me" type of person. They never remember your name, because there's no interest in you, or your insignificant name.

Burt was just the opposite from the start. Despite his gruff style, heavy smoking and swearing, he was an exceptionally sensitive listener. It was obvious, by the nature of his comments and questions, plus his riveting eye contact that he was always trying to grasp every word and idea. That was another aspect of his charm.

Chatting away over a half dozen cups of coffee and

Calistogas, Burt and I lost track of time. Everything I said seemed important to him, and he was never challenging or patronizing. We shared treatment biases, endless Tenderloin street stories, jokes and even political views. I was beginning to sense the onset of a long, lasting friendship. I knew I could learn a great deal from a man who devoted half of his life to using drugs that practically killed him, and the other half in trying to save other drug users from killing themselves.

Burt didn't know it at the time, but he was also a true pioneer. He was a forerunner and champion in the field of drug substance abuse and alcohol treatment. He talked of such insightful, sophisticated concepts as holistic programs with mega-vitamin therapy, work and education projects, social transition groups, AA, etc. He also clearly recognized that no two abusers were the same. He used to say, placing all clients in the same treatment program was "stupid." He was right.

Burt knew that a comprehensive psychosocial profile was needed to provide each client with a program that only fit him as an individual. Ironically, it's clear to parents that not every kid likes *m & m*'s as a reward. That simple notion is still unclear to treatment programmers who believe every alcoholic likes AA.

Burt had spent years preaching those ideas to anyone willing to listen. His sermons were widely known long before comprehensive drug programs were fashionable, financially profitable or—his biggest stumbling block— politically endorsable. He was an alcohol and drug substance abuse treatment activist. Even though no one seemed to care, he kept talking, arguing and pleading with any audience, especially politicians. Burt's mission continued until the day he died.

📖   📖   📖

Characteristic of his crusty candor, were Burt's many stories about the "good old days." It didn't take much to get him started. Once when I complimented him on how young he looked, he dimmed his smile with a frown.

"You should have seen me twenty-five years ago, covered with my own shit, crawling with lice and almost too weak to take another hit on the jug. Lying there in some fucking Tenderloin alley, I finally figured I'd either blow my brains out or get out of the shit hole I'd buried myself in."

Burt moaned and complained a lot about his self-destructive past and life's many injustices. Yet, it didn't take long to realize that his complaints were honest expressions of frustration, not self-pity. Discussing some of his more painful self-disclosures, Burt used to frequently heave a deep sigh, throw his head back and with hands in the air, ask the ceiling why he had become so "damned introspective" with age.

Then he'd glance at me with a big grin. It was so clear to Burt, he had been there, at the very bottom of the heap and he knew what needed to be done to help others climb out. Burt also knew that, as director of a treatment and monitoring program, the bureaucrats were more concerned with monitoring than treatment.

📖 📖 📖

The dinner patrons were starting to mosey up to the bar when Burt and I realized our initial noontime chat had blossomed into a riveting four and a half hours.

"Have you run out of gas?" Burt playfully asked.

I looked around the barroom, whimsically feeling I had been in an exciting time warp for several hours. "Not me, I'm thoroughly enjoying this."

The more Burt engaged me and others that first day,

the more I liked him. Also, the more he told me about his life, work and goals, the less interested I was in a conventional and possibly prestigious career in psychology. Burt left no doubt about what he needed in a psychologist. His requirements would have provoked a hardy laugh or a whimpering retreat by most psychologists I knew.

I've always supported the underdog, maybe because I was always the underdog as a child. So, when Burt stressed his need for a clinical advocate for those poor skid row bums and not a "rules and regulations drone," I was hooked, and not on drugs. In the same breath, he said he wanted a "street savvy shrink who wouldn't take any shit from Tenderloin hustlers." I was still hooked.

As I recall, Burt never formally offered me the job, which isn't too surprising since Burt wasn't a fan of formality. He told me later that once he decided he liked me, all he had to do was honestly explain himself and the type of program he wanted. "I knew you'd accept," he added, "I just knew."

During our many years together, the pay was MediCal and Medicare low, the surroundings were usually the Tenderloin and the biggest irritant was combat with bureaucratic regulations. In retrospect, working for Burt was always a challenge, typically frustrating and never regrettable.

⌨ ⌨ ⌨

When I started, our office was on the second floor of an old Clement Street building. Directly below, on the first floor, was a grocery store. Next door, was a boutique, then a flower shop, another grocery store and a dry cleaner. Businesses didn't seem to last long there, which may have had something to do with our smelly, grubby-looking clients. They frequently paced, stumbled, staggered and occasionally urinated in front of the various businesses, while awaiting their appointment.

Upstairs there were seven large offices accommodating four counselors, a secretary, receptionist and me. Burt's room, in the front, was more than large, it was mammoth. His mahogany desktop was as large as some small dance floors, and his wall-length couch could comfortably seat seven or eight. The office contained several other enormous leather chairs. Sitting on one shrank you to the size of a tiny dwarf. Also, his super thick wall-to-wall carpet seemed to give everybody a stumpy look as their shoes were sucked beneath the long, loosely-woven fibers.

Then there was his ashtray. It was about the size of a manhole cover. I doubt if anyone had ever seen the bottom of it. That enormous ashtray always had about a four inch covering of cigarette butts. I estimated 10,000, and Burt never debated my guess. He would just look disgustedly at the huge heap of ashes and butts. "I kicked heroin and booze, but not these."

A little less conspicuous, but no less imposing in size was his enormous baseball bat, leaning against a wall behind his overstuffed chair. The bat was of the "Louisville Slugger" period and it represented the street-survival side of Burt. It was a weapon.

"If any of these drunks pushes me too hard, I'll crack their fucking heads open," he would growl. Rumors were that he had busted plenty of kneecaps in his early Tenderloin days.

I uneasily remembered those same rumors one busy Monday morning when Burt was handling a frustrating client. It was a hectic day for all of us, with ten to fifteen clients awaiting initial interviews or psychological testing and an assortment of special interviews by Burt.

Three closed doors and about twenty-five feet of hallway separated my office from Burt's. It was a sturdy, thick-walled old building that blocked normal adjacent room sounds from penetrating my office walls. That provided a nice confidential setting for clients being interviewed by counselors or myself.

I quickly learned, however, that Burt's more explosive outbursts were anything but normal sounds. When enraged, Burt's voice could erupt into wall-piercing volleys. His bellows could trigger a tsunami wave of undulations that shattered everything in its path, especially eardrums.

On that particular Monday, his rage was unnerving to everyone in the office and probably some innocent bystanders outside. I could practically feel, as well as hear, Burt's ragings—an unsettling clue that his decibel count was off the scale. I again thought of his baseball bat, those kneecap rumors and his precarious short fuse.

Barney was a big hulking, brain-damaged shell of a man. He resembled a huge empty oil drum or an ex-professional boxer who had lost too many fights by knockouts. Years of alcoholism had seriously damaged his short-term memory and decision-making processes, as well as his balance and general orientation. His stumbling, shuffling gait, with a tendency to sway side-ways in a zigzag fashion, was typical of burned-out skid row drunks. Poor old Barney looked drunk even when he was sober, and his damage was irreparable.

Although ornery in his younger days, at 50 he was meek and mild-mannered. He looked 90-years-old and he could barely handle his life, let alone his finances. Like a child, he would sometimes harmlessly shout if denied a request or when scolded. He still shared a bottle with other Tenderloin winos. Barney also had frequent epileptic seizures that were beyond the control of medications because of his continued drinking. It was apparent, Barney would have been better cared for in an institution, yet it was equally apparent he might not have been better off.

I knew Barney was Burt's first interview and when I felt and heard those thundering salvos, I thought, *poor Barney.*

Barney's slurred words were barely audible, while Burt's voice crackled cleanly through my wall like machine gun bursts.

"You God damn bastard, you've blown every cent of your money..." "Don't give me any of your bullshit..." "Not a fucking cent..." "You're a loser..." "Horse shit..." "Shut up..." "I said shut up..." "This bat...break your head."

After a brief silence it started again.

"A what? Keep your God damn mouth shut... or detox...you asked for what you got..." "After I bust your skull and throw you down the stairs; I never want to see you again..." "Why you..."

Then there was an alarming dead silence like the eye of a hurricane, followed by some crashing furniture and even a deeper silence.

I and some of the counselors had on a few occasions muscled a drunk or belligerent client out the door at Burt's request. This time, however, was different. I'd never heard such rampaging anger coming from Burt's office. I also knew better than to interrupt. He'd always said he'd call if needed, but in this case I was more worried about the other guy.

About ten minutes later, while in the hall on my way to a filing cabinet, Burt's door flew open and out staggered old Barney. As he shuffled by me, I flashed a concerned smile that Barney returned.

"Hiya, Doc Wundalun."

After asking about his health and getting his usual, "I allays fine," I was relieved.

"Do you have enough money to get you back to the Tenderloin?"

With another of his bewildered-looking smiles, Barney said all there ever again needed to be said about Burt's temper or what happened in his office, "I don' stan too good. I fell on his table an broke sommin. I'm OK, I guess I ain't got no mo' money 'is month, so Burt gave me twenny dolla."

📖 📖 📖

Like an old gunslinger, Burt died several years later at the age of 78, with his boots on, cigarette in hand, bitching about something, while preparing for another of his endless drives to Sacramento to fight for his Tenderloin drunks.

His dream was for a large treatment facility where no drug abuser, no matter how broke or hopeless, could be denied admission. He had envisioned a retirement home type community atmosphere, where every burned-out drunk was given a job to match what was left of his abilities. It was going to be a sheltered place to share in developing their own personal treatment plan, while learning how to care for each other.

Burt's dream never materialized, maybe because it was too early or too ambitious. But then again, speculations don't really matter. It was Burt's chosen destiny in life; and his influence is still felt in the Tenderloin drug treatment community.

During his memorial service at the San Francisco General Hospital, there was an unprecedented standing-room-only crowd of Tenderloin drunks, police, medical personnel, politicians and, of course, barmaids, all expressing their sorrow through tears and eulogies.

Burt was a father-surrogate to his skid row family. He was a perpetual irritant to the Washington, D.C. and Sacramento bureaucrats who had vainly tried to ignore him. He was a pioneer in the treatment of drug substance abuse long before it was either fashionable or profitable. Burt was also a true friend, who taught me a great deal about honor, compassion and courage. He's still my hero.

I'll bet one reason I included Burt in this book was to keep him alive and heroic in the minds of all who knew him. Printed true stories tend to immortalize their characters; otherwise the "Burts" I have admired would vanish—as if each of those heroes hadn't existed at all. The heroic deeds of Gandhi, Martin Luther King, Jr. and Rosa Parks may live on forever; while lesser known heroes are forgotten without reminders. So, seventeen years after his death, Burt Trammel remains alive and well in my book of memories.

5

RJ

The Exception

Can a psychotherapist ethically develop a friendship with a client, hire a client to do some work or report exaggerated psychological symptoms to help a client keep his disability benefits? Whereas, the *letter of the law* shouts "absolutely not," the *spirit of the law* says "sure."

Similar to all professionals serving people, psychotherapists have a code of ethics and rules of conduct. Those represent the *letter of the law* established to protect the people. Yet, why do clients need protection from the professionals rigorously trained to care for and protect them?

The answer seems imbedded in the term "risk management." It is a professional liability concept that isn't particularly concerned with client protection. It's about protecting the psychotherapist from lawsuits. Risk management has absolutely nothing to do with effective psychotherapy. Even a beneficial therapeutic session in a restaurant can be potentially harmful—to the psychotherapist. Whether such treatment helps the client is irrelevant. That underscores another flaw in those rules of conduct to protect "people." Psychotherapists don't treat "people;" they treat individuals.

The term "people" is an abstraction—only the individual is a real person. So, in treating the individual, there will invariably be exceptions to those exhaustive people rules. Mandates for the good of the people rarely fit the needs of the individual. No one knows that better than a psychotherapist trying to help each client.

As I look back over the many years of my practice, it's all too obvious. I could have never totally complied with the *letter of the law*. Too many of my unique individual clients were those "exceptions" to today's written rules of treatment conduct.

◫ ◫ ◫

Just before passing on my practice to a colleague, I sat alone in my office reminiscing about past clients and their frequent need for treatment exceptions—especially those of the Tenderloin. Gazing at the empty leather armchair directly in front of me, I felt a sense of loss. I had bought the chair in San Francisco over twenty years earlier. It was light cream then, with a rich immaculate look and the unmistakable odor of newly-tanned leather.

The chair is much darker now, like the indelible shadows of clients etched into its grain. Over a hundred clients of all sizes and shapes sat in that chair uneasily—staining the leather with tears, smiles, laughter and endless stories. That was my clients' chair during their fifty-minute therapy hour; and yet, many died before they were ready to relax in the chair, feeling better about themselves. The old chair revived memories of my years with Project Title XVI; the first federally funded agency monitoring substance abusers receiving Supplemental Security Income (SSI).

When I first started working with my friend, Burt Trammel, most of our clients were considered unamenable to any form of treatment. Virtually all had gone through every available program with no significant changes other than further brain damage—as they continued to abuse drugs.

Those clients were housed in Tenderloin flophouses. They didn't mind. Most of them were beyond the point of caring where they lived or whether they lived. They were all different, yet similar in their sense of hopelessness. Complying with the letter of the law hadn't worked. Those were the exceptions to the rules.

My old, tired leather chair had also cradled clients with strange behaviors unrelated to drugs. Those clients weren't necessarily psychotic; they were just exceptionally peculiar. They were usually referred by other agencies or professionals who didn't know what to do with them.

Betty was one of those peculiar exceptions. I easily remembered her by the two missing leather buttons on an arm of the chair. Wearing her blue crystaled armor, Betty would pick nervously at the buttons until they fell off. She was a loner who believed in white magic. Betty knew a horrible death awaited her without the protection of the blue crystals she had sewn into a full-bodied undergarment. It must have weighed fifty pounds.

Then there was George, in his late twenties. He had epileptic seizures during every session, followed by an impulse to steal items from my office.

Today, the old chair represents a huge scrapbook of memories. It's difficult not to remember retarded Jerry, in his fifties. He would approach women anywhere to play with their breasts while he played with his penis. He also liked sitting in the chair, playing with his penis.

The old chair dredged up dozens of other exceptions, including Jack the finder, Pete the peeper, Dennis the flasher and RJ, a special exception who had managed to survive, despite overwhelming obstacles.

◫　◫　◫

My first office on Clement Street with Burt Trammel was nicer than I had expected, especially when I added those two brand new leather chairs, one for me and the other for my clients.

I had barely finished arranging the chairs when I got my first seven Tenderloin referrals. All had been treatment failures. Those were the first of many clients to occupy my new chair, and when writing the first edition of this book, RJ was the only one of the seven still alive. It just doesn't seem like nearly four decades have passed since I first met RJ.

◫　◫　◫

Historically, that was when George Moscone, an old high school pal, was a charismatic, happy San Francisco mayor; and Harvey Milk was a courageous member of the San Francisco Board of Supervisors, loved by his gay community. That was also about the time I happened to see the mayor in Polo's Restaurant in the Tenderloin.

"How do you like being Mayor?" I asked.

"It's really fun, Larry." he replied.

A few days later, both Mayor Moscone and Supervisor Milk were slain in their City Hall offices by

Dan White, a disgruntled ex-supervisor.

Supervisor Dianne Feinstein was appointed mayor, and I was becoming a therapist and advocate for Tenderloin drunks and crazies on SSI.

On the fringe of the Tenderloin, the once
popular Polo's Restaurant–now closed

"An RJ is here to see you." The receptionist was trying out the new intercom system linked to each office.

"Thanks send him in." Waiting for him, I was wondering what he would be like. Would he be drunk or sober, aggressive or passive, obnoxious or pleasant?

"Thump, thump, thump," it seemed like one of those faint knocks of hesitancy. I'd find out in a moment. *If I'm right about his hesitancy, I can't blame him*, I thought.

"Come in," I shouted, using my kindest voice. After one of those interminable pauses, I figured he might have changed his mind. Then the door began to creep open, like the reluctance of his knock. I decided not to ask him in again. He might panic and run for it.

Finally, as the door inched along the hardwood floor, four fingers of a hand appeared on the door's outer edge, followed by half a head.

"Dr. Wonderland?"

By that time, I was out of my chair trying to assist with the door opening drama. "That's me. Come on in. I promise I won't bite."

Standing awkwardly in the middle of the room, RJ stared at the floor with a vague, embarrassed smile.

"Here, sit in one of my new leather chairs," I added with more kindly encouragement.

He quickly complied with an obedient, "Yes sir," that could have been "Yes officer" or "Yes warden."

This, I thought, *is a guy who knows how to approach anybody who seems like an authority, with caution, respect and a lot of distance.*

Sinking into the new chair, RJ looked around the room, still gazing well below my eye level, and I pondered his shyness. At least physically, he had no reason to be shy. He was a nice looking man, in his twenties, of average height. He had a solid, well-proportioned build and smooth coordinated movements.

He certainly doesn't look disabled, I thought. I had noticed, however, a missing index finger on his left hand, well-chewed fingernails and sweaty palms that practically dripped.

As I explained my readiness to help him make a more satisfying life for himself, he seemed to listen carefully yet without any eye contact or reply. I wasn't sure he understood what I was saying. Then I realized that what I had just said was a bit presumptuous.

"Maybe your life is quite satisfying now. Is it okay as-is?" I asked.

RJ looked directly into my eyes and paused thoughtfully. "No, not really. Not at all."

That was my first hint that he might be motivated to change despite his many treatment failures in the past. His brief comment also suggested he clearly understood what I was saying. I was starting to feel good about RJ's potential and curious about his initials.

"What do the initials RJ stand for?" I asked.

After soberly pondering the question for a few moments, he raised his hands slightly and shrugged his shoulders, like a kid who didn't have the correct answer for his teacher. "That's really the only first name I know," he finally replied.

By the fourth session, my notes were beginning to form a behavioral portrait. I considered him a soft-spoken, mild-mannered, unusually timid person, with average intelligence and retarded social skills.

Shy, quiet and uneasy relating to others, RJ spent much of his time in the Tenderloin falling down drunk. His index finger had been amputated a year earlier. He had failed to care for an infected cut during one of his prolonged drinking episodes. He had been in many residential alcoholic treatment programs, each one followed by an immediate drunk when released.

RJ's arrest record contained three pages of misdemeanors for public drunkenness, and his employment record was equally long and disastrous. He had been repeatedly fired for intoxication, while the longest job he had held in three years was for six days.

There, in agency records and my notes, was the sadly obvious conclusion. For RJ, alcohol was a disinhibitor. It enabled him to be more relaxed and gregarious around people. There was simply no reward for lengthy sobriety. His "unamenability to treatment" designation was understandable. There's just no fun being shy, socially awkward and sober. Along with shy and awkward, comes the inevitable lack of self-esteem and confidence. That made sobriety even worse.

In four sessions, I thought I had a firm grasp on his problems, even though his records began only three years previously. What he was like before that period was a mystery, but I assumed it wasn't much different from his current lifestyle.

RJ had also been vague about his past. Yet, I figured that wasn't particularly unusual for alcoholics with limited memories and plenty of shame. In any event, it was apparent that all those expensive alcoholic treatment programs in the past hadn't worked. "Staying sober," not "getting sober" was the immediate problem. Until he could find satisfaction in sobriety, RJ would keep retreating into booze. Being sober because one is supposed to isn't a good reason for anything, especially for staying sober.

Nevertheless, I was thrilled with RJ's improved eye contact, spontaneity and openness in such a few sessions. Like magic, psychotherapy seemed to be working.

Later, however, I learned progress had nothing to do with magic or psychological theories per se. It was really all about two people talking and listening to each other. Playing therapist didn't work either. After repeatedly bungling attempts to mimic my clinical heroes, it gradually dawned on me, being a therapist was being myself—the only role I really knew how to play well.

Then, after three months of treatment, I was disappointed to learn his progress was confined to the office. A few nights after RJ's twelfth session, I had a satisfying Italian dinner at Original Joe's on Taylor Street. Returning through the Tenderloin to my car, I noticed somebody staggering toward me, which isn't unusual in the Tenderloin.

Poor guy, I thought, *I wonder if he could be one of my clients.* Then I saw his face. "Damn it all," I said to myself, "it's RJ."

"Dr. Wonnerlan, Dr. Wonnerlan," he slurred as he lunged forward, grabbing a nearby pole to keep from falling, "I dinna wan to see you like this." Disheveled, glassy-eyed and swaying on the pole, RJ managed to remove his old watch. "Pleash, Dr. Wonnerlan, I gotcha have a couple dollars…heresh my watch, take it, I can't hock it…pleash."

I quickly gave RJ a five-dollar bill, took his watch and offered no therapeutic comments. He was too drunk to reason with. Anyway, the last thing he needed was a sermon. He needed a drink.

Two weeks later, RJ crept into my office sober, contrite and very apologetic. "I'm really embarrassed, Dr. Wonderland, I'm sorry you saw me like that."

I removed his watch from my desk and read aloud the inscription on the back. "I'm proud of you. Mother."

"Here's your watch and I need five dollars. Then why don't we talk about your mother and why she was so proud of you?"

RJ gave me the five dollars, slipped his watch back on his wrist and told me about his single parent mother, who had attended all of his high school basketball games when he was a star. He talked of a drunken father he never knew, a younger brother who was murdered and the woman he intended to marry. She OD'd on heroin during one of their many drug sprees.

Those were personal, painful disclosures I didn't know and RJ had been reluctant to tell. Surprisingly, finding him drunk in the Tenderloin marked the real onset of therapy for him. Even with his re-start, there were no quick fixes, no sorcerers' magic and no shamans' healing incantations. There was just a unique relationship between client and therapist, which may weave a bond of trust—that gateway to eventual progress.

Almost a year after RJ's Tenderloin drunk, I was waiting for some clear signs of improvement. There weren't any. Instead, there were more relapses and increased withdrawal from social activities when sober. He was uneasy in any group and so shy, he quickly backed down in any argument. Awaiting signs of therapeutic progress is like watching the proverbial grass grow. If the seeds are nourished with trust and patience, change will happen—eventually.

At least, RJ was exposing painful bits and pieces of his struggle, but only within the safety of my office. Gradually, I had become a special friend. He was learning that I was trying hard to understand, help and never hurt him. Other faint wisps of progress were the tears of frustration when he shared memories of his past. Somehow his errant behavior had contributed to his mother's despair and to the death of his woman and brother.

Seeing RJ cry was a privilege for me and a right of passage for him. Tears are not necessarily beneficial in treatment. Some clients routinely cried their way through years of therapy. Others associated emotions with weakness, which blocked any thoughts that might beckon tears. After a dry year of therapy, RJ's tearful comments were a relief to both of us.

Transferring just a fragment of his trust to others was still a major therapeutic obstacle. He hated the Alcoholics Anonymous (AA) meetings he was required to attend. At meetings RJ coped with his resentment in silence by avoiding all confrontations. He also sat near the exit, so he could be the first out the door after a meeting.

Herded into a room jammed with strangers in various stages of alcoholic recovery, was below the bottom of the list of helpful therapy for RJ. AA is an exceptionally beneficial treatment adjunct for many and a disaster for others. The trick is knowing the difference. That didn't matter much in California. All SSI alcoholics were forced to attend AA meetings.

Timid, mild-mannered RJ rarely blamed others for his problems. Yet he often mentioned his urgent need for a drink after AA meetings. For years he had been listening to confessions, testimonies, incomprehensible mumblings and sermons. Those speakers were advocates, born-agains, falling down drunks and overbearing extroverts who just liked to talk.

They were irritants he managed to tolerate, until it was his dreaded turn to say, "My name is RJ and I'm an alcoholic." That was his moment of terror, when usually his awkward decline mercifully satisfied the group. Sometimes, however, his request was unmercifully challenged. Some insensitive secretary (the AA person in charge of the group) would badger RJ into introducing himself. After such a meeting, he ran for the nearest bottle.

AA in the 60's was the premier treatment for alcoholics, even if those classified had other diagnoses. At that time, alcoholism wasn't the central problem of most of my clients. Their drinking was symptomatic of more severe psychological disorders. Some of those clients were so withdrawn, they were afraid to leave the security of their room. Others had terrible paranoid suspicions. Regardless, they were forced to attend AA, in a room filled with menacing-looking strangers. I finally decided I had to do something about it. I first launched a campaign of letters and phone calls to the Department of Social Services (DSS). My request was simple and my reasoning clear. Waive the AA requirement when a therapist believes a client is harmed by the meetings.

After numerous calls to anyone, followed by numerous referrals to everyone else, I was finally able to talk to someone who actually listened. She must have been where the "buck stops."

The voice was soft, soothing and disappointingly patronizing as she droned her reply, "I'm sorry, sir, we don't make the rules, we follow them. Try contacting your state legislator."

A few days later, a letter from DSS had the same message. *A dead end,* I thought. Then the big contradiction dawned on me.

Although AA is supposed to be anonymous, many clients were ordered by SSI or the courts to have their attendance verified. Those clients were required to have a card signed by an AA secretary after each meeting. I had assumed the success of AA, "Friends of Bill," was based on anonymity and free choice. At meetings, it was ludicrous to watch the majority of attendees line up at the end of the meeting to have their cards signed. So much for the "anonymous" in AA.

Responses to calls and letters to the AA national headquarters in Washington, DC were gratefully prompt and frustratingly vague. The agency agreed that their success had a lot to do with its anonymity and voluntary attendance.

The director added, with a big however, "We can't defy the orders from courts or states." Then the director explained absently, that each AA chapter could refuse to sign cards—"even though most comply."

My next question was instantaneous, "How does one start a chapter?"

A week later I announced to RJ and other clients the official opening of our own AA chapter. Adding a dash of ceremony, I decreed that their cards would be signed by me, even if they never attended. I found a small basement meeting room a short walk from the Tenderloin. The room was available one hour a week and, to my astonishment, RJ and four other clients began attending the newly formed "Sober Fun" AA chapter. Their comments reassured me that I might have made the right decision.

They came for a variety of personal reasons. There was no religious emphasis, the group was tolerably small, they didn't have to go if they didn't want to and the goal of this new chapter made sense. "How can you enjoy sobriety in San Francisco, alone and on a small income?"

Quietly listening to the other four members, RJ offered his opinion with a gentle, reflective smile. "Besides, Dr. Wonderland, it's really our chapter."

Attendance was never a sellout crowd, twelve or thirteen at the most. Yet in over the twenty years of my practice, attendance never fell below the original five, all of whom had become good loyal friends. It wasn't long—a matter of a few months—before I realized that the core group really didn't need a leader. They had learned to rely on and help each other.

Shortly after the start of "Sober Fun," some mysterious elf-like things started happening. My car that was dirty in the morning was shining clean when I left my office. Although I had no janitorial service, my office was mysteriously clean.

I was beginning to wonder if elves existed, until I returned to my office one evening for some papers.

RJ was the elf. Embarrassed, he pitifully tried to convince me he hadn't taken anything.

"RJ," I said, "each time I learn something else about you, I'm amazed."

RJ blanched, "I just had to do something to repay you, Dr. Wonderland."

As RJ became increasingly secure in the "Sober Fun" group, he was faced with a dilemma. His benders diminished—while his social timidity intensified. Drunk, he could always find a loose woman who enjoyed his happy temperament and good sense of humor. When sober, he bored loose women and when drunk, he annoyed the proper ones.

After a long pause, RJ raised his eyes to the ceiling with one of his thoughtful smiles. "You know, Dr. Wonderland, when I'm sober, I can't even buy a shirt in a nice department store without getting all shaky and smearing everything with my sweaty hands."

Something was still blocking his sober, social development. It was obvious to me, conservative "risk management" treatment strategies just hadn't worked. He needed a gradual, safe exposure to situations he feared—a sort of "desensitization process." That's when we decided to move our office sessions to the streets. There would be field trips to department stores, shopping malls, marinas or anywhere else he chose.

I appreciated RJ's elfish expressions of gratitude for the new AA chapter. So, as our first field trip, I wanted to repay him with a dinner.

RJ agreed to meet me at Original Joe's, one of my favorite nearby restaurants. When I approached, he was squatting against the restaurant wall, staring vacantly between his knees at the sidewalk. I could practically feel his uneasiness, yet once he saw me, RJ leaped up with a toothy smile.

"Dr. Wonderland, I just got here. I appreciate this. I was waiting for you..."

His nervous chatter was a reminder that, away from the security of the office, he needed my support more than ever. I had never seen him wearing a tie or sport coat, and on that particular occasion, I wished I still hadn't. Those old, used clothes were as out-of-style as he no doubt felt. Standing next to RJ, with my casual leather flight jacket and Levi's, I was starting to become upset as well. I realized I hadn't adequately prepared him for such an experience. Dining at a nice restaurant was comfortable to me and alien to him.

Still a fine place to eat, unless you've swallowed the Tenderloin's reputation

"Did I dress right for the restaurant?" he asked.

"Fine," I replied, as I patted him on the back with a gentle nudge toward the entrance.

Thankfully, the restaurant wasn't crowded, which permitted quick seating at an obscure booth away from the bar and waiting area. The last thing either of us needed was loud, pretentious barroom banter or idle waiting area indignities about Tenderloin bums.

RJ stared unfocused at the back of the waiter's head as we were escorted to the end booth. When I sat down, RJ paused for a moment, until I nodded in the direction of the seat opposite me. He quickly complied with a slide into the seat, while looking startled when the waiter said, "Bon appetite."

RJ gave me a wide-eyed "what did that mean?" glance.

"That was French," I explained. "Some waiters get a little fancy. It means something like 'have a good appetite.' But most waiters just say 'enjoy your meal'."

RJ paused for a moment as he played with his napkin, "I heard something like that on the TV or radio. I never knew what it meant. Thanks, Dr. Wonderland."

Although I gave RJ the seat that provided an overall view of the restaurant, he rarely looked up, other than a sheepish glance at the occasional hovering waiter or busboy. I had also anticipated his reluctance to order. He looked carefully at the menu with no comment. Finally I had to ask the critical question.

"What would you like to eat and drink? Remember, this meal's on me and it's just a small payback for all your work."

As I expected, he was only willing to mention the least expensive and most familiar item. "I see they got hamburgers and French fries. Is that okay, with some coffee?"

"Sure," I said. "If it's okay with you, I'll also order you a plate of spaghetti. Don't worry, if you can't finish it, you can take it home."

RJ ate everything around him, including the bowl of grated cheese. Instead of sprinkling the cheese, he hungrily poured it on his plate of spaghetti until the bowl was empty—several times.

He was probably the most grateful guest I've ever had, with his "Boy this is good" and "Thank you, Dr. Wonderland," between mouthfuls.

I had the big platter of spaghetti and raviolis; and between us, we probably munched away ten pounds of sourdough bread, a couple of pots of coffee and enough grated cheese to serve the entire restaurant.

That first session out of my office started a bit shaky, but once it turned into an eating frenzy, I was delighted with the first field trip choice. RJ ate with the enthusiasm and energy of a sumo wrestler. As he ate, there was no timidity or inhibition, no holding back. He was just having a great time shoveling in the food.

By the time we had downed our last morsels, RJ even seemed genuinely content, without a trace of un-easiness. His hands were surprisingly dry as he offered a self-assured smile and thank you when a waiter brought another serving of bread.

When all the food was gone, however, his spon-taneity and self-confidence followed. He sank lower in his seat and resumed speaking with a soft hesitancy. He also avoided eye contact with any one but me.

As I looked at his hands, he turned his palms toward his face. Then he nodded slowly. "They're getting kind of damp again, huh."

I agreed, but with a dash of reassurance. "Yeah, but don't forget your hands were dry in this restaurant for over an hour. That must be some kind of a record for you."

It was dark when we finally left after two hours in Original Joe's. While I was paying the check near the front counter, RJ had already escaped. He had slipped outside unnoticed, where he stood against the wall waiting for me. He looked worn out, yet relieved, as if he had survived an ordeal.

"Well, what do you think of these field trips?" I asked, noting his hasty retreat.

"I'm sorry I left before you, Dr. Wonderland. I really needed some fresh air fast." Then he added in nearly a whisper, "I guess being in places I'm not used to is helpful, and the food was sure great. Maybe not as long the next time?"

Again, I had to agree.

We walked up Taylor Street in silence for the next three blocks. RJ turned left on O'Farrell toward his nearby apartment, as I continued to walk up Taylor another couple of blocks to my parked car. We shook hands and I couldn't help notice, his palms were still wet.

"Take care, RJ. Call me if you need me. Otherwise, I'll see you next week."

Typical of him, his reply was meek and cheery. "Great, Dr. Wonderland. Thank you for everything."

I wondered if he had always been that polite and submissive. I was soon to get an answer that ranks as one of the most unexpected and incredible of my personal and professional life.

📖   📖   📖

It was one of those rare, crisp San Francisco nights, when the fog strayed well beyond its usual Bay trek along the Marina and Embarcadero. Thick ghostly vapors of grayish, white fog were slowly oozing down the old Tenderloin buildings, while shrouding the neon signs and street lights with splashes of dull, glowing shadows and eerie images.

As I zipped up my leather flight jacket to repel some of the penetratingly damp cold, I was startled when four vague silhouettes appeared in front of me through the swirling white mist. Resembling sentinels spread evenly across the width of the sidewalk, they were tall, husky black males in their late teens or early twenties. Their crossed arms and wide stances hinted they certainly weren't waiting to welcome me. I knew I had to either walk between them or cross the street to avoid them. I decided to cross the street—but it was too late.

"You got some money, man?" was the opening request that promised me I was in serious trouble.

In all my years of activity in the Tenderloin and other so-called dangerous areas of the world, I had never been challenged, let alone mugged. True, I had clients who were victims of muggings, many of whom had been badly injured. But those clients were usually vulnerable prey—not like me. I also realized muggings can occur anywhere, even in "safe" neighborhoods. All of those ruminations scrolled through my mind, along with the surreal quality of the situation. I still didn't believe this was happening.

"Hey, honky mother-fucker, we talkin' to you."

That comment quickly burst my denials. I was again standing in the foggy Tenderloin with blotter-dry mouth and racing, thumping pulse. I then decided on one attempt to out-bluff them. After all, they were just kids.

Conjuring up all the authority and casual indifference I could muster, I finally replied, "How ya doin' guys. I'm not sure I heard right, what do ya need?"

As I spoke, I noticed a semi-circle forming around

me, with two of the black youth brandishing knives. I knew then I couldn't out-bluff them. They weren't bluffing. "I've got about eighteen bucks if that'll help." I really didn't want to know their next reply.

"Let's get the money and hurt the honky."

That's when I heard the footsteps behind me, followed by a bellowing warning. At first I thought it was a police megaphone, but the words didn't fit.

"Whatcha doin' niggers? Why you chompin' on my main man? He ain't no honky and he ain't no jive-ass punk like yous."

Out of the dancing mist stepped RJ, all five feet ten inches of him. Yet, at that moment, he was a giant. As he strutted by me to face off with the four youth, RJ placed his hand on my shoulder with a firm, gentle pull that sent me behind him. His demeanor sent a clear message that he was in full control. I was to obediently comply, by staying out of his way and keeping my mouth shut.

Although the four were over six feet three inches tall, they seemed to shrink in the face of RJ. He reminded me of a western gunslinger. There was a brief silence while RJ seemed to be staring each one down—known as dog-eyeing.

Then he moved close to one of the biggest youth, holding a knife. "You wanna get it on, mother-fucker? Either come on in or stick that shank up your black nigger ass."

Without a pause, RJ shot a glance at the other knife-wielding youth. "You too, fool. Yeah, I'm lookin' at you. You wanna be my bitch? You gonna be a mother-fuckin' punk?"

Both knives seemed to gingerly retreat beneath heavy coats, and for a moment, I thought the showdown was over.

Then the apparent leader of the four garnered the courage to question RJ. "Hey bro, who ya think ya are? He's no blood. We ain't fuckin' wit you."

RJ's reply was explosive. "This ain't no shuck and jive mother fucker. Run you mouth again nigger and you gonna be my bitch. You fuck with him and your sorry punk ass is mine."

With heads slightly bowed, each of the four slowly turned away from RJ and shuffled up Taylor Street. In a few moments they had disappeared and it was so quiet I could nearly hear the fog whispering around us.

My head was pounding with a volatile mixture of relief, confusion, gratitude and sheer astonishment. I must have looked stupid standing wide-eyed, speechless and stunned.

In contrast, when RJ turned toward me, his entire demeanor seemed riddled with self-disgust. With sagging shoulders, dangling arms and head thrown back in some sort of supplication, his lower lip kept quivering as he spoke. "You should have never seen me acting like this. I'm really sorry, Dr. Wonderland. I guess now you know."

His remarks deepened my bewilderment. "No I don't know, RJ. You never stop surprising me. Every time I think I've got a handle on you, you zap me with another riddle. But I do know one thing for sure; you rescued me from injury and possible death at the hands of those kids I didn't even know. I'll be forever grateful."

I grabbed his hand between both of mine and shook it long and hard. RJ began to smile shyly and I broke into a grin, as my knees started to shake. Through shy smiles, grinning, shaking knees and quivering lips, the whole frightening episode seemed to hit us both at once.

We just couldn't hold back those intense, pent-up

feelings any longer. Our grins and smiles erupted into uncontrollable laughter and tears on the fog-swept Tenderloin street. Hysteria? Perhaps, but so what. It felt good!!

"Wow. What a night," I exclaimed. That comment unleashed another torrent of laughter. We were safe and uninjured. Everything was hilarious. It must have taken another ten minutes of sidesplitting roars before the adrenaline receded enough for some calmer comments.

"I'm still pretty wired and loaded with curiosity. Got time for a quick cup of coffee, RJ?" I asked.

He offered a slight grimace before staring at the wet street. "Do we have to go back to the restaurant, Dr. Wonderland?"

"Of course not, two ordeals in one night are enough. How about Jim's Coffee Shop on Eddy Street?"

RJ lifted his eyes and sighed with relief, "Sure, Dr. Wonderland."

📖 📖 📖

Jim, the owner, was an enormous man whose thoughtful, compassionate manner was as impressive as his size. He also had plenty of Tenderloin street-savvy. Those qualifications attracted Tenderloin prey and repelled the predators.

Jim's Coffee Shop represented a safe haven to pensioners and derelicts who knew they were protected from the street hustlers. They could sit all day, even into the evening, inexpensively drinking coffee, eating sandwiches, telling stories of the good old days and playing chess.

Jim was truly a rare, gentle giant, who was ironically once a street hustler, thug and heavy boozer. He seemed to know everyone in the Tenderloin. He even referred a couple of his vulnerable patrons to me when he realized they were eligible for disability benefits.

"Well, I'll be damned. What are you two doing out in the fog so late?" Jim was busily cleaning the small counter overlooking the eight or ten empty tables. Other than a big wooden sandwich menu on the wall, the place was Spartan. It had the basics for those days: a jukebox, shuffleboard, pinball and cigarette machines. What it lacked in elegance was abundantly replaced with a down-home, friendly atmosphere and a feel of cleanliness.

Wiping his huge hands with a towel, Jim shook our hands heartily. "It's good to see you, Lar; you too, RJ. Now I don't have to waste my last pot of coffee. Grab a table."

RJ and I smiled. "It's really good to see you too, Big Jim," I said. As we sat at a corner table, Jim poured us two mugs of coffee.

"Stay as long as you like, I've got a lot of cleaning up to do."

When Jim resumed cleaning, RJ softly cleared his throat. "I guess you want to know about the other guy." His reluctance was a little sad.

"Sure I do, RJ, but only if you're ready."

RJ looked around the coffee shop, avoiding any eye contact as he talked.

Born in an Oakland housing project and raised in the ghetto area of San Francisco's Hunters Point, RJ adapted so well to tough, black youth gangs, he became a leader of a notorious Hunters Point gang at the age of fourteen. He believed then that a poor black had three avenues to success—education, professional athletics or leader of a ghetto gang.

He never felt bright enough for the first or big enough for the second. Well-liked by his black peers and pit bull tough, he was a natural gang leader. It wasn't long, however, before he realized being tough and fighting his way to the top weren't enough. He had to stay tough, fight whenever challenged and maybe even kill, if necessary.

The rewards for a young ghetto black were well worth the risks and dangers, at least for a fourteen-year-old. Any loot or drug money went directly to the leader, who was always entitled to the largest share before dividing the rest equally.

"I guess I was on the top," he added. "I even got my younger brother in the gang."

RJ took a huge gulp of his third cup of coffee.

I was on my second cup, quietly listening to his story.

"For two years it was an exciting, prosperous game, until I saw one of the gang stabbed to death. Yeah, I used drugs and beat up a lot of guys, but I'd never seen someone die, all bloody. There were also a couple of older guys in the gang, eighteen or nineteen, who wanted to be leader. I had to watch my back every minute and I couldn't trust anyone."

RJ stopped talking for a moment, staring vacantly at the ceiling. His eyes seemed to redden as he managed a deep breath before continuing.

"In just two months, Dr. Wonderland, I was like in a coma, dead; and when I came to, I could hardly recognize me. My goals, values, my identity could have belonged to somebody else."

RJ went on to explain that, during that two month period, at the age of only sixteen, his fifteen-year-old brother was shot to death by some rival gang members; and his sweetheart died in his arms of a heroin overdose while he was helping her fix.

No wonder he ran from himself, I thought. *Barely a*

teenager, RJ had survived a situation as deadly as any combat. Add the loss of two loved ones and a tortured sense of responsibility for their deaths, and it's amazing he had any personality left.

I finally needed to say something. "I'm deeply grateful for your trust, RJ, and I'll always honor that trust."

RJ then closed his eyes and smiled faintly. "Dr. Wonderland, you're the only person I ever trusted besides my Momma."

It was midnight before we left Jim's Coffee Shop. This time the walk up Taylor Street was exhilaratingly uneventful. No ambushes or shocking surprises, just a brisk walk through the icy layers of fog—reminding me just how fragile and fortunate I was.

📖 📖 📖

During the next few months, each session was a new experience for RJ. We met in Ghirardelli Square, the Marina Greens, the Emporium on Market, the Cliff House and the Embarcadero, where we took long walks.

Despite his street savvy, RJ had led a cloistered, one-dimensional existence in San Francisco. Most of the field trip locations were well beyond the ghetto or Tenderloin's invisible boundaries. Amazingly, he had never heard of Ghirardelli Square, and although he knew of the Cliff House, he didn't know what it was.

RJ remained nervous and sweaty-palmed with each new exposure. The big difference, however, was he looked forward to those field trips. He was finally discovering San Francisco, learning that he was free to follow his curiosity anywhere. He was also rediscovering himself, which offered me a deeper understanding of his earlier mistrust and resistance.

When RJ withdrew from the ghetto subculture, he

was convinced he had nowhere to go. This is probably why most ghetto youth rarely venture beyond their ghetto. Conventional middle-class lifestyles were as alien to him as a foreign language or "the Cliff House." Yet, he hated the black "super flies," hard drugs and ghetto gangs.

He explained that even finishing high school at the multi-racial Polytechnic was tough. Most of his black brothers shunned him as an "Oreo," while middle-class whites and blacks mistrusted him.

"If it wasn't for sports, I couldn't have stayed in school," he acknowledged. "I guess Momma was my real inspiration." RJ was an outstanding high school athlete in both baseball and basketball. His mother never missed any of his games.

For RJ, graduation was a major triumph, followed by cruel disappointments. His size and poor grades eliminated athletic scholarships, he lacked the money for junior college, his fair-weather high school chums had vanished and job opportunities for him were nil. To make matters worse, he still hated ghetto blacks, and middle-class society had no interest in him.

RJ was alone, except for his mother. He was drinking heavily and felt he didn't belong anywhere in San Francisco. That's when he found the Tenderloin.

"I was accepted there, no questions asked. I guess I became a Tenderloin wino, Dr. Wonderland, because no wino judged me. Most of us just shared a bottle to fight off our miseries and no one bothered us."

Ironically, about the time RJ was confronting the past and controlling his drinking, his progress became the problem. He no longer matched the California State disability standards. The letter of the law was unequivocally clear—no exceptions. You either fit the disability criteria, or you simply weren't disabled. That meant you were able to work full time. Again, RJ was the exception. He wasn't legally disabled or clinically capable of regular employment.

State disability evaluators and review panels were not hired to help the exceptions. As RJ's therapist, that was my job. Many of his disabilities were gray areas. He lacked the mental stamina, emotional control, flexibility, intelligence and frustration tolerance to cope with the pressures and stresses of regular employment, especially in a society where he still didn't quite fit.

I was also aware that, without his SSI and MediCal benefits, his further deterioration was inevitable. My clinical decision was clear. When the State requested an evaluation of RJ, my report lied. Perhaps that's a bit harsh. I simply gave them the clinical jargon necessary to conveniently fit RJ into their disability rules.

📖 📖 📖

I finally met RJ's mother when she was in her late 70's. She was a wonderfully tough, caring, clear-thinking woman who wore her finest every Sunday as she sang in her Baptist church. She has never given up on RJ, or me. During an occasional dinner at her home, she always mentioned how she knew RJ would be fine as long as he kept seeing me. Then, with hands on her big hips, she would look me over carefully, shaking her head.

"Honey, you're too thin. You've got to eat more."

As for a middle-aged RJ, in recent years he was inducted into the high school Athletic Hall of Fame. He has become a world-class ping-pong player, and he continues to assist disabled people in the Tenderloin who can't manage on their own.

That small group alternative to AA remains a vital part of his weekly activities, and they haven't missed giving a Christmas party for the poor in over twenty years.

RJ is still on SSI, he rarely gets drunk and he devotes much of his time to caring for his aging mother. I'm no longer his therapist, but we remain trusted friends, with a long relationship that has benefited both of us. However, there is one old habit RJ can't seem to break. He still calls me "Dr. Wonderland."

In 2005 I learned that RJ's mother had died peacefully at home with a caring son at her bedside.

Then, in 2006, his phone was disconnected and I lost all contact with my old friend. Other than a few vague rumors about him staggering drunk in the Tenderloin, no one had actually seen him in months. He was no longer at his last address and in searching the city for him, I also sadly discovered that his "Sober Fun" AA group no longer existed.

I hope he's all right.

6

SANDY

The Price of Freedom

As a social identity, the moral majority had labeled Sandy a homosexual or transvestite. As a psychiatric classification, the professionals had diagnosed her as Gender Identity Disorder with Suicidal Ideation. As a human being, those who knew Sandy viewed her as a warm, generous and very sensitive woman—with the body of a man.

Aside from big feet, big hands, small breasts and protruding genitals, Sandy was probably never a man. What we think we are is infinitely more powerful over our behavior than what our physical appearance tells us we should be. Despite her biology, Sandy was a female from the beginning and for her, nature versus nurture or biogenic versus psychogenic debates were irrelevant.

She was raised by a loving grandmother following the death of her parents. They had been killed in a drug-related shoot-out when Sandy was four. Characteristic of little girls, she was a bit shy and bashful around boys, loved dolls and walked hand-in-hand to school with her girlfriend.

Most of Sandy's pre-puberty years were a bit puzzling to her, but not really frustrating. At that stage of her development, she was experiencing gender anomalies, not sexual ones.

Anatomically, there was definitely no question about her gender, even though she was more comfortable with anything female. Her grandmother and birth certificate clearly validated her gender and her given name was Sam. Yet, she could only remember being called Sandy, a name of unknown origin that matched her identity as a female. She preferred all that was feminine even though, as a child, she uneasily used the boys' restrooms and knew better than to wear dresses. But clothes were never a real problem as a kid, since most of her girlfriends also wore trousers.

By the time Sandy entered high school, her anatomy and physiology became serious burdens. She was experiencing sexual urgings that were destined to be satisfied only with males. Her body had finally become grotesque and alien to her.

Sandy once asked me if I had ever awakened in the morning with bad breath, messed hair and huge bags under my eyes; and if I looked in the mirror in disgust with my appearance.

When I said, "Sure," she replied with a wry half-smile, "Multiply that disgust by a hundred and that's the way I feel about my whole body every day."

Sandy quit high school in the tenth grade when no longer able to endure the jokes and ridicule she received from boys. Although intellectually bright, she had no developed skills, no trade and no tolerance for the intolerance of others. Despite those obstacles, she kept trying to adjust to situations that never let her belong.

After losing numerous unskilled jobs and commitment to psychiatric wards because of botched suicide attempts, Sandy sought refuge in the Tenderloin—where misfits are always accepted. At that point in her life, she cherished her woman's identity and despised the taunting and mocking of her male body.

📖 📖 📖

I met Sandy very early in my career, when most of my clients were living in the Tenderloin—their refuge as well. Sandy was doing some volunteer work at the Tenderloin Outreach Clinic, where I worked as a consultant a few hours a week. She filed a few papers, made lots of coffee and illuminated an otherwise depressing, drab hangout and refuge for an assortment of physically and mentally ill addicts, pensioners and parolees. It would have been difficult not to notice Sandy by the feel of her warmth, the subdued fragrance of her perfume and her good-natured, genuine laugh that resonated happy melodies throughout the clinic.

Physically, Sandy wasn't particularly attractive, even for a man. At a glance, a rough, slightly blemished skin covered her square face and rather harsh, chiseled features. She had chipped teeth, a thin body with no noticeable curves and her shoulder length hair was showing signs of thinning. She wore no make-up that might have camouflaged some of her physical flaws, perhaps because behaviorally she didn't need it.

Nothing about her appeared strained or excessive. Her movements were ballerina graceful and pure feminine, while her smile radiated a glow that seemed to relax her skin into a smooth, delicate, rosy softness. Her cheerful greetings bedazzled everyone, including me.

No matter how I felt, I found myself smiling back at her, hoping some of her nurturing, feminine charm would embrace me as well. She didn't have to try being a woman or beautiful. She was both.

Sandy also seemed to grasp the essence of anyone she met, as if she were clinging anxiously to each word with deep love and compassion. I used to think that any woman who seemed to care so much for everyone, couldn't possibly have any personal cares or problems. She was constantly cheering up somebody, encouraging, supporting or simply listening with affectionate tender concern, as others belched their complaints, problems and rage. Sandy seemed to calm the most bizarre and angry person with her gentle, non-judgmental listening.

During one of my visits to the clinic, I was both surprised and delighted when Sandy asked to see me in private.

"Dr. Wonderling," she said, "you deserve to know that people here both like and trust you, so I have no reason to search any further. I need to see a professional, and I would deeply appreciate having you as my therapist."

Characteristic of Sandy, her gentle and clear request was preceded by some positive feedback that simultaneously put me at ease with her and made me feel good about myself.

"Of course." I replied. Then, trying to be too cavalier and without much clinical thought, I blurted out, "You're the last person in this office I would have imagined seeking psychotherapy."

Her smile dissolved into a sober silence that was a scolding of telegraphic clarity. It wasn't some whimsical request. Sandy was in pain and pleading for help.

"I've tried to kill myself twice. Do you think that's serious enough, Dr. Wonderling?" she asked.

Sensing my embarrassment, Sandy very tenderly added, "I'm sorry, how could you have known. I put up a good facade here, don't I?"

Sandy taught me a lesson I've never forgotten. Listen carefully to the words and the music, and don't ever back away. The pain is somewhere or your help wouldn't really be needed.

During our first session, I quickly discovered just how troubled and complex that sweet, delicate woman really was. People usually enter therapy to desperately talk about things they desperately don't want to talk about. It may take several sessions before there are self-disclosures of any significance.

Sandy, on the other hand, had barely sat down when she tearfully declared, "I have a man's body." That was a gut-wrenching acknowledgment she had to announce to her new confidant. The message was like telling a respected relative you have syphilis, while watching for the slightest change in expression that might signal your relative's alarm or repugnance. Sandy simply had to share this secret and assess my reaction before therapy could begin—but therapy had begun.

Although not particularly eloquent, my reply was direct and honest. "Wow, what a mouthful. Now we can get to work."

She smiled and nodded approvingly, "Yes, we really can, can't we?"

Sandy was always early for her appointments and once in the office she would begin each session with her adopted phrase, "I'm ready to go to work." That favorite phrase of hers was a major understatement, not a playful joke.

She used virtually every minute of each session examining every remembered childhood event, every interaction, relationship and friendship. She explored early aspirations, later disappointments, desperation and suicide efforts.

She recounted physical illnesses, hospitalizations, social workers, counselors, psychiatrists, psychologists, hypnotherapy, electroshock, legal drugs, street drugs, happy times, sad times and boring times. All of that and she was only 25.

She detailed self-sex, same-sex, other sex and kinky sex; the beginnings, middles and conclusions of her few romances, employment attempts, hobbies and religious activities.

Despite her hard work, after a year of psycho-therapy, there were no apocalyptic insights, no enrap-tured sighs of relief that it all finally made sense, no born-again salvation, no one to blame, no savior to the rescue and no end to her torment.

There were, however, somewhat inexplicable hints of positive change, even progress. Sandy had remained in therapy with me four or five times longer than ever before. Three months was usually her limit before she'd run for cover, escaping into drugs or other self-defeating street activities.

We had also developed a solid trusting relationship. She was no longer intimidated by my masculinity, and her thinking wasn't muddled by the overwhelming "love-versus-hate" ambivalence that she had exper-ienced with other male therapists. Most important, Sandy hadn't been hospitalized or preoccupied with suicide for over a year.

Then there were the more pitiful aspects of her daily life. Each day, dressed in jeans and sweater, she would give her love to all those in the Tenderloin Clinic in search of help. Each night, dressed in skirt and blouse, she gave her body to others on the Tenderloin streets in search of love for herself.

Sandy would slowly roam the Tenderloin streets until the bars closed at 2 a.m. It was a terrible irony that she had to dress like a woman to attract men, even though she was a woman. Worse, she had to act less like her feminine self and more like a prostitute or men on the streets wouldn't approach her.

She frequently pondered this dilemma in my office concluding, "Even physical women mask themselves in all kinds of make-up and apparel to look more alluring to men."

At least therapy seemed to be realistically reminding her that maybe there were no profound reasons or clinical solutions to be uncovered in therapy. Just maybe it was simply a case of a mind/body mismatch. She was a congenital anomaly of nature—no one's fault; and she might as well get used to it.

But Sandy wasn't getting used to it. She was accepting the absence of an underlying psychological disturbance, but what she couldn't accept was the absence of love. She was a freak of nature, like Wolf-man or the mermaid lady, yet no circus would ever hire her.

So Sandy continued to roam the Tenderloin streets at night, which typically meant engaging men from the waist down. She masturbated them in alleys, orally copulated them in their cars and sometimes let them sodomize her in the dark shadows of an empty doorway. Sometimes they gave her money, occasionally they slapped her around, yet they never kissed her, hugged her or showed her any signs of affection.

📖　📖　📖

One of Sandy's most nightmarish horrors was the possible discovery of her genitals by a man who expected her to be a woman. Paradoxically, one of her most hallowed desires was the discovery of her genitals by a man able to love her as a woman.

This dangerous masquerade finally became her "nightmarish horror" during her second year with me in therapy. While standing on a street corner one lonely midnight, she was approached by a tall, handsome-looking man who wanted sexual intercourse in a hotel. Knowing that was far too risky, she finally talked him into anal sex in the back seat of his car.

As Sandy lifted her skirt and slid her pants down low enough to expose her buttocks, the man began kissing her on the neck. She could also feel his hard penis sliding toward her anus. She was more carelessly responsive than usual, naively thinking, *maybe this is the man who will understand and love me.*

Caught up in rare feelings of affection, she let him slide a hand into the front of her panties. Expecting a moist vagina, he jerked back the instant he felt her testicles.

"You fuckin' queer bitch," he shouted.

Sandy was so humiliated and disgusted with herself, she lay silently on the back seat of his car while the man punched and kicked her until she was about to lose consciousness. After dragging her across the seat and throwing her from the car, he kept kicking her until she mercifully lay unconscious.

She was hospitalized for several weeks, with broken ribs, internal bleeding, a badly damaged, nearly dis-lodged right eye and a severe concussion.

Although I visited her regularly in the hospital, we never discussed the beating in detail. She was terribly ashamed. She also never clearly described the man to the police. It was her fault, no one else's. Her physical pain was just no match for her guilt-laden torment.

Sandy's injuries healed over the next few months, but she never fully recovered from the emotional trauma. Her childish fantasies of some romantic rescue faded, along with her open wounds. She was also noticeably sluggish and lethargic, as if not particularly moved by anything. She had become resigned to a solitary, stolid life, without magic or miracles.

Even those at the Tenderloin Clinic noticed the change. She was still very helpful and supportive, yet conspicuously less soft and caring. Her laughter seemed courser, less melodic, more superficial—like church bells forged in tin.

Sandy also experienced her first of many seizures during one of our sessions. We were talking about her disinterest in sports, and as I was suggesting some kind of hobby, I noticed an unfocused, fixed stare, muscular rigidity and an unresponsiveness that signaled the on-set of an epileptic seizure. Her sightless eyes rolled mechanically up toward her forehead, her body stiffened into grotesque jerks and her head shuttered violently as foamy saliva splattered her chin. Sandy was out of control.

At that point, protecting her from injury was all I could do. No words would ease the seizure activity, so I quietly held her firmly by the sides of her upper arms until she finally relaxed. Then I guided her limp body onto the floor as she slid off the chair. This entire episode, from the time I noticed her vacant stare until her first focused awareness, was no more than a couple of minutes. For those who have never seen a seizure, that time can be easily exaggerated into what seems like a half hour or so.

Lying on her side, with heavy breathing, Sandy appeared to be in a deep relaxing sleep; when, through her fluttering eyelids, she looked at me sitting on the floor next to her. She very haltingly asked the classic seizure wake-up question: "Wha…what happened?"

She was still confused and not fully recognizing me. After explaining what happened I sat with her on the floor until the ambulance I had called arrived.

Once alert and aware of her seizure, Sandy not surprisingly objected to a hospital examination. Reluctantly, she finally agreed when I reassured her that the Department of Social Services would be more inclined to award her permanent disability status if she had hospital verification of seizure activity.

Sandy was also not surprisingly disappointed when hospital tests were negative for blood clots, tumors or other damage that could hasten her death. It was highly probable that her street and legal drug use and abuse, previous electroshock therapies, her concussions and even emotional stress contributed to the seizures.

Epileptic seizures have the unpredictability and fury of one of their clinical nicknames, "Electrical Storm," and their origin is too frequently a mystery. For her, seizures continued to occur several times a week despite medication.

📖   📖   📖

For the next eight months, Sandy's life remained a humdrum, barely tolerable, routine struggle. She continued to pursue her volunteer work at the Tenderloin Clinic with a deep concern for others. Although she still deeply cared for those at the clinic, her cheerfulness was more strained, less natural.

Otherwise, guaranteed weekly seizures, by-weekly therapy sessions with me, lonely sexual liaisons with strangers, constant fear of exposure and pervasive despair exemplified her life.

"I feel numb," she once explained, "no desperation, anticipation, hope or inspiration—just numb."

Then she met Pete, who gave Sandy in a week what psychotherapy couldn't provide in several years. All those manifestations of lethargy, depression, indifference and her constant self-loathing burst into virtual meteors of sparkling optimism, vitality, forgiveness and a renewed belief in miracles.

Sandy felt more like a total woman than ever before. Her smiles and laughter again echoed resounding melodies of love and compassion. She even enrolled in a cooking class, and seizure activity decreased in frequency. Sandy was in love.

Pete was a parolee, whom she met at the Tenderloin Clinic. He was a big, rugged-looking, heavily-tattooed recent release from San Quentin Prison, where he probably did much of his time lifting weights. His thick black hair was braided into a shoulder length ponytail. His deep-set eyes were so concealed beneath bushy brows it was hard to tell what his eyes were saying.

His big scarred hands, however, did have a clear message. On each of the four knuckles of his right hand were the crudely tattooed letters F - U - C - K. On his left hand, inked on three knuckles was the end of the message: Y - O - U.

Sandy couldn't wait to tell me all about Pete. Everything she said about him was enthusiastically positive. She could see nothing else and I wasn't about to question, let alone challenge, any of her sometimes naive comments. She deserved a taste of happiness, at least for the moment. Besides, I reasoned, maybe the relationship would work. For her, it was certainly worth a try.

"He's so handsome and funny, with a wonderful sense of humor," she raved. "Everybody likes him and he only uses a little pot," she added proudly.

"I'm happy for you Sandy," I grinningly replied. She simply couldn't handle another hurt, so rather than warn her about Pete, I could only offer her the supportive comment, "I'll always be here if you need me."

Pete was a street-wise ex-con with more years in prison than out. He had learned early in life that sex in prison was inescapable. You play passive or active, sadist or masochist, child or adult, master or slave. He happened to like it all. Pete was an animal.

At the Tenderloin Clinic, Ben, the director, was a bit tense when Pete was around. Pete would wander the clinic, picking up things that didn't belong to him; and several times he was found in a back office going through drawers.

When confronted, he always had a smiling excuse; and once when Ben asked him to leave, Pete looked him straight in the eye and said coldly, "Man, that wouldn't be cool."

Intimidated, Ben walked away and Pete stayed.

Scarper, a scrawny ex-convict and reliable police informant, was terrified of Pete. Years earlier, at a juvenile detention facility, Scarper had been gang-raped by Pete and his buddies.

Even then, Pete was the bully leader of the pack; and although Scarper tried to avoid him in the Tenderloin, Pete was unavoidable. He had been out of prison only a few weeks and already Pete was at the top of the Tenderloin thug pecking order.

All of the lesser thugs told Pete everything of any significance including the location of "wimps" and "marks" like Scarper. Pete didn't need to accost or physically threaten Scarper. His presence was enough.

He would just appear with a leering smile, "Hey man, where ya been hidin'?"

Scarper knew better than to resist when Pete invariably asked for cigarettes or money. He knew what the consequences would probably be.

📖 📖 📖

Sandy couldn't wait to tell me that Pete had moved in with her. Her eyes were wide, bright and filled with hope as she told me about his helpfulness in rearranging some of her furniture.

She also told me about her cooking class, his first home-cooked meal with her and how they satisfied each other sexually.

If I started to ask about their financial harmony, however, her eyes would narrow defensively. She was obviously paying all the bills, so I stopped asking.

Sandy also stopped coming to see me as frequently. Her sessions dwindled to once a month. That can be a positive sign of remission.

For her, however, it was more likely a negative sign of denial. She spent most of each session defending Pete, even though I never questioned her about him. It was painfully obvious that she was really defending herself. Again, the magic had begun to collapse, along with her belief in miracles. I was really worried, but felt powerless to make it better.

Between sessions, Sandy maintained a friendly, cheerful facade at the Tenderloin Clinic, and on the streets, we would always greet each other with a wave or brief friendly chat. Even Pete waved at me once and after a few months; it was a relief to conclude I might have been over-reacting to the possible sinister aspects of their relationship.

Then one afternoon, Sandy canceled her next appointment, explaining that she really didn't need to see me professionally any more.

"I feel fine," she said reassuringly.

Again, I felt powerless, and all I could add was, "I'll be here if you need me."

□   □   □

Sandy needed me sooner and more urgently than I could have ever anticipated.

A week after canceling her appointment, I heard hurried footsteps up the front stairs of my office. Those sounds were followed by unmistakable deep sobs, heavy pounding on the door and a frantic rattling doorknob with futile attempts to open the door.

As I opened the door, Sandy fell across the threshold. She was covered in blood and crying hysterically.

Her hands were so bloody I thought they had been crushed, until she screamed, "I killed him; I killed Pete, the dirty bastard!" Sobbing, she cried almost as if mumbling to herself, "I killed him, I stabbed him all over his neck, his stomach, his prick—all over."

Sandy had returned to her apartment from the clinic about an hour earlier. She was going to fix a spaghetti dinner for Pete and one of his friends. When she opened the door, there were two men locked in oral sex, another man engaged in oral sex with a woman and Pete sodomizing the same woman. They were all naked and, except for Pete, all strangers. Sandy was completely ignored until Pete shouted, "Strip and get some, you freak bitch, we can eat food later."

They all looked up and laughed, except Sandy. She had just been disemboweled, and the wrenching stomach pains were unbearable.

Some primordial instinct seized her mind, and she knew she must kill him before he finished her off.

Sandy hypnotically walked to the kitchen, grabbed two butcher knives, returned to the orgy and practically cut Pete's head off with two slashes to his neck. Pete fell over the woman he was sodomizing and the strangers finally took Sandy seriously by grabbing clothes and fleeing out the open door.

Sandy kept slashing and stabbing Pete's body until there was no solid flesh to cut.

"He was peacefully dead and I was miserably alive." Sandy sobbed. After retelling every painful detail, she collapsed in my arms with deep hysterical sobs.

In another half hour of just sitting and holding her, she seemed quite calm and alert, stating that she was ready to turn herself in, after she showered and changed clothes. She was a bloody mess and to help her regain a bit of her dignity, I agreed she should clean up before her arrest.

Sandy called a street-wise woman friend from the Tenderloin who would let her shower and change clothes. We hugged a long good-bye, and when she left, I called the police about her plan to surrender herself at a friend's house.

That was my last session with Sandy. When she left my office, she had walked straight to her apartment and jumped off the roof to her death.

When Scarper called and told me, my whole body shuddered, and then I smiled.

Sandy was free of conflict and torment. She no longer had a man's body. She was finally at peace.

In retrospect, should I have kept her in my office until the police arrived? I suppose as a debatable issue, it depends on one's frame of reference. As a rigid "Letter of the Law" issue, the answer would be a resounding "yes." From a textbook clinical perspective, I would imagine a more flexible "probably." As for me personally, it's still a compassionate "no."

Sandy's last day on earth remains crystal clear and hard to forget.

7

ANDREW

The Announcement

One of the least puzzling reasons I chose psychology as a profession is because I'm a people-watcher. I've always enjoyed watching people, perhaps because I'm one of them. Then again it may be related to our extraordinary complexity along with our transparent simplicity. We may be tall or short, white or black, fat or skinny, yet we're more the same than different. We walk, eat, laugh, cry, sneer and flirt alike. People are easy to figure out, however, just examine yourself and extrapolate—not really.

Like a fingerprint, we're also profoundly different from each other. This individual uniqueness is our personal essence and our resultant complexity as humans. Uniqueness is easy to notice but difficult to figure out, especially when it's unique behavior.

If we all looked and acted exactly alike, we would never be remembered, let alone ever noticed. We are set apart, spotlighted, aggrandized and immortalized by our uniqueness. Paradoxically, the absence of any uniqueness can be tragically memorable; at least it was to me.

📖   📖   📖

Andrew's third week of membership in my Tenderloin therapy group was the dawning of one of those memorable events in my life. In existence for about one month, the group was held in a small barren basement room. The meeting place was in one of the old decrepit Tenderloin buildings that was sadly destined to be leveled in a few years.

Those once magnificent, historical buildings frequently ended up as high rise office buildings or parking lots for downtown shoppers. The room was donated by the Tenderloin Community Center with only one condition, that I would let them try a few of their clients in my therapy group. I had eagerly agreed to the free room and occasional referrals, all of whom were receiving Medicare or MediCal—my main source of income.

The group started with six of my own clients and one from the Tenderloin Community Center; which brought it to seven members. Yet strangely, I could only remember six. There had been some lively discussions during those early group sessions. Although poor, disabled alcoholics, they were uniquely different from one another, with memorable features and opinions—well, most of them.

At the end of our fifth group session, when all the members were heading for the Tenderloin streets, I began scribbling a few notes about group objectives, goals and other reminders to facilitate the next session. Following ten minutes of writing, I happened to notice a pair of shoes and pant legs directly in front of me. A little startled, I looked up to see a male figure looking down at me. It was Andrew.

"Hello, Dr. Wonderling, I didn't want to bother you."

"Hey, no problem. How long have you been standing there?" I asked with a grin.

"Since the group ended," he answered.

Wow, I thought, *he was standing over me for ten minutes and I didn't notice, nor did he say a word.*

"Dr. Wonderling," he repeated, as if following a prepared script, "I would very much like to see you as my therapist."

He was still standing over me motionlessly, not even a twitch. "Grab a chair and let's talk."

He obediently and quietly walked to the circle of chairs that had contained the boisterous group. Andrew took a chair slightly to the rear of the other chairs and returned.

"Where shall I put the chair?" he asked, practically whispering.

"Right here is fine." I pointed to where he had been standing for ten minutes.

As Andrew sat quietly, still without even a twitch, I smilingly asked, "So, you'd like to join our little group?"

"I'm in the group," he said dryly.

Wow, I said again to myself. *How in the world did I miss him, I know everybody else.*

"Did you start today?" I hoped.

"No, this is the third time I've been here."

I was afraid to ask any more questions, since it was getting worse every time. I decided it was useless to even try to conceal my embarrassment beneath my red faced, startled expression. "Gosh, I'm really embarrassed and terribly sorry, I ah…"

"That's all right," he graciously interrupted, "it happens."

Andrew explained that he had been receiving Supplemental Security Income (SSI) for several years, "because I get depressed sometimes." He thought therapy might help, instead of the "pills" a doctor prescribed that, "made me feel worse." He added, "The clinic suggested I sit in your group for a while and I'm glad I did." He made the last comment with a near smile that was quickly erased by the repeating of his earlier request, "I would very much like to see you as my therapist."

How could I refuse, even if I wanted to? Although I knew nothing about him, I figured I'd learn during our sessions. He was also a Tenderloin Community Center referral and a member of my group, even though I was convinced I'd never seen him before.

"I would be delighted to see you on a one-on-one basis," I replied with an air of absolute confidence in my decision.

His response resembled a grin that never quite achieved smile status. "Thank you, Dr. Wonderling; I'm certain we can work well together. Oh, yes," he added, "would it be OK to terminate my group participation?"

"That would be fine," I said, thinking—*what participation?*

☐ ☐ ☐

During our first individual therapy session, I finally had an opportunity to begin observing Andrew closely. I quickly learned why I hadn't noticed him in nearly three hours of group sessions. Physically, he appeared to be average everything, except for his excessive girth. There was nothing particularly distinctive, ugly or offensive about his appearance. Those, of course, weren't noticeable characteristics.

Andrew wasn't very noticeable. He was just unobtrusively plain and consequently very hard to describe. He was big-bellied, fleshy and soft looking—but so is half of America. His beady, grayish little eyes, tiny pug nose and thin lips occupied a small part of his head; leaving vacant an excessive area for a dome-like forehead, pudgy cheeks and a flaccid receding chin that blended with his sagging neck. His thinning hair was kind of a non-color, somewhere between black and brown, and his unblemished skin was an obscure pale. His clothes were also unremarkably colorless, including old brownish-laced boots, faded jeans and shirt. His belt was well concealed under his portly belly.

Behaviorally, he could have been clinically described as reticent, soft-spoken, unspontaneous, unanimated and dysprosodic; which translates into a flat, monotone without melody. In layman's terms, Andrew was boring. However, he was never boorish.

He tended to speak only when he was spoken to or acknowledged and then he gave only the required information with no embellishments, levity or other nonessentials. Andrew seemed acutely aware of all aspects of his surroundings, and his responses or rare comments were typically crisp and relevant. He was also very polite, considerate of others and articulate. No, he was certainly not a boor.

After eight months of individual psychotherapy, I still didn't know much about Andrew's underlying problems or the nature of his SSI disability. No one seemed to know. The Department of Social Services couldn't locate his records. Previous psychotherapists were either no longer practicing, had moved or were unavailable. The Tenderloin Community Center knew less than I about Andrew.

According to Andrew, his SSI benefits were associated with "mild depression," which is not a debilitating
enough diagnosis to warrant SSI benefits. Probably none
of that should have mattered to me anyway. Even
though he displayed a critical absence of charm, or for
that matter, personality, he was ironically one of my
favorite clients.

Noticeable clients are often visibly obnoxious, with
neurotic or psychotic traits that I personally can barely
tolerate. Yet, as a therapist, I must try to understand
them. Neither threatening nor noticeable, Andrew never
generated any negative energy.

Intelligence testing was not necessary to determine
that Andrew was exceptionally bright and very well
read. A full battery of psychological tests wasn't necessary either. Andrew said he was feeling fine, with no
noteworthy depressive episodes. The Department of
Social Services was not concerned about a diagnosis,
and he was receiving all of his benefits with meticulous
regularity. Furthermore, psychodiagnostic testing is very
expensive. So, I continued to treat Andrew without
really knowing what kind of problem I was supposed to
be treating.

I never knew when Andrew was in the waiting
room, since he never announced his presence, even
though I had an office bell for that purpose. I learned,
however, that once in my office, he would sit silently
until I asked him a question. Then he would obediently
respond clearly and concisely. When he completed his
monologue, Andrew quietly awaited the next question.

At the end of our first year, I still knew very little
about Andrew as an individual. I only knew what he did.
I knew he read the newspaper daily, from the front page
headlines to the back page weather. He got the paper

free from his hotel lobby.

I was aware he walked around the Tenderloin, sometimes dropping into the Tenderloin Community Center to peruse their new batch of secondhand books. Wandering through Market Street department stores was an important part of his afternoon, and when he wasn't reading, his evenings were utilized watching mainly news and various documentaries on his nine inch black and white TV set. Additionally, I knew he ate well, slept well and never complained about any medical problems.

I had also learned that even though his life seemed secure, eventful and satisfying, he was essentially a spectator. Aside from his professional relationship with me, Andrew seemed to have no social life. He never mentioned friends, acquaintances or even relatives. He appeared to always be watching, observing, reading or learning, but never interacting with others. Even our sessions were rarely interpersonal. We didn't speak about each other or our feelings about issues. We just impersonally talked about issues.

"Yes, Dr. Wonderling, the paper said yesterday there was a serious waste of oil in the United States...." "The Time magazine had an article last week about more political corruption in Washington."

Andrew was indeed a wonderful source of information about current events, which happened to be one of my major interests. It was a symbiotic relationship. I looked forward to his reports, and he looked forward to my questions. Neither of us seemed interested in pursuing Andrew's personal preoccupations, whatever they were.

During the second year, however, I felt a bit guilty that I was learning more about worldly events than about Andrew; and despite his reassurances that he was fine, he agreed to set a few simple goals.

I was concerned that he was on a treadmill to nowhere, in a rut, and that expanding his vistas might somehow enhance his sociability.

His first goal was to explore the diversity of San Francisco by simply increasing his walking boundaries beyond his usual Tenderloin and Market Street route. As part of that strategy, Andrew obediently, albeit a tad reluctantly, consented to therapy sessions in a hotel lobby instead of in my office.

Office visits can become a nonproductive routine to any long-term client. Meeting such shy or paranoid clients in pleasant public places had proven in the past to be a safe field trip experience, as well as therapy. We chose the Jack Tarr Hotel because of its location and comfortable lobby.

It has more recently incorporated as the Cathedral Hill Hotel. The sofas and lounge chair arrangements were sufficiently spaced that even the keenest of eavesdroppers couldn't hear our conversation. The Jack Tarr was located at Geary and Van Ness Avenues, only a few blocks from the Tenderloin. Hotel security barely noticed and never bothered two people chatting away in comfortable chairs. It was a pleasant setting for both of us.

Andrew gradually seemed to enjoy his new therapy location. He usually arrived long before our scheduled time. As I entered the lobby, I would look for Andrew in his preferred chair adjoining another chair in the corner of the lobby. There were no other chairs nearby and he could sit unobtrusively with his back to the wall, watching guests or reading the paper.

Typical of Andrew, the adjacent chair, the one he left for me, was the most invitingly comfortable looking. Also typical, he kept those sessions impersonal by reciting straightforward, articulate local, state and national news events. He described guests and their interactions with other guests.

"Just before you came in, Dr. Wonderling, there was the tallest man I've ever seen, he must have been seven feet tall. He was with a woman about five feet one. From what I gathered, they were going on a bus tour."

His reports were becoming increasingly spontaneous. It was gratifying that he no longer needed permission to speak. He was also becoming a little more visible—at least to me.

Aside from a newspaper, Andrew usually carried an old red, white and blue folder filled with papers. He never discussed them and I never asked. When, however, he accidentally dropped an envelope from the folder at one of our Jack Tarr sessions, he seemed compelled to tell me, even though I still hadn't asked.

"It's a letter from one of the children I sponsor," he said uneasily, as if caught doing something wrong.

Andrew was receiving about $520 per month in benefits, which barely covered his basic survival needs. Nevertheless, he was sending $100 a month to several orphaned children in Africa. He admitted feeling guilty.

"This is not my money to give to others."

I promised not to tell a soul.

For the next several months Andrew continued seeing me, exploring San Francisco and avoiding social interactions. He also kept reassuring me that his life had never been better. I wasn't convinced. There were still no smiles, no frowns, no melody and no friends. Something was wrong, and during our next appointment, the underlying drama began to unravel.

The entrance to the old Jack Tarr Hotel was impressive.

Sequestered from San Francisco's heavily trafficked streets, a semicircle driveway arched its way off Van Ness, up a slight hill until it crested under an enormous marquee, supported by huge polished brass posts. Leaving the Jack Tarr was a gentle "S" curve descent onto Geary Street. A sidewalk, adorned with colorful flowers, traced the driveway's meanderings on and off the main streets.

The doorman, resplendent with gleaming epaulets, gold braided deep green cut-away, white gloves and ornate visor on a gilded crowned hat, orchestrated the activities of endless cabs, tour buses, guests and awaiting bellhops with their luggage carriers.

As I ascended the flower-lined walkway on a crisp October afternoon, I was about ten minutes late for my appointment with Andrew. That wasn't particularly disturbing, since I was rarely late. Anyway, Andrew would be enjoying the newspaper or people-watching.

Nearing the entrance to the Jack Tarr, I noticed a large group of people, which is not unusual. In this case, however, the group seemed focused on something in the center of their circle, rather than the doorman. *Must be a tour director*, I thought, until I glanced at the circle's center of attention.

It was a clown, just standing there, while all the animation and laughter was coming from the crowd. Then I noticed a familiar security guard standing next to the clown. He was holding an old red, white and blue folder that I recognized. Looking more closely at the clown, I shuddered with a shockwave of dread and surprise.

It was Andrew all right. Weaving my way through the crowd, I was intercepted by the security guard, who was fortunately more of a decent person than a law enforcing cop.

"Are you Dr. Wonderling?" he asked.

As I said yes, the security guard quickly added, "There's no charge or anything." Then gesturing toward Andrew, "He was creating too much attention sitting in the lobby. He told me he was waiting for you."

I thanked the security guard, accepted the folder and walked the still silent Andrew down the walkway to Geary Street.

Andrew's clown costume was more than an "Emmett Kelley" sad. It was pitiful, almost tragic. Maybe because he wasn't an actor telling a story, he was the story. He had used charcoal, lipstick, mascara, nail polish and a tennis ball to create his clown face. Pathetically, the tennis ball with a hole for his nose and red paint still looked like a poorly painted tennis ball, askew and sagging off his nose.

The rest of his face was anything but a creative array of colors. It was a smeared mess that ran together with his perspiration, staining his shirt. His clown suit was torn and frayed and so small, about twelve inches of pant leg and shirtsleeves, as well as his shirt collar, were woefully visible.

Once seated in my nearby-parked car, I had to ask as gently as possible, "It's a little early for Halloween isn't it, Andrew?"

Looking straight ahead and gazing out the passenger window, Andrew spoke in a slow, articulate monotone. "I'm gay, Dr. Wonderling," he began. "Before I met you, I lived with my friend. He died and I'm HIV positive. I have a mother, father, sister and brother— they're younger. My whole family has disowned me. They will no longer talk to me. I'm so afraid of infecting somebody; I have no social life, no friends or anybody to talk to except you.

"I don't mind being alone, but sometimes I do need

to be noticed. So I put on a costume and everybody notices me."

Andrew gazed silently out the window for a few minutes, and as he turned toward me to speak again, his eyes glistened and a single tear trickled down each stained cheek.

I could feel his deep sorrow and my deep sympathy.

"Those costumes really announce my presence, don't they, Dr. Wonderling?"

I remember my quivering voice, "They sure do Andrew, they sure do."

Andrew died of an AIDS related illness less than a year later. He was 24 years old at death and still un-noticed—except by me.

❋　　❋　　❋

So many people I have known from my Tenderloin days have profoundly influenced my life—including Andrew. Ironically, through the years I have become much more acutely aware of the painfully shy, unobtrusive person who fades into the woodwork. I believe I try to listen harder to them because I know that inside they are probably screaming to be heard.

8

ODY

A Quart of Milk

Whenever Ody was out of prison, he was in the Tenderloin—his second home. Similar to prison, the Tenderloin was a special place for Ody, for no special reason. Concrete 8 x 10 prison cells or sheetrock 10 x 10 hotel rooms were identically immaterial. He just needed a place where he could be left alone, where no one could bother him. Locked cells or locked hotel rooms were essentially all the same.

As long as he wasn't bothered, the social characteristics, dress style or the appearance of people didn't matter either. Black jackets with turned-up collars over gray shirts with pocket numbers, black work shoes and gray creased work pants were his prison wear. Those made him invisible in prison, since everyone wore the same thing. For different reasons the same clothes, without pocket number and crease, made him invisible in the Tenderloin. There, everyone dressed differently and no one seemed to care how they dressed. He knew that in the Tenderloin, clothes had little to do with status or identity. Most were bought at Salvation Army or Goodwill stores. Some women wore men's clothes, some men wore women's clothes and none of it really mattered, since the main purpose was just to cover the body.

Ody's logic seemed a bit peculiar at times but it was so sprinkled with a pragmatic common sense, it was difficult to argue with him. He just didn't want anyone, as he put it, "messin" with him, while assuming everybody was trying to "mess" with him. Some institutional clinicians had diagnosed Ody as a sociopathic personality with strong paranoid tendencies. I viewed him as a crusty old ex-con who didn't want anyone messing with him.

Ody was a prototypical ex-con. He was the kind you see in old Edward G. Robinson movies. He occasionally talked out the side of his mouth like they used to do in the old days when prison inmates weren't permitted to talk in lines. He sometimes even used old convict words like "bonaroo" (anything cool or sharp), and if introduced to a stranger, especially one who might be an official, Ody would respond with a flat, mechanical "all right," if asked how he was doing. In the old days, any real convict never related to guards or officials. So, "all right" didn't mean all right. It was simply a forced acknowledgment that meant nothing.

Despite his extensive prison background and convict expertise, Ody especially hated ex-cons. "You can't trust 'em as far as you can throw 'em," he'd grumble.

Practically raised in prisons, it was also obvious that he wasn't very good at his chosen profession as an armed robber. He was usually caught within hours after a robbery, at least in part because he was drunk. But in those days Ody didn't drink for courage, he was an alcoholic who didn't need a reason to get drunk. He was also a pretty good street fighter with a hot temper. That provided him with plenty of fights, both in and out of prison.

As a youth, Ody quickly gained a reputation that lingered throughout his prison career. He was an independent, self-reliant loner who never joined or sided with any prison gang, never submitted to any pressures, never bullied anyone and he never had a "kid" for sex. In convict jargon, he did his own number and never finked (informed) on anyone.

According to other ex-cons living in the Tenderloin, when Ody was in his fifties he clearly earned the fiercest of fierce reputation. He was in the maximum security Folsom State Prison then, and because of his constant fighting, he was placed in the "Adjustment Center." This is a small prison within Folsom Prison that housed the most uncontrollable, violent inmates in the nation. Those were the inmates who couldn't live in any general prison population without hurting someone.

Despite close security in the Adjustment Center, inmates managed to play Dominos or Checkers for cigarettes. Ody enjoyed the gambling. He never cheated and always paid up when he lost. He expected the same, and when another Adjustment Center convict tried to cheat him out of ten cigarettes, Ody was enraged.

Group counseling in the Adjustment Center was mandatory at that time; and during a session, Ody told the group of convicts he was going to kill the cheater. After a long group discussion of alternative sanctions, Ody decided to just hurt the guy.

Sure enough, a week later, during a brief unlock, Ody anesthetized the cheat with a knock-out punch. Then with his big hands, he methodically broke the guy's two thumbs and eight fingers. From then on, no one in prison ever tried to cheat him. He also gained the respect of other convicts, which never really mattered to him.

📖   📖   📖

When we first met, Ody had been discharged from Folsom Prison for the fifth time and living in the Tenderloin for two years. Needless to say, he didn't want to meet me, but his Supplemental Security Income (SSI) was contingent upon such a get-together. When released from prison, he had been adjudicated disabled by the Department of Social Services as a result of physical and behavioral problems. One condition of his SSI was by-weekly sessions with a psychotherapist.

Ody had successfully maintained his benefits for almost two years without a psychotherapist. He had given social workers endless spurious excuses, but the day of reckoning had finally arrived. He was advised in a letter from the Department of Social Services that he would forfeit his SSI checks if he didn't see one of three designated therapists within a week. Ody had to immediately decide which was the most important—his absolute independence or his SSI checks. He pragmatically chose the checks and randomly chose me.

Ody was 72-years-old when he grumbled, growled and groaned his way into my office for that first meeting. He was about 6'3" and barrel-chested, with a few faded tattoos, a craggy weathered face and heavily scared brows and knuckles. Although sagging flesh clearly marked his age, he still had all of the residuals of a once powerful man and formidable opponent.

Ody was indeed an ex-con, with fowl temper and cranky aggressive mannerisms, yet he was no fool. He knew when he was licked and that the most common sense way to deal with "officials" he could no longer avoid, was to patronize them with the neutral "all right" treatment.

"It took me an hour to find this place," he smilingly bellowed as he opened my office door. Those were the first words out of his mouth. That's before he knew for sure he had opened the right door and that I was actually his therapist.

That first session was very brief, about fifteen minutes. I introduced myself and gave him the ground rules which included never showing up stoned or drunk, never telling me anything I would be compelled to report to the police and never expecting me to lie for him. I further explained he was free to talk or not talk about whatever he wanted and that, because I was an independent contractor, our sessions were totally confidential—even to the Department of Social Services. He liked that. I also told him I'd be his advocate if he had SSI problems. He liked that even better. Then I added that I could listen to his complaints, but couldn't do anything about them. He didn't like that.

"I don't complain," he argued, "people just don't know how to leave you alone." His leering smile not too subtly hinted the last remark was meant for me.

It took several sessions before Ody stopped flavoring his comments with bits of sarcasm about my meddling with his private life. That change began to occur after he asked me, with a genuine show of curiosity, "How come you're not checking on my private life?"

I replied with a special display of my brand of professsionalism, with the hope of teaching him something about therapy. "I'm only interested in what you want to tell me. I really don't care to know what you do with your private life."

"Hmmm," he mused, without offering his usual token repartees of the "gottcha" variety.

Ody eventually began to portray me as only a minor annoyance, who could be helpful at times. He told me once; I didn't really threaten him and didn't "meddle" after all. He even showed subtle signs of disappointment that I didn't probe into his private life.

"How much do you get for seeing me?" he queried rather inadvertently during a lull in our usual conversation about sports.

"Twenty-seven dollars," I answered casually.

"And you don't even pry into my private life. That's a pretty easy way to make a livin', huh?"

Resuming my special professional mode, I offered another therapeutic rejoinder. "Some people really make me earn my money by confronting their personal problems and asking for help," I explained.

That, together with my earlier "private life" comment, probably contributed to his increased openness and diminished resistance during his second six months of therapy. Characteristic of Ody, he often intimated that he was "gonna make this guy work for his money," and he did.

He still complained a lot, but he also talked a lot about his worries and even his fears. One of his first acknowledgments involved his intense uneasiness around people. In order to survive in prison, you either "bend over" or become a "gunfighter like in the west," he would explain. Other convicts never left you alone unless you were "crazy" or a "tough, fearless fighter."

Ody had learned how to be both, which was effective most of the time. Sometimes, however, a real "crazy" or young fighter would challenge him anyway. That's when bluffing didn't work.

His reputation followed him into the Tenderloin, where he was generally left to do what he pleased, at least until that occasional new combatant would try to take him on. Ody always won those fights, along with more prestige as a "gunfighter," a reputation he didn't really want.

📖 📖 📖

Since his discharge from prison, Ody finally "hung up his guns." He realized he was too old and afraid to fight when challenged. He was also tired of committing botched robberies that would return him to prison, the next time probably for life. All he wanted was to live peacefully the remainder of his days in the Tenderloin without any hassles. That created one major problem.

Ody had a huge Tenderloin reputation that didn't easily allow a quiet retirement. Any show of weakness would provoke challenges and fights from all of those who had been afraid of him. He felt his only choice was to keep bluffing as a dangerous crazy. That was a real dilemma for Ody and he felt trapped. Finally in his life, he was unarmed, easily stressed, mostly sober and vulnerable. Nevertheless, he still had to pretend he was a top gunfighter.

During the next few years, Ody kept working on his dilemma, as he unwittingly kept mellowing with age. Strangely, it helped that his old reputation had exaggerated him into a monster. Effortlessly, he had become a legend that other old grizzly thugs dared not test. As for the younger thugs, Ody was considered simply too old to matter.

Since no one seemed to be bothering him anymore, Ody was able to drop his masquerade. He was finally free to be the mild-mannered, laid-back nice guy he had secretly always wanted to be. He could either walk the Tenderloin streets, stay in his room or go to a movie and no one seemed to care. He wasn't that important or infamous after all. He was really just an old man who was experiencing an honest contentment and piece of mind for the first time in his stressed-out life.

Only Ody and I knew his real history and even then, well into his 74th year, he could be intimidated under certain conditions. If it happened, he would be propelled back into his crazy, violent role.

Ody had also adapted so well to our sessions, he wanted and usually received the last appointment of the day so he could stay a little longer. Satisfied with himself and his life, Ody had lost the art of complaining and the need to worry. At least he thought he had. He typically chatted about impersonal, situational things— like the poor prostitute who was hit by a car running across Taylor Street to see a potential customer; or the fire in the apartment building on Jones and Eddy that left dozens of disabled homeless, including his crippled friend, Martha. He was proud that he had gotten Martha a room in his building and helped her to obtain food from Meals on Wheels.

The nearby grocery store, where some of the Tenderloin old-timers hung out, was another topic he frequently brought up. He liked the Chinese who ran the store, even though he couldn't understand them. He had even developed a friendly, nodding relationship with the old-timers who crowded around the front door.

When the Chinese gave up their lease to some "Arabs" and the old-timers disappeared from the front of the store, Ody was not terribly concerned. "They seem nice enough," he said in referring to the new operators. Then with a big grin, "Can't understand them very well either."

Ody loved milk when he was drinking heavily; and now that he no longer drank, he loved it even more. Despite contradictory evidence, he was convinced that whole milk soothed his stomach ulcer. He called it a "curse" that had been bothering him for years. Those little pills he took couldn't possibly do the job—it was the milk that helped. Besides, Ody couldn't stand physicians or their advice.

📖　📖　📖

Not long after the new operators took over Ody's Tenderloin grocery store, he arrived at my office for his bi-weekly afternoon chat. He looked alarmingly like an old rerun of the cranky, stressed-out gunfighter, forced into another shoot-out.

"How you doing, Ody?" I asked, offering a big cheerful smile. His pacing, deep signs and frowning silence were a clear message I had dreaded hearing.

"Damn it all," he shrieked, "I bought a quart of milk at the grocery store, and when I got home I couldn't drink it 'cause it was spoiled." With flaring nostrils and gnashing teeth, he continued to pace all over the office.

"Just take it back," I said, as if I were talking to a rational old friend.

Such words were much too quick and challenging. They sent Ody reeling backwards, angrily reaching for the gun he didn't have. Clinching his fists and tensing his already taut jaw muscles, Ody shot back, "Don't you see, Doc, they're settin' me up. This never happened when the Chinese were there; you're a big help! It's some kind of test. If I go back and complain, they'll deny it and force a showdown. If I don't go back and complain, they'll know I rolled over. Then they'll know they got me."

In his own vulnerable way, Ody was absolutely right. I had responded to his concerns as an acquaintance, rather than as a therapist. That sour milk was a serious threat to his peaceful way of life and I hadn't taken it seriously.

"Ody," I said apologetically, "we'll handle this together and I promise you there'll be no confrontation or backing down."

"But, what if…"

"Ody," I gently interrupted, "if it doesn't work out, I'll be there to resolve any dispute." By then, Ody had learned that, although I expected him to cope with life's pressures and annoyances on his own, I was always there to guide him and even defend him if necessary.

We spent the entire session and more talking about his options—the other nearby Tenderloin grocery store, the less expensive Safeway several blocks away from the Tenderloin, a written complaint to the owner of the grocery store building, buying another quart of milk from the new Arab operators or returning the sour quart of milk, were just some of the possibilities. The options seemed endless, as did his arguments against them.

Ody finally agreed to call the next day with his decision, and I agreed to support whatever decision he made. Very early the following day, Ody called. He hadn't been able to sleep all night and at that point, he was so upset and angry, he didn't care what happened. He was going down to the store with the sour milk, demand a fresh bottle and tear up the store if they refused.

"Ody," I admonished, "that's not necessary. I'll meet you at the store, you go in and if they resist, I'll come in and back you."

A few hours later, I met Ody in front of the grocery store. I could virtually hear his knuckles crack as he tightened his fists. His jaw became one huge muscular spasm. He was ready. Like a fighter entering the ring, he smiled at me, sneered at the open door and then walked into the store with the sour quart of milk under his arm.

I apprehensively waited outside for about two minutes, when a red-faced, very relieved Ody left the store with a brand new quart of milk in his hand.

"What happened?" I asked.

"When I got inside the store, two of the Arabs were behind the counter talking their foreign language. I put my sour milk on the counter and told them that the quart of milk I bought yesterday was sour. Without even looking at me, one of them said, 'Well go get another one'."

Ody never forgot that incident and frequently reminded me how we spend too much of our lives "worryin about nothin," Then, he would invariably add, with a broad grin, "What a waste of time, huh Doc?"

✳   ✳   ✳

I've had a few of my own "quart of milk" experiences in the many years since writing this story. Yet, thanks to Ody, my initial grimacing at the thought of a dreaded showdown invariably morphed into a reminiscent smile.

In trying to locate Ody's whereabouts for the second edition, most of the old Tenderloin regulars who knew him agreed that he had died. When, where and how he died was open to long debates and no clear consensus. Apparently he died "last year" or "a few years ago" somewhere in the Tenderloin.

I'll bet he also died alone, drinking milk until the end.

9

KENNY

Six Letter Word

Before HMOs, traditional psychoanalysts spent several days a week with their "analysands" exploring dreams, probing transferences, unearthing repressions and chasing insights. They collected $250 a session.

The traditional psychotherapists were spending one day a week with their "patients" spotlighting unacceptable behaviors, uncovering denials, reducing symptoms and re-shaping personalities. They received $125 per session.

There was also a more pragmatic, common sense group of clinicians. Those psychotherapists had bi-weekly sessions with "clients" to help them stay out of trouble and better cope with the stresses of every day living. I was one of those therapists. We got $27 per session from MediCal.

All of those therapies had a few things in common. They served customers (analysand, patient, client). The therapist did a lot of listening and, of course, there was that fee for services. Research has indicated that what constitutes the best therapist has nothing to do with education, therapeutic discipline, amount of fee, etc. Hence the best therapy may well be the cheapest that can help the unique struggle of the customer, as a client. Those are affordable, no frills, no trendy theories and sometimes, no office therapies. Kenny was one of those clients. In retrospect, Kenny was the epitome of all of my clients.

📖 📖 📖

Kenny was a Tenderloin resident, an occasional victim, part time drunk and periodic mark, with plenty of street savvy to protect his naive innocence. He had never learned how to say "no." That can be a severe handicap in the Tenderloin, where everyone is constantly asking for something.

"You got an extra cigarette, extra dollar, extra joint, extra beer, extra food?" were some of the more typical requests.

That was no problem for Kenny, he just grinned a big "yes."

With a fixed Supplemental Security Income of $600 a month, he managed amazingly well. He kept extra everythings, except money. He was always broke, but never needy. Kenny supported two cats and a goldfish in his little room. He also helped care for his deaf mute, mentally retarded girlfriend. She lived down the hall.

Kenny was very much Tenderloin. He didn't just live there; he felt he belonged there. He really liked it. He liked the people, including the ones who liked using him. He liked the grocery store on Pine Street, and he even liked his local reputation as an amateur hustler and easy mark. He was accepted by Tenderloin toughies as both harmless and useful. He was trusted to mind his own business and keep secrets. In some ways, he was the Tenderloin water boy—always on the sidelines, running errands for the big game hustlers.

When not busy with his Tenderloin chores, Kenny engaged in two cherished hobbies. He loved puzzles and walking. Funny paper puzzles, like finding hidden objects in pictures and Hangman, were his favorites. He also liked doing easy crossword puzzles, even though he never finished any without looking up the answers.

Puzzles were usually followed by long walks, well beyond the Tenderloin perimeter. Many of the Tenderloin "hard-core" envied those walks since, for them, the Tenderloin was not just a place to live, but also a refuge. It was a safe haven where no one was labeled strange, odd or inferior. Those Tenderloin residents considered themselves an extended family of displaced persons. They felt protected by an invisible wall that borders the unfamiliar, where they believed they were not wanted.

Kenny's friends were amazed that he was as comfortable in unfamiliar territory as he was in the Tenderloin. He could be spotted merrily walking Market Street, the Embarcadero, North Beach and such distant areas as Golden Gate Park.

He roamed the city with grinning "How are you today" greetings. He even braved the big department stores, especially nearby Macy's. Those stores were off-limits to most Tenderloin people because they fit the stereotype of what Tenderloin people should look like. They were profiled as shoplifters and usually shadowed by security personnel, who had arrested many of them. Kenny was never rousted or arrested by security; maybe because he blended so well or maybe because he never shoplifted. He just walked around and handled merchandise, tried on clothes and dowsed himself with sample colognes. His scent was recognized long before he was seen.

Cruising the hotel lobbies for complimentary meals was another of his pastimes. That was probably his most legendary activity, one that won him honorary hero status in the Tenderloin.

Kenny's creative success was his ability to look and smell familiar to the unfamiliar. He would don one of his Goodwill suits, hit Macy's for a quick dowsing and infiltrate the Jack Tarr or Hilton lobby in search of a free meal.

He usually began by scanning the hotel convention directory with other conventioneers. The conventions with the biggest buffets were his first choice. Those were "easy pickin's" as he casually smiled to others who were more concerned with the food decorating the tables than another friendly colleague.

Security and convention hosts were rarely a problem. He simply looked and acted too much like the average conventioneer. He even smelled like most of them. Kenny did, nevertheless, avoid sit-down meals. Some of his closest calls occurred when sitting at a table with "pretend" colleagues. That was much too close and personal, especially since he didn't have a meal ticket. Conventioneers generally got their meal tickets in the mail or at the reception booth where they paid their fees. In his more daring days, Kenny might even sift through convention packets left on chairs during breaks. He also tried plucking at an occasional pocket. Kenny soon discovered he was a terrible pickpocket with a conscience. Besides, it was too risky.

Even with a meal ticket, the conventioneers seated at his chosen table, were often too friendly. "Hi, I'm Dr. Smithers, what did you think of the lecture on the use of Ciprofloxacin in place of Cephalexin? …" "What school did you say you graduated from…?" "Where did you do your internship…?" "You must have known Professor Strudel."

Knowing he was an impostor, Kenny viewed these friendly questions as interrogations. That tended to spoil the best of luncheons as he gulped, nodded and tried to smile his way through each course.

📖 📖 📖

I heard of Kenny before I ever met him. One of my clients told me about this Tenderloin legend, who dined for free at all the big hotels, ran drugs for the Mafia and was Macy's most notorious shoplifter. He was a legend all right. More accurately, another client said that Kenny was looking for a therapist and would like to interview me. I, of course, agreed to the interview. After all, he was a potential customer who had every right to look me over.

The "legend" arrived at my office on time, holding a half-filled cup of coffee and wearing an ear-to-ear grin. I'm not sure what I expected, but he wasn't very legendary-looking.

Moderately short and thin, Kenny probably weighed in at about 140 pounds. His clothes were very clean, well-pressed and very second-hand. His green 1950's style sport coat, with huge lapels, dangled loosely over his narrow shoulders, and the collar of his red shirt neatly overlapped his sport coat collar, also 1950's style. Clearly visible argyle socks suggested that his gray polyester bell-bottoms were too short. His big, shiny, buckled brown high tops were reminiscent of an earlier decade's stylish fashion. His thick, curly, dyed golden blond hair matched his second-hand clothing. Yet below his long Roman nose was a natural graying handlebar mustache—20's style.

Despite those old-fashioned time-lapse contradictions, Kenny looked dapper, even handsome, especially when one was distracted by his sparkling clear blue eyes that constantly smiled along with the rest of his face.

Kenny would have been a charmer in any historical period. He always seemed comfortable with himself or others, no matter who they were or what he wore. Much of his charm was his childlike exuberance and open delight with games of all kinds. Dying his hair and wearing obvious second-hand clothing weren't feeble attempts to disguise himself, it was "himself." He was like a kid dressing up as a cowboy or a Frankenstein monster. He wore whatever pleased him, except at conventions, when part of the game was a more conservative suit and tie.

During that first interview Kenny sat back quite relaxed in his chair with hands clasped behind his neck and left ankle resting casually on his right knee, wrangler style. He asked me all kinds of questions about my hobbies, interests, marital status, preferred restaurants, etc. Interestingly, he asked nothing about my experience or background as a therapist, other than a grinning, "Do you accept MediCal?"

Then, less than a half hour through the interview, Kenny readily agreed to see me bi-weekly. He coyly explained that therapy was a condition of his SSI benefits. He could have obviously survived without treatment, but not without his benefits.

Many Tenderloin residents receive SSI benefits for physical or mental disabilities. Those benefits entitle them to a bare-bones survival income and MediCal or Medicare health insurance. Mental disabilities that qualify include drug substance abuse, emotional disorders and any other conditions that preclude regular salaried employment. One of the requirements attached to those benefits was psychotherapy or counseling. That was an aggravation to many, a nuisance to some and a blessing to the remainder.

Aggravation, nuisance or blessing, the fee was the same, $27 per session. MediCal or Medicare paid the fee, while the customers were charged 50 minutes of their time every other week.

Those qualified therapists, with their higher fee "patients," rarely accepted MediCal clients. The two main reasons were obvious. The State or Federal government was paying about one-sixth of the amount therapists were receiving in the private sector. MediCal clients required an enormous amount of paperwork and regulations before collecting the meager fee. There were also arbitrary payment denials for the slightest typographical error.

I was one of those rare therapists willing to endure the low fees and excruciating paperwork, while Kenny was one of those rare customers who found psychotherapy neither an aggravation, nuisance nor a blessing. He just enjoyed it.

In fulfilling treatment requirements, he needed a therapist who wouldn't demand conventional therapy and wouldn't try to change him. He really wanted an advocate and companion, who knew the social service system well enough to keep him in the system.

As a psychotherapist with very little professional Tenderloin experience at the time, I had a lot to learn. Tenderloin people are simply people with a complete range of problems, indicative of persons anywhere. I was also acknowledging that psychotherapy is only a word, encompassing a broad range of activities. It has something to do with favorably altering one's self-image and coping skills. This boils down to increasing a client's degree of comfort with life.

In the Tenderloin, there couldn't be much comfort without a roof over one's head. Consequently, as a Tenderloin psychotherapist, helping clients pay their rent by keeping them on SSI was probably my greatest therapeutic contribution. Even today it seems obvious that a top priority in any therapy for the poor is ensuring a client's basic survival.

Once we agreed to a $27 therapeutic relationship, Kenny unclasped his hands from behind his neck, dropped his left foot to the floor and leaned toward me with his elbows on his knees. His narrow-eyed, casual grin rearranged itself into a wide-eyed, boyish smile.

"Is it okay to call you Larry?" Like bright blue stars, his eyes seemed to openly twinkle with my answer.

"Of course," I said half jokingly, "that's been my given name since birth."

Professionally, what I was called by Kenny didn't matter. How we got along and how he felt about himself did matter. As we smiled at each other, I asked, "Do you have any more crucial questions before we wrap up today's session?"

Kenny quickly whipped out a thick packet of papers from his back pants pocket. "Did you ever try to solve one of these?"

"One of what?"

My question was all he needed. He soberly leaped out of his chair and spread a cartoon-like puzzle on the table in front of me. Then he carefully explained the object of the puzzle. "There are twenty animals hidden in this picture. See if you can find them."

After a couple of minutes of searching the cartoon picture, I told him I could only find eighteen.

Kenny was ecstatic. He had just challenged and beat his newly acquired therapist. Beaming with pride, he cocked his head to one side and gently placed a hand on my shoulder.

"Larry," he said, with a confidential whisper, "it has taken me years of practice to get all of them. You got more than most. Do you want me to show you the two you missed?" he practically pleaded.

"Oh yes!" I begged.

He gleefully showed me the two undetected animals, and with a "there, there" pat on my shoulder, he offered a few pointers on how to find the hidden objects "next time." He kept his promise. Every session was a "next time" for Kenny. He brought old, classic hidden object puzzles that I never successfully completed, Hangmen I never solved and crossword puzzles that always stumped me.

Kenny just loved therapy. It guaranteed his rent, and he had a bi-weekly companion whom he could trust and respect. He also loved supporting his disabled lady friend down the hall. He loved posing as a conventioneer for free food that frequently yielded a bonus of pens, key chains and other advertising trinkets. He loved smelling good from Macy's perfume samples and he especially loved his cats, Fluff and Rags.

Aside from his puzzles and puzzle lectures, Kenny affectionately devoted some session time to his cats. Both neutered females, they had been rescued by Kenny from abusive owners who decided they no longer wanted the responsibility of caring for an animal. Sadly, such owners also shunned the responsibility of finding a new home for their castaways.

When the family next to his room moved, they abandoned Rags, half starved, in the hallway. That was two years earlier. More recently, he heard a desperate meow, echoing through the garbage chute on his floor. Each chute ended in a closed trash box in the basement of the building. That's where he found Fluff, terrified, dirty and bloody from scratching open wounds.

Rags and Fluff were now well-fed, physically healed and recovering emotionally. Rags couldn't be dragged from the security of her home without a clawing, scratching fight. She could happily spend the rest of her life sprawled on the windowsill or on Kenny's lap. Fluff, on the other hand, was most content wandering the Tenderloin streets, perched safely on Kenny's shoulder. She playfully nibbled either earlobe, hissed at passing dogs and meowed gleefully when someone stopped to pet her.

That was a pleasant life for Kenny and his little family. The only real problem, he could always use more money. That need applied to most Tenderloin residents, who were constantly so broke they tended to idolize money. The lust for money intensified as it neared extinction toward the end of each month, when pension, welfare and SSI checks were depleted. During that dreadful last week, pawnshops flourished, St. Anthony Dining Room bread lines lengthened and bartering was everywhere. Some of the shyest of the poor just quietly got hungrier.

It was during one of those "end of the month" weeks when Kenny missed his appointment with me. He had decided to take a walk with Fluff before our session. That wasn't really unusual. While merrily walking down Jones between O'Farrell and Ellis, he and Fluff noticed a man lying on the sidewalk, halfway up an alley. Part curiosity and part compassion led him into the alley. He could smell those familiar alcoholic fumes as he approached the snoring body.

He's just another drunk sleeping it off, Kenny thought. He noticed the man was better dressed than most Tenderloin bums. As Kenny was about to leave, he unfortunately saw a cluster of green paper, more out than in the coat pocket.

He could clearly see two twenty-dollar bills, a ten and two five's working their way out of the snoring man's pocket. Down to his last fifteen cents, that was just too much for Kenny to ignore. Nervously he carefully removed one of the five-dollar bills, while pushing the remaining bills deeper into the man's pocket. Kenny felt that was a moral compromise. Any nicely dressed drunk with all that money at the end of the month wouldn't miss five dollars.

As Kenny started to walk away, the snoring suddenly became a clearly articulated, "Don't move, this is the police." The snoring man was an undercover cop who, along with his partner hidden behind some garbage cans, arrested Kenny and Fluff.

During his one phone call from the city jail, Kenny's somber explanation ended in a tearful plea for Fluff's release from the animal shelter. I assured him I'd retrieve his cat. Fair-weather therapists, like fair-weather friends lose their reliability if they disappear in a crisis, especially in the Tenderloin, where crises are frequent. Part of therapy was helping clients out of jams, and Kenny was a well-qualified client in a jam.

After managing Fluff's release from the San Francisco Animal Control, I contacted a friend of Kenny's who was willing to care for both cats until Kenny returned. That was a huge relief for me since my dog happened to hate cats. Kenny was so relieved his cats were safe, he must have thanked me every five minutes while we talked within the city jail holding tank. He would be arraigned the following morning for robbery.

📖   📖   📖

The receptionist was bent over, shuffling official looking papers when I approached her desk at the District Attorney's office. It took about eight calls to get an appointment with the deputy district attorney handling Kenny's case.

"Good morning, I'm Dr. Wonderling," I announced a bit timidly, as I gazed at the top of the receptionist's head.

There was no response, nothing, not even a grunt. All I could hear were the muffled voices from rear offices, phones ringing and occasional laughter from the nearest office.

"I'm Dr. Wonderling," I repeated in a bigger voice. "I have an appointment to see Mr. Smedley."

Again there wasn't the slightest upward head movement, not even a head tilt. "Take a seat and Mr. Smedley will be with you in a while." I heard from somewhere beneath the top of her head.

About a half hour later, the nearest office door partially opened, producing a more audible exchange of jokes and laughter. Mr. Smedley and another deputy D.A., both with big grins, strolled through the now fully opened door.

Recognizing Smedley, I leaped to my feet and passively blocked his intended exit. "Mr. Smedley, I'm Dr. Wonderling. I believe we have an appointment."

His grin seemed to automatically shift to an authoritative stare, "We do? Oh yeah. Come into my office." As he gestured toward his open door, he gave his deputy buddy a knowing nod. "I'll see you in a while at Polo's."

The receptionist was still a top of a head without a face. I wondered if she were all right.

Mr. Smedley frantically searched through dozens of arrest reports until he finally found Kenny's report near the bottom of a foot high pile. Softening a little, Smedley apologized for not having time to look over the report.

As he read, I recounted the entire incident, as explained to me by Kenny and the arresting officer. Police, probably worldwide, are prone to exaggerate an arrest report in order to strengthen their case. Weak cases are routinely dismissed or never heard and more critically, the arresting officer's credibility is damaged. Even overworked public defenders were aware of those exaggerations, which invariably invited back room deals and pleas to lesser offenses.

Serving as Kenny's therapist, advocate and defense attorney, I argued that Kenny still needed therapy; he was harmless and entrapped by the police. "Besides," I said, trying a bit of levity, "who intends to commit robberies with a cat on their shoulder?"

Prepared for an officious legalistic rebuttal, I was delighted with Mr. Smedley's comment as he glanced at his watch, "Don't worry, this case will be dismissed tomorrow."

I never did see the receptionist's face.

📖 📖 📖

After nearly two days in jail, Kenny was released, feeling freer and happier than ever. Reunited with his cats, he swore to never jeopardize their welfare again. He would also walk by fallen bums unless he knew them, and he assured me that any pickpocket urges vanished with his release from jail. Kenny was the same little guy, only with more resolve to stay out of trouble. He still loved puzzles, our sessions, his cats and caring for others less fortunate. He continued to smell like Macy's cologne samples, but he cautiously avoided convention sit-down meals.

I was delighted he was free and hadn't changed much. He was a caring person who never hurt anyone or expressed any anger. Blaming others tends to trigger anger. He never blamed anyone for anything. Some of the well-fed, middle class might have complained that Kenny had no business receiving SSI benefits. He wasn't psychotic, neurotic or an active drug substance abuser. He was also pretty much a conniver who could manage his life in the Tenderloin.

What the righteously indignant didn't know was that Kenny, like so many other SSI recipients, was simply incapable of competing for, or maintaining, regular salaried employment. No one has a perfect brain, whatever that is, and Kenny's brain was significantly less than perfect. The average I.Q. is 100. His was a borderline 68. The average person can remember what they ate yesterday for breakfast. Kenny could barely remember what he had for breakfast a half hour after breakfast. His attention span was seriously compromised, as well as very sluggish motor ability and concrete-type thinking.

In other words, Kenny had difficulty following simple instructions, sizing up social situations or sustaining attention for over several minutes. What was clear and obvious to the average person was confusing to him. He just couldn't figure things out like most of us. Kenny was just a kind person with a perfectly compassionate heart and an imperfectly wired brain.

Kenny could always marginally get by in the Tenderloin, simply because he blended inconspicuously with so many others who were socially ridiculed, scorned or even feared in more conventional communities. The Tenderloin was indeed his home, a secure haven where he contributed as friend, jester, sometimes hustler and—even as victim.

"Payday," as SSI recipients call it, was a first of the month event. It was a busy time for Tenderloin residents who paid their rent, shopped at their favorite grocery store, paid off small loans and even tried to figure out a budget for the next month. Kenny was as busy as anyone, except that he was interrupted more than most with repaid cans of food, cigarettes and an occasional dollar or two. He rarely remembered to whom he had loaned what, and it probably didn't matter. He was always thrilled to have any of his loans repaid.

The short, two-block walk to his Tenderloin grocery store was pleasant for Kenny, especially on payday. He had taken that stroll hundreds of times and looked forward to greetings from friends on the street. Repaying his grocery tab, generally about $25, was another first-of-the-month pleasure.

On that rather cold, rainy first of February, Kenny left Fluff at home in anticipation of a wet walk to the store and a load of groceries to carry back to his room. On his way to the store, the wet, chilly streets seemed deserted, except for two young guys he vaguely recognized from the south of Market area.

He spent about a half hour at the store chatting with the clerk, cashing his check, paying his bill and buying enough groceries to fill two big brown bags. Gripping a bag under each arm, Kenny was only several steps from the store when one of the young guys he'd noticed, emerged from a shadowy doorway directly in front of Kenny.

"Got some extra change?" the kid nervously demanded, while shifting his eyes up and down the barren streets.

Before Kenny could answer, his arms were pinned by someone else, probably the other young guy. Both brown bags crashed to the wet curb and Kenny felt a sharp pain as a knife blade pierced his lower abdomen. The assailant then sliced upward, ripping a five-inch gash. Kenny slumped to his knees with the knife still in his stomach.

After removing everything Kenny had in his pockets, the knife was pulled from his stomach and both thugs disappeared down Leavenworth Street.

Clutching his intestines, protruding from the open wound, Kenny fell backwards over broken jars and soggy, bloody groceries that had torn through the bags. The entire assault probably lasted ten seconds and, fortunately for Kenny, the grocery clerk called the police while the assault was in progress. An ambulance arrived in a few minutes and Kenny's life was mercifully spared.

Although that traumatic incident occurred very early in my Tenderloin practice, I'll never forget one of his comments after surgery. Kenny had been in the recovery room for just a few hours when I arrived at his bedside. A newspaper was draped over his covers and tubes seemed to be exiting his body from everywhere.

"How are you?" I asked very solemnly.

Kenny clutched the newspaper as if looking for something. "What's a six letter word for cat?" he solemnly replied.

The young thugs were never arrested and from what I've heard since my retirement, Kenny walks to the same grocery store every payday. He still loves puzzles, and he rarely goes anywhere without a cat called Fluff perched on his shoulder.

Six years later and no one in the Tenderloin seems to know what happened to Kenny. Hopefully he simply moved to another area where stray cats, puzzles and big department stores with samples of colognes are readily available.

10

JOHN

A Personal Choice

Much of our society still demands that we stay alive until we die naturally—whatever that means. Many hospitals are reluctant to administer too many pain-killing drugs to the dying, because such drugs are addictive. Some hospital staff even think they know that the dying patient isn't really in that much pain. Such traditional and irrational nonsense placates and protects the medical institution while devastating many of the dying. Societies don't experience pain, nor do they have thoughts or feelings. Only humans can experience their own consciousness, and only the individual can decide how much dying to endure.

Once we agree that each of us, as individuals, know our tolerance for both pain and life better than any society, it becomes apparent that only the individual is qualified to manage dying and time of death. Yet, tragically, too many of our social institutions translate this humane logic of suicide or euthanasia into some form of murder.

Throughout the centuries, wars have killed millions of precious lives for their country's political and religious institutions. They think they know when the time to die is moral. Medals and a hero's burial are even given to those individuals who die righteously for their country's debatable beliefs. The logic of that reasoning is as sour as its message is absurd.

There is something terribly wrong with reasoning that even hints you're a hero when you die for your country and some sort of lunatic when you die for yourself. Social policies and politics, allies and enemies, even right and wrong may change from one country or decade to another. But your responsibility to yourself never changes, even in the Tenderloin, where bums may also prefer to die with dignity.

📖   📖   📖

John was one of my special clients. He lived in the Tenderloin, complied with all aspects of our treatment program and never seemed to complain. He clearly understood that his Supplemental Security Income was contingent upon his program compliance, and he took his responsibility very seriously. He attended Alcoholics Anonymous three times a week, kept his appointments with me in therapy every other week and volunteered his services two times a week at St. Anthony's, where he generally helped cleaning up the kitchen.

John was the ideal client—mild mannered, co-operative, non-aggressive yet assertive and helpful. He was the kind of person who lingered after a group meeting to help fold and stack chairs without being asked. During group meetings, John showed a reticence that might have been interpreted as being shy or withdrawn. Neither was accurate, he was simply a good listener, who preferred not to talk unless he had something to say or contribute. He had no interest in performing for the sake of impressing anyone or winning an argument. All that seemed to be irrelevant to him.

Sometimes, near the close of a boisterous group session, tangled in opinions, counter-opinions, threats and challenges, John would articulate a clear summary of the group interactions to the astonishment of everyone. It also became increasingly evident that when John offered one of his occasional comments or summaries, the whole group listened—even those loud-mouthed "performers."

John's physical appearance and mannerisms fully supported his crisp insights, an ability to expose non-issues that so frequently sabotaged group progress. All of John's features radiated a gentle strength, sound health and normality. Over six feet tall, slender yet solidly built and well-coordinated, John could have been easily believable as a retired champion athlete, college coach or any profession requiring intelligence and outdoor activities.

Underlying his reddish, slightly veined, ruddy complexion was the straight, well-sculptured bone structure of a very handsome younger man. At 50, his hair had remained thick and sandy brown, with a few hints of gray. His clear brown eyes always seemed relaxed and unchallenging, even while darting about in search of direct eye contact with others.

To the average observer who didn't know him, he was invariably regarded as a still handsome man who had spent too much time in the sun. Those who knew his history, however, would clearly see the vestiges of a handsome man who had spent too much time in taverns.

In short, John probably looked more self-contained and reliant than most therapists, which is actually a terrible obstacle in life for someone on disability. People expect too much of them and resent disabilities they can't understand. There was a time before John began receiving SSI benefits that the only thing expected of him was a wretched early death.

He started drinking with his abusive father and phlegmatic mother in his early teens. His parents were both alcoholics and attorneys. Well-liked in high school, John graduated with academic honors and athletic scholarships, yet, after one year of college, he was expelled as the school drunk. After losing several jobs, he apparently hit the alcoholic bottom with incapacitating Delirium Tremens (DT's). That condition resulted in acute care hospitalization. Later, John frequently needed detoxification, and was placed in several residential treatment programs, to which he was totally unresponsive.

John's clinical history further included near endless, between treatment public drunkenness arrests, multiple job loses after less than a week or two and several failed marriages to alcoholics he met in bars or treatment programs. He had also experienced some nasty head injuries during drunken falls, and by the time he reached his middle thirties, John was having severe epileptic seizures, probably related to alcohol and head traumas.

John's downhill spiral gained momentum in his forties, when he plunged into the bottomless abyss of a skid row wino existence. That stage is generally terminal within a few years with causes of death ranging from cirrhosis, suffocating seizures, strokes, pancreatitis, to drunken exposure. Such a history, with its inevitable slide into further deterioration and death, was characteristic of too many of my clients from Project Title XVI—sometimes.

Crawling with lice and scabies, intestinal parasites, seizures and a painfully swollen cirrhotic liver, John was barely surviving. The Tenderloin was the only place in San Francisco that could tolerate his tortured dying.

"I have never experienced such agony and degradation, and I hope I never will again," he often said to me.

Those, like John, who have been there, fall so far into misery and despair; they give up ever finding their way back. John was one of those rare exceptions.

It was during that critical period, between dying and death that John, with the help of some Tenderloin Clinic counselors, was awarded his life-saving SSI benefits. His clinical diagnosis was Alcohol Dependence, Severe, with Organic Brain Syndrome, Unspecified (epileptic seizures associated with alcoholism). His first SSI check was a tiny ember that seemed to ignite a fragile spark of hope for one last chance—to find his way back. His most urgent needs were medical and with newly authorized MediCal benefits, John was hospitalized for two weeks. When discharged, he was again able to afford a small Tenderloin hotel room, clean clothes and nourishing food.

John had another chance, with only a glimmer of promise. He had failed during this recovery period too many times before. He knew too well that when alcoholics like him begin to feel better, they celebrate with a disastrous binge that pulls them further back on the street or into the morgue. He also clearly recognized that he must avoid another insidious alcoholic pitfall of over-ambition.

Many recovering alcoholics in remission entertain an unrealistic surge of confidence that they're capable of working and competing in competitive society. Invariably those alcoholics are overwhelmed by the stresses and pressures of everyday living, resulting in another failure and retreat into alcohol.

During the ten years following his near fatal relapse, John had managed to solve those obstacles realistically and quite effectively. By the time he met me, John had created for himself a safe cloister and stable lifestyle within the Tenderloin.

Oddly, he had adapted well to an environment that most San Franciscans would find too unstable or distasteful to even consider as home. That was one of the many clinical lessons I learned from John and other clients.

Conforming to the demands of conventional society is never a tenable treatment goal. Sometimes the most "socially acceptable environments" are just too psychosocially toxic to nourish anyone. Yet, making the best out of a shaky situation by finding a protective "fit" for your abilities and interests is vital. John found the right "fit" in the Tenderloin. In addition to his treatment program routine, he functioned best as a loner with numerous acquaintances and no friends. I once asked him if he were ready for another woman in his life.

John offered a smile of understanding along with a clear, simple explanation. "I can hardly tolerate or manage myself. I think it's best I leave well enough alone. Don't you?"

I had to agree.

John had never even considered abstinence as one of his adaptive solutions. He was still a heavy smoker and he continued to drink. Yet he had managed to regulate his alcohol to a "maintenance level." For him that represented about ten beers a day, no wine and no hard liquor. It was certainly a biological stabilizer in the sense that he had no more binges, incontinence, lice, bloated liver or detoxifications. Even his seizures were less severe.

When not involved in treatment activities, his day was occupied leaning over a beer at his nearby Tenderloin bar on Leavenworth Street. Like so many others, he would engage in shallow bar room banter about sports, weather or politics. Sometimes those discussions would evolve into heated arguments, but almost always at a safe, friendly distance.

On his way home, he frequently ate at one of his favorite Chinese cafes, where the food was, as he used to laughingly put it, "good and cheap." His last stop was typically for a six-pack that he generally polished off alone in his hotel room, reading or listening to the radio. He couldn't stand TV.

Those were John's Tenderloin activities, his way of life; and in therapy, he was always quick to agree that his life wasn't very exciting or inspirational.

"For me, it's safe and predictable, with very few demands and no stress. I'm even healthier than I ever was."

It was really hard to find a flaw in John's reasoning, except when he would sometimes add, "It's tolerable, Larry."

That's when I would reply, "Gee, John, just tolerable? No risks, no surprises—no fun? What would make your life more than tolerable?"

Staring at the floor, John always gave me the courtesy of a long reflective pause before repeating essentially the same message. "I've taken too many risks and always end up with emotional or physical pain. I'm finally safe and secure."

After knowing John for several years, I summarized his progress in my therapy notes. "John is exceptionally cooperative and amenable to treatment; however, one of his major defensive strengths results in his noteworthy unresponsiveness to change. He is his own person, earnestly believing that he knows himself better than anyone and accepts responsibility for caring for himself. He tends to rationally weigh advice before making his own decisions. John's reasoning has merit, and I intend to continue supporting his position…"

I wasn't particularly worried when John missed an appointment. He was still predictably self-contained, stable and one of the least likely of all my clients to relapse. Besides, after five years, he was entitled to a day off now and then, and if he had a problem, he'd certainly call. He did.

"This is John, sorry I missed the appointment. I've been in the hospital for several days. They say I have some kind of throat cancer. They're going to give me some chemical treatment and maybe an operation. The oncologist told me that surgery, chemical and radiation treatments have an 80% success rate for this type of cancer."

John accepted those odds, and after several months of extremely painful treatment, he gradually recovered with a gravelly voice and the loss of about 35 pounds. He also looked older, with sunken eyes, deep wrinkles, pallid complexion, the temporary loss of all his hair and a generally gaunt, fragile appearance.

John resumed his voluntary kitchen work at St. Anthony's, group participation and his visits to my office. During the following year and a half, he was again a regular at his local Tenderloin bar, with evening meals at the Chinese cafe and a six-pack to his hotel room, where he read and listened to the radio, as he had for so many years. He was still a maintenance drinker, and although he often acknowledged to me he really missed smoking, he hadn't had a cigarette since his hospitalization over two years before.

John continued to be the easy-going, cooperative client who amazed his group with rich clinical insights. He never troubled anyone. The possibility that the throat cancer would reemerge had long faded from our conversations—until he arrived one day for what turned out to be his last session with me.

His oncologist had advised him that the cancer had reoccurred. John looked directly into my eyes, as he explained in a clear, articulate, almost pleasant fashion that he just didn't want to endure more cancer treatment.

"At best," he said, "it might prolong my obscure and monotonous life for a while longer." He had decided to kill himself.

When asked about any unfinished business in his life, he said he hadn't seen his father, who lived in Oregon, for over five years. So he agreed to visit his father before suicide.

Three weeks after his final session with me, he shot himself in the head, causing instant death.

His father later called me with expressions of gratitude for his chance to say goodbye to his son, and he tearfully added that he understood his son's decision.

Comparisons aren't fair, but neither is prolonging painful dying just for the sake of living, while hastening dying just for the good of another debatable war. For the individual, dying for the good of the self is much more rational.

John was no lunatic, blowing his brains out because of some fleeting whim, momentary rage or hallucinatory voice urging him on. His decision was reflective and rational. And, according to his father and my observations during that last session, he had begun his dying with a calm serenity and sense of dignity that was curiously comforting to observe. There should be no argument, no controversy about his death. Anyway, he's not alive to defend himself, and if he were, he would probably respond with nothing other than a reflective smile.

What really matters is that neither the Tenderloin nor I could protect John any longer from life's pain and torment. He needed to die.

It's 2007 and many years since I accepted John's death by suicide. Fulfillment of his decision, especially while in therapy, no doubt remains embroiled in heated controversy. Too many mental health professionals view suicide as clinically unethical even if it were a well-thought out last resort, rational decision by the client.

Unfortunately such professional opposition too often seems to be based less on ethics than possible litigation; which is more concerned with protecting the therapist than the client from intolerable suffering.

I hope some day the mental health profession will at least acknowledge that not all individuals in therapy are *incapable* of deciding when enough is enough.

11

EDWARDO

The Handshake

The Gettysburg Address offers comforting assurances that "All men are created equal." Over a hundred years later, while leaders are still echoing equality for all, there are nagging questions that keep challenging those echoes.

All men are equal? To whom? Why weren't women included? How come some people always seem better off than others? In fact, why do social scientists refer to some people as the "disadvantaged" if we're all created equal? The reality seems to be that equality is a wistful myth, leading to false hopes and unexpected failures.

It would be wonderful if all of us began life's journey at the same starting line, with the same bag of marbles and the same support systems to spur us onward. Then we might all truly be responsible for our successes and failures. In such a just, fair world, we could all be given a thousand credits. There would be

200 points each for a series of perfections, including perfect physical appearance, a genius IQ, perfect physical and mental health and exemplary parents of excellent genetic endowment.

This Utopian credit system would tend to eliminate imperfections and even differences. There would be no need for the normal distribution curve (bell-shaped) since there would only be "the advantaged."

But that's not how it works. There are glaring individual differences in everything that defines each individual. Our abilities, capacities, aptitudes and talents are as dissimilar as our fingerprints.

Some of us are naturally endowed with the speed of a cheetah, while others can barely make it across a boulevard by noon. The "gifted child" may be favored with natural brilliance or burdened with a natural gift of stupidity. There are the cruel variations in our health, and there's certainly nothing equal about our physical attractiveness. Birth gifts can only provide differences in opportunities, not equality.

More typically, a person starts life with a so-so appearance, an average IQ, vulnerable physical and mental abilities, flawed parents with imperfect genetics and a lower middle class socioeconomic status. In our Utopian system, those features would amount to about 495 credits; which would be characteristic of an Anita Average or Mike Mediocre. They could hardly share equal opportunities with Bill Brilliant and Betty Beautiful, both in the high nine hundreds.

📖 📖 📖

This is the story of Edwardo, who began his life's journey with credits somewhere in the "low 70's." From his beginning, there was nothing easy about Edwardo's struggle and nothing fair about his endowments. Sensing what was in store for him, he was reluctant to enter the world. Edwardo's delivery was long and difficult, until virtually yanked from the womb, into an early life of poor health, poor vision, poor parents and no opportunities.

During adolescence he was still small, sickly and partially blind, with no encouragement and no friends or guidance. Even his school experiences were preparing him for a gradual withdrawal from most of life's challenges.

By the time he approached his twenties, Edwardo had learned how to rebel against failures, taunts, rejections and criticisms with anger, mistrust, alcoholism and an inherited skin condition gone wild. As an adult, nothing about him was open, relaxed or accessible. He was a shadowy little nobody who creeped around the Tenderloin where he just wanted to remain safely unnoticed.

Suspicious of everybody, Edwardo never wanted participation in any kind of treatment program. But he had no choice, since treatment was jammed down his throat by the Department of Social Services, who controlled his meager disability income. He was diagnosed as an alcoholic, with partial blindness and all sorts of psychological disorders.

I first heard of him through the courts in late 1987. I didn't actually meet him, however, until the middle of 1988. He missed his first half dozen appointments. When he finally slinked into my office on a warm summer day, I understood why.

I saw his heavy tattered clothing before I noticed his face, probably because his face was too pathetically repulsive for me to notice. He wore an old, frayed sailor's cap—the kind you used to see in the five and dime stores, with a cloth anchor emblem glued to the crown above the cardboard visor. There was also a shiny red star carefully pinned to the anchor.

Long, stringy, dirty, black hair dangled beneath his sweat stained hat brim. The rest of his hair hid inside his turned up pea coat collar that served to obscure much of his face. Old denim bell-bottomed trousers hung loosely below his well-buttoned pea coat and combat-type, round-toed boots supported the bundle of clothes that effectively concealed Edwardo from others.

As he slouched into the chair I had offered him, the sun hit his shadowed face; and I clearly saw what I had tried not to see. Imagine cloves of garlic, wrapped in thick scars and festered pieces of skin, with a nose that looked like an old ginger root. Behind glasses as thick as telephoto lenses, his darting, evasive eyes seemed grotesquely sunken beneath thick jagged crests of dried pus and scars. Even his lips were drawn tight by scars creating a fixed ghastly snarl. Years of erupting acne cysts had produced layers of coarse, scar tissue that cruelly sculpted a hideously disfigured face. That was the cruelest of all his disabilities. Mercifully, at least his poor vision probably spared him a distant stranger's shocked glances or morbid stares.

During that first visit to my office, Edwardo tried hard to avoid any eye contact with me. I tried even harder to look directly at a face I really didn't want to see. As his eyes shifted from floor to ceiling, my greatest concern was losing him to shallow, patronizing words, strained, excessive smiles, or worse, a show of revulsion or rejection. So, I just let myself look sympathetic and sad, both of which were very genuine feelings at the time.

There was no dialogue that day, nor was there my usual orientation monologue. I did introduce myself, explain that I would try to help him in any way I could and that our first goal was to get to know one another.

He had no questions or comments. He certainly didn't know or trust me, and in using his major defense, he simply kept a safe distance. He offered one "no," two "yes sir's" and two "OK's" during our entire first session.

"Did you have any trouble finding my office?"

"No."

"How are you today?"

"OK."

"Do you still live on Eddy Street in the Tenderloin?"

"Yes sir."

"Would you like to leave now?"

"Yes sir."

"Will you come back next Thursday at 10 a.m.?"

"OK."

During the next half dozen sessions, Edwardo remained essentially inaccessible with more OK's, no's and not even a glance in my direction as he looked around the room. He seemed to look at everything but me. I used to think telephone sessions would have been easier for both of us.

There were, however, encouraging hints of some progress. Edwardo hadn't missed any appointments. His pea coat was unbuttoned by the third session, exposing his khaki, military type sweater and, most important, more of his face was showing. He was becoming increasingly comfortable with me as I became used to his face. He probably sensed that I could finally gaze at him without staring.

By the third month, Edwardo's silent defensiveness became more open and gratifyingly verbal. A new plateau was achieved. Dialogue! His OK's, yes sir's and no's gradually shifted to sarcastic questions, flavored with traces of paranoid suspicions.

"What did you mean by that?" or "Why are you asking me all these questions?" were his favorites. He was also beginning to look at me instead of around me, as if he finally knew I was thoroughly accustomed to his face and that my casual manner wasn't faked.

He told me over the next few months, that he loved to cook and had even tried cooking school. He added that he flunked cooking school because of poor vision and his incompatibility with supervisors and students.

Even though I just listened with an occasional, "uh-huh" or "I see," Edwardo would try to provoke me into an argument. He complained that I didn't understand his problems with people.

He threatened to stop coming because he "wasn't getting anything out of the sessions." "They're a waste of time," became one of his choice closing comments.

"I'm not going to fight you, so don't use me as an excuse to quit," became one of my choice replies.

Seven months had elapsed since our first session, and still there were no significant changes in his daily routine. No miraculous insights. No reduction in his drinking and plenty of anger, mixed with depression and distrust.

On the other hand, Edwardo was actually opening up. He was discharging intense, pent-up hostility that had been smoldering and festering, like his acne, for most of his life. Edwardo was finally able to vent his blocked inner rage in a safe place. He was also beginning to talk about topics he didn't want to talk about—like his face. It was more of an oblique question than a disclosure, but for me, a real breakthrough.

He casually asked, "Some people say alcohol is bad for acne, is that true?"

Psychotherapy is rarely magic. If it works, it starts

with a relationship that takes time to develop. Such progress has traditionally been called rapport or trust, and the bottom line is its very foundation to the therapeutic process. If that client sitting by you never develops any positive feelings for you and if you're not really liked, respected or trusted by your client, you will be approached or avoided like everyone else in the client's life. That means no honest expression of feelings and no progress.

During his initial sessions, Edwardo wasn't even expecting any positive changes in his life. He was just trying in his own seclusive way to survive the torments of another day. Then, gradually feeling increasingly comfortable with somebody, he seemed to be scenting an aroma of hope that something more than survival might be available to him. He was also experiencing a more healthy impatience instead of bitter resignation. He could finally express his frustrations to someone who would caringly look and listen.

It was time to do more than look and listen, no matter how caringly. Edwardo needed some tangible show of progress, something he could grasp. There was nothing more tangibly pitiful or therapeutically demoralizing than his face, which became my major goal and his major hope.

MediCal doesn't cover cosmetic surgery, especially for an alcoholic with no viable future. So, it wasn't unexpected when several months of formal requests and pleas to countless health agencies and charities, resulted in generous sympathy without assistance.

Then one night while having dinner with a physician friend, I shifted our conversation to Edwardo's face, and my face flushed with glee when I discovered help had been as close as a friend.

My friend, Marty, contorted his face into an almost

devilish grin as he said, "I'm not a plastic surgeon but I'll give it a try with a sanding process that should help."

"For free?" I asked.

With another big grin, he confessed that MediCal could pay for it under another billing code.

Thanks to Marty's compassion, friendship and his larcenous, creative billing, Edwardo got his face sanded. The process was long, frustrating and painful. Sand until you awaken feeling like you've been dragged through gravel on your face. Healing into a huge scab face, and once the scabs fall off, more sanding, pain, and scabs.

Six months after the first sanding, Edwardo's appearance was no longer grotesquely disfigured. Although far from handsome, he could at least walk relatively unnoticed with a face that was tolerable to view. That may not seem like much of an improvement without a before and after comparison of his face, but it was astonishing.

At last, there was no longer a hideous face in Edwardo's mirror, but it would take him months to lose sight of the old horrors of that face in his mind. Mind healing usually takes much longer than body healing, and even after abstinence from alcohol, a more nourishing diet and nature's constant tissue replacement, his self-image would lag behind his improving face for many years.

There were still residuals of his seclusive, insecure behavior. His reflex tendency to avoid eye contact with others was a reminder that old habits are hard to break and old appearances are hard to forget. Yet, Edwardo continued to honor his appointments and discussions gradually shifted from his face and life's many irritants, to his interests and life's possibilities.

📖 📖 📖

It was four years since I first met Edwardo. At that time he was a withdrawn, emotionally fragile, intensely wary, grotesque little guy whose only expectations were to maybe survive another day in the Tenderloin. Mind progress is indeed slow, but the effort is more than worth it.

Edwardo was beginning to feel content as he strolled the Ocean Beach. He was satisfied with himself and a face he no longer hid. Even more rewarding, was meeting a women he liked, especially when she smiled and he could smile back.

That may seem like a fitting end to this true story, but it gets better. During that fourth year, I learned one of Edwardo's secrets. Since childhood he had day-dreamed about working aboard ships and sailing to exotic ports of call. Private day-dreaming was a safe, secret way to hide the day's ugly realities. It was a time when no one could ever laugh at or mock his dreams because no one knew—no one until now.

Knowing that I could keep his secrets, Edwardo spent many sessions talking about his sailing fantasies, which just happened to be some of my fantasies. I had once planned to sail a small sloop around the world. Plans sometimes need to change, but I still loved talking about anything related to sailing. We shared fantasies, stories and the reality that San Francisco was more than a safe haven for him in the Tenderloin, it was a seaport city where he could actually touch the things his dreams were made of.

I remember when in school, there were few assignments as gratifying as those I had always wanted to do but never had the courage or encouragement to try on my own. Edwardo was ready for such assignments that would take his therapy beyond the safety of my office or the familiarity of his Tenderloin—out there, where there were greater risks and infinitely more gains.

His first assignment was easy. Just silently explore all the San Francisco marinas and piers. The second assignment was tougher. It involved his major hang up, interpersonal skills. He was still too outspokenly candid and could easily offend people without trying. Edwardo initially even balked at approaching some sailor with the intention of asking a question. That was too giant a leap for him, so we compromised. He agreed to simply try out his two new skills of making eye contact and flashing a smile at someone working on a boat.

He quickly learned that when you smile at someone, that someone invariably smiles back at you, which is usually followed by a greeting. Edwardo did his home-work well, and within a couple of months, his eye contact and smile paid off when an old seaman told him about the SS Jeremiah O'Brien.

The O'Brien was the last operational Liberty Ship out of thousands that braved the oceans during World War II. Those venerable and very vulnerable ships had been virtually defenseless as they carried essential cargo to allies in fighting areas throughout the world. The O'Brien had survived, but was in desperate need of volunteers to refit the historical ship for San Francisco Bay cruises as a floating museum.

Edwardo and that steel gray relic became insep-arable pals. They took good care of each other. He started his volunteer work as a general helper with the dirtiest clean-up jobs, then paint chipping and sanding. As the old ship grew more presentable and confident, so did Edwardo.

His tattered old wool pea coat, that had hidden his face and shielded him from the world for so many years, probably had to be surgically removed before he could wear his new, polypropylene jacket. It was dark blue with the proud words "JEREMIAH O'BRIEN CREW" emblazoned across the back. That jacket was Edwardo's new skin. Those words must have been grafted to his mind's eye. I never saw him drop his eyes again.

S. S. Jeremiah O'Brien

By 1993, Edwardo had been elevated to third cook on the O'Brien, and in another year he had a chance to experience the journey from his dreams.

The fiftieth anniversary of the end of World War II was nearing, and the O'Brien was to be honored at an international ceremony for heroic ships, to be held in France. Edwardo was still receiving SSI benefits as his only source of income.

During one of our sessions about three months before the ship's departure, Edwardo mentioned he had been offered a berth as one of the crew. He added, through misty eyes, it was a real honor even though he couldn't go to France without losing his SSI.

"Hey," I said, "I'm not even going to ask you because I'm telling you. You're going on that ship if it's the last thing you ever do. As far as SSI is concerned, it's part of your treatment—the most important part. Get it?"

Like an echo from his first office visit, Edwardo's only reply was a barely audible, "yes sir," accompanied by a rare sight. Edwardo sobbed.

The O'Brien returned to San Francisco toward the end of November 1994. It was a day for celebrities, and Edwardo was one of them. As the old liberty ship was escorted under the Golden Gate by those huge fireboats, there were hundreds of small boats to greet her. I watched from the Aquatic Park pier, and when those great plumes of water covered the O'Brien in a rainbowed mist, I knew that Edwardo was somewhere on deck, bundled in his polypropylene crew jacket, feeling very proud and fulfilled.

One of my most cherished gifts is a large picture of Edwardo shaking hands with President Clinton on the deck of the Jeremiah O'Brien. On the back it says, "Dr. Wonderling, Thank you for your friendship and for helping me through the many years. Sincerely yours. Normandy '94."

The Edwardo I first met in the eighties had tenaciously survived into the 21st century. A reunion with him on the O'Brien, still moored in San Francisco, was a real treat. He was self-assured, engaging, spontaneous and without a trace of the old habit of questioning all of my comments. So I figured now it was my turn for a question. Just what did he and the President of the United States say to each other?

When I asked him, Edwardo flashed me a mischievous smile and his answer should have been obvious to anyone who knew him, "I just told Mr.

Clinton I never voted for him. The President kinda laughed and said he hoped I'd vote for him next time. I probably will."

Edwardo no longer needed the Tenderloin. He continued to work as a volunteer third cook on the O'Brien and he lives contentedly with his lady friend in the Mission District. He went back to cooking school, pursuing an earlier dream, and constant reminders of his past have encouraged volunteer work with the disabled.

Remarkably, Edwardo felt fulfilled and grateful for his prosperity, despite daily dialysis during the past five years. When I heard of his need for daily treatment, the flaw in the 1,000-credit system dawned on me. If resilience, determination, courage and gratitude are included in my credit system, I realized Edwardo had been destined to succeed after all.

President Clinton and Edwardo on the deck of the
S. S. Jeremiah O'Brien

❋   ❋   ❋

It has been nearly seven years since I wrote about Edwardo, and his spunk hasn't changed. Shortly after the first edition of this book was published, I called Edwardo to check on his health. His answer was an invitation to a day long San Francisco Bay cruise on "his ship," the Jeremiah O'Brien.

Then he added, "Oh, I'm great."

I had a fun day enjoying the Bay on that revered old piece of World War II history. Edwardo, of course, couldn't have felt too great with useless kidneys and daily dialysis.

I never expected that my transition from middle age to old age would trigger guilt about my exceptionally healthy kidneys. It did. So I made the big decision, yet not too surprisingly, he declined my kidney offer with an awkward smile. Admittedly, I experienced a mixed sense of relief and disappointment—I've always hated hospitals and procedures. Anyway I might not have been a match.

Finally, after seven years, Edwardo topped the donor's list and received a kidney late in 2003. As of May 2007 he's doing fine and still third cook volunteer on "his ship."

If there were a Hall of Fame award for resilience, Edwardo would be my choice. Even today I can easily spot him a block away with his white seaman's cap and polypropylene O'Brien crew jacket.

12

BOB

The Prophecy

People choose to live in the Tenderloin for as many reasons as there are Tenderloin residents—escape, anonymity, affordability, acceptance, protection, etc. Beneath those choices are the strong fibers that bind them together. Those are the expectations that the Tenderloin will somehow enrich their lives by strengthening their survival struggle. Unfortunately, in some cases those new residents rely too much on either the Tenderloin or themselves. Then those strong fibers snap.

Expectations play a vital role in our lives. There's even a psychological theory relevant to this notion and story. One of the endless ways to sort people is by their dependency. In the extreme, "Field Dependent" individuals rely on their surroundings for success, and "Field Independent" persons rely on themselves.

We need both our environment and ourselves to succeed; and when we expect too much from either, there's trouble ahead. That's when we start beating up our surroundings or ourselves.

📖   📖   📖

A crisp clean booming bass resonated the closing lines of a play at the Curran Theater, located near the Tenderloin. Opened in 1925, the Curran was an invitation to success for any actor who performed there. Bob had performed exceptionally well. After bowing gratefully, he accepted several curtain calls. Then he angrily stomped his way back to the dressing room. That was his last performance for American Conservatory Theater (ACT). His director considered Bob a brilliant actor with an intolerably bad attitude. Bob considered himself a brilliant actor, hampered by the director's intolerably bad attitude. Perhaps, in actuality, they just didn't get along.

That was young Bob, in the early 50's. At that time, he had the singular burning ambition of becoming an accomplished professional actor. He had numerous acting awards and endless accolades in high school drama. Upon graduation, he received a prestigious ACT scholarship. Bob assumed he was on his way to a successful acting career, and his optimism sometimes bordered on arrogance. Yet his over-confidence didn't seem unreasonable considering his physical talents, intense motivation and early successes.

He had inherited a magnificent voice that commanded attention, even when he whispered. It was a deep thundering voice of power and an imposing, passionately expressive voice of wisdom. Those qualities made just about everyone who heard him, his audience. Bob's voice could invite tears, chills or blind obedience.

He was also strikingly handsome with strong, well

sculptured features, thick lively black hair over matching bushy eyebrows and dark brown penetrating eyes. Bob's physique was equally impressive. Broad-shouldered and narrow-waisted, he moved his six foot four frame in a surprisingly light, graceful fashion. His striking physical appearance complimented the allure and authority of his voice. Bob had everything going for him; he was a shoe-in, a sure thing, a winner. Maybe that was his problem.

Perhaps success was premature and out of sequence. He discovered too early and erroneously that all he had to do was try hard and the environment would reward him. Bob hadn't learned about failure up to that point in his young life, because he hadn't known any failures. He didn't know you needed to be knocked down a few times before you could practice getting up and trying again.

A ski instructor once told me he first taught his beginners how to fall. He knew the snow and terrain weren't always smooth and protective. "If they fall well, they learn how to ski well," he said. That seems to apply to all aspects of life. Apparently, Bob must have missed that lesson.

There's something else about Bob worth considering. That Adonis, with a powerful Herculean stature, was irreversibly gay. He was probably born gay, and was thoroughly comfortable with an identity his hulking, former pro athlete father couldn't stand. Bob adapted well to his homosexuality, while his family had increasing difficulties adapting to Bob.

As the rift widened, his loving mother lavished tolerance and sympathy on Bob, who didn't need sympathy for a sexual problem he didn't have. At the same time, mother was showing her brooding disapproval of father's attitude. Bob was squeezed in the middle. He was a problem child, without a problem, and worse, without the genuine support and acceptance he would need in growing up.

Leaving ACT was an early trauma for him as well. Another problem never really resolved. He was throbbing with mixed feelings about an acting career, authority and self-confidence. Bob made a terrible decision. He retreated to his family and their cold war. There, he was suffocated by an overly protective mother and rejected by a macho father. Bob had no one who would try to understand and help him deal with critical growing-up issues.

His father coldly ignored or belittled Bob's frustrations. Like many other insensitive fathers, he argued that he had always been a good provider. Bob lived with an unspoken message from both parents. Acting was a high school fad he no longer needed.

"You'll always have a place to live and a good job here with us," was his father's pledge. He kept his promise.

For the next ten years, Bob worked on and off at his father's prosperous second-hand furniture store in San Francisco. He continued to live at home where he was infantilized by mom and criticized by dad. The family was a dysfunctional mess.

Time sometimes has a curious way of rescripting previously painful experiences. Bob couldn't accept constant compliments from co-workers, friends or even store customers about his great voice and acting talents. He believed he could never return to a business that had refused to acknowledge his talent. It simply wasn't his fault. To try acting again would be disastrous. Nevertheless, those shallow rationalizations didn't help much. Bob felt miserably bored, unfulfilled and unappreciated.

Old wranglers displayed clinical insights when they

used to say, "Get right back on 'ur hoss if ya'all fall off." They knew then what Bob never seemed to figure out.

When you avoid a once distasteful situation, you're setting yourself up for a phobic thorn in your side. Worse yet, you may get a delusional stake through the heart. The longer you avoid some feared event, like falling off a horse, the more you'll convince yourself that your continued safety depends on avoiding "the horse." Bob's "horse," of course, was the acting business, and after seventeen years of avoidance, he acquired another horse—his family. He was safe as long as he avoided both.

When liberal San Francisco encouraged an "open closet" policy in the 70's, gays began to materialize everywhere. Bob, still a physical hunk, left his home, his parents and his job in pursuit of a gratifying gay relationship. His new illusion was eternal happiness and fulfillment in the gay community. He just needed to stay away from his parents.

The next few years offered Bob an abundance of sexually exciting sorties, but no gratifying relationships. He lived with twenty or thirty men in as many months. Temporarily exciting, none were satisfying. Still miserable, Bob was at least safe from parents whom he considered as potentially dangerous as acting.

That was about the time Bob's clumsy attempts to avoid his problems were contributing to recognizable depression. Over-indulgence in sex, food and escape into activities are some defensive strategies of the clinically depressed. Bob seemed to practice all of the above.

📖   📖   📖

When I met Bob, he was living and working in the

Tenderloin. He acknowledged for the first time in his thirty-seven years that he needed to talk to a professional. In six months he had ballooned from a solid 230 pounds to a blubbery 295. His last lover had left him and their Tenderloin apartment in search of a more attractive partner. In tears, Bob called an old friend and ex-lover, who called me.

Our first session occurred a few days after the referral call. As Bob nervously entered my office, his appearance was still impressive, excessive weight and all. Raymond Burr probably wouldn't have argued about their striking similarity, nor would the voice of James Earl Jones. Bob was a big handsome man, with a formidable voice that filled my office. As I looked around, my office suddenly seemed much smaller.

"I'm a little embarrassed," he softly boomed, "I've never been to a psychiatrist before."

That was my chance to reduce initial tension with a dash of levity. "You still haven't, I'm a psychologist," I chuckled.

Bob replied with kind of an awkward half smile, and I figured my humor didn't work. He had remained standing all this time, which was straining my neck. As I leaned back toward the ceiling, there was "Gulliver." He was sheepishly looking down at me.

"Please sit down, Bob, and I'll explain the difference between a psychiatrist and a psychologist."

Bob sat quietly and listened intently as I explained that psychiatrists were physicians who chose treating the mind, after years studying the body in medical school. Their M.D. degree was in medicine. Psychologists, I added, studied principally the mind, human behavior and its physiological correlates. I further explained that, as physicians, psychiatrists dispensed drugs and psychotherapy. Psychologists, on the other hand, dispensed psychotherapies in addition to extensive diagnostic testing. Psychologists have a Ph.D., doctor's degree in psychology.

Bob rumbled a deep sigh of relief. "I feel better now. I just don't trust medical doctors, and I was afraid I'd have to take pills." Bob's new, broader smile verified his sigh of relief. Hopefully, we were off to a good therapeutic start.

The remainder of the first session was fairly routine. Included was an overview of confidentiality, a description of the therapeutic relationship by me and sobs of frustration by Bob. He was an enormous young bull, buried deeply in a quagmire of torment. As he bellowed cries of blame, pity and pain, his desperate thrashings buried him deeper.

Such a beginning of psychotherapy is much too often a last resort for a new client who can no longer deal with life's problems. It's like some of us who tolerate the terrible pain of an abscess long before we seek a dentist. Bob had waited too long, and any progress was going to be agonizingly slow.

I was also concerned that Bob wouldn't respond too well to a straight male, who was also an ex-athlete, like his father. Such an initial obstacle, I figured, might thwart a positive relationship that is so vital in treatment. Thankfully, I was wrong. Other than my sexual orientation and sports background, I was completely different from Bob's father. The most important differences were my unqualified acceptance of Bob, and my need to understand him by listening carefully.

Within a couple of months, Bob began to trust, even respect me. He seemed to realize that not all straight, ex-athletes were bigots. He was relieved to discover he could tell me just about anything without being scolded or interrupted. I had become a unique friend who wanted nothing from the relationship but to help him.

Sometimes Bob dropped his eyes along with his constant, strained smile. He would sit quietly, as if in deep thought, before saying a word. "You know, Dr. Wonderling, I can depend on you to be here every other week. I can depend on you to listen and I can depend on you to try your best to help me, even if you don't understand me yet. I also know that whatever I say will be between us and no one else."

Those words were so gratifying to hear, I wrote them into my records. He had clearly described what any effective psychotherapy is all about. He knew there was no magic. He was learning that progress can be discouragingly slow. His self-confidence was shattered, he felt worthless and out of control. *At least he's still working,* I thought.

📖 📖 📖

Bob had a job that matched his self-image. Although he hated his job, he was convinced he wasn't worthy of anything better. He had been hired to manage one of several Tenderloin gay/porno stores. Those stores sold everything from magazines to S & M chains, whips, handcuffs and leathers. The main attraction was the store's five private booths with gay/porno videos of sex between couples, groups, slaves and masters.

Each booth also had a "glory hole," where one customer could insert his penis into a hole in the wall in search of a mouth or anus in the adjoining booth. Those through-the-wall sex partners never saw each other. That was apparently part of the thrill. If there were no willing participants in the adjacent booth, the sexually excited customer would masturbate himself while watching the rest of the videos. Bob described his working conditions and job description with wails of self-debasing disgust.

"Before closing I had to clean all five booths. The floors and chairs were always slimy or sticky with cum. It sickens me to even think of cleaning cum and sometimes it had blood or shit in it."

Bob was anything but a sexual prude. He had engaged in every conceivable type of sex play, including intercourse with a few females. He had tried glory holes in both directions. None of that disgusted him. "I disgust myself," he once argued. "I was the performer, not the clean-up crew. It's like being a surgeon, then being reduced to an orderly, cleaning up the mess after the operation."

Bob was a master at proving his self-depreciating point. Proving anything positive was another matter. What he saw in the mirror was proof enough. "I'm a fat, ugly toad," he used to say. Clearly, losing weight was critical, and I became Bob's trainer.

Gradually, Bob's dieting and exercising sent his weight slipping below 230. Once again, he was that gorgeous hunk with the commanding voice. To my chagrin his weight loss therapeutically backfired. I had hoped his trim appearance would serve to lift his self-esteem and reduce his depression. Weight loss would offer proof he could change other aspects of his life. Instead, only part of the strategy worked exceptionally well. His sex life and self-esteem soared, while his interest in therapy plummeted.

Dieting was a quick fix that sent Bob the wrong message. He told me he felt so much better, he could finally resume a satisfying life.

"Thank you, Dr. Wonderling, you saved my life." That was Bob's thundering farewell. He happily retreated from a therapeutic process that threatened to eventually open up old wounds.

As Bob left my office, with squared shoulders, head high, quick bouncing stride and a handsome Herculean presence, he paused at the door, tilted his head to one side and winked.

"Goodbye, Dr. Wonderling, take care of yourself."

Clients often terminate psychotherapy during a temporary spike of improvement in a process filled with peaks and valleys. They are also inclined to run for it during some painful confrontation. That's one of those valleys. Come to think of it, it's astonishing that anyone stays in psychotherapy long enough to benefit.

Premature termination of psychotherapy is curiously more of a conflict for the therapist than the client. If the client terminates therapy by never showing up again, the conflict is resolved. Case closed. In Bob's case, he bid a happy farewell to me—too soon. When that occurs, what's the therapist's responsibility?

Since therapy is as much an art as science, the decision to terminate is the client's—not mine. Therapists don't always know what's best. I certainly didn't. One exception is when a client is ordered to remain in treatment by the court. There are also cases when a client asks my opinion. Then I'm delighted to tell them what I think.

In private practice, there's another touchy issue when clients announce their treatment termination. A client may believe that the fee is the main reason therapists encourage continuing therapy. After all, in private practice therapists need "customers" to pay their bills. So, when clients voluntarily end therapy, I shake their hand and offer a smiling comment.

"Good luck, Bob. If you need me again, just give me a call."

Bob finally returned—two years later. With a busy Tenderloin practice, I hadn't thought of him in months. I did learn from some of his old friends that he had moved from the Tenderloin well over a year before. As I answered my office phone for about the tenth time that August morning, the voice was unmistakably familiar.

"Hello Dr. Wonderling, it's Bob. Is there any way I can possibly see you again?"

The deep, resonant voice with the crisp clarity was certainly the same Bob I had gotten to know during our earlier sessions. Yet something was missing. Bob's voice sounded flat, almost lifeless except for a slight tremor. *A voice of desperation*, I thought, *or maybe he's just given up.* The second possibility seemed less likely. After all—he did call me.

Although it's generally gratifying when an ex-client resumes treatment, the gratitude is always mixed with some apprehension. Is the client better or worse off now than when he terminated?

The moment Bob walked through my office door a week after his call, there was no question why he had sounded different. One look at him and a medley of old images flashed through my mind: the joy of watching the dancing elephants in Fantasia when I was a kid, those prize hogs at the county fair, the old Goodyear blimp at Moffett Field, that beached and dying gray whale along the coast of California.

Bob could barely fit through the door as he struggled with heavy breathing to enter my office. *My God*, I thought, *he must weigh almost 400 pounds.* I was close. He weighed 430 pounds.

There were other obvious changes in Bob. During our earlier sessions he was consistently well-groomed and fastidiously dressed in slacks, sports coat, turtleneck and shined dress shoes. Now he was barely recognizable as he squeezed into my office. His once clean-shaven face was stubble below scraggy hair. He was also covered from neck to tennis shoes with a fully buttoned old beige raincoat, about the size of a car cover. His fixed smile was more strained than before.

Sensing Bob's intense uneasiness, I leaped to my feet with the biggest smile I could tease out of my stunned expression. "Gee it's good to see you, Bob," I shouted enthusiastically while trying to look at his eyes and not his mass. My greeting released in him a torrent of pent-up emotions.

"Thank you, Dr. Wonderling; I'm so glad you could see me again. You must have known I wasn't ready to leave. Now look at me." Tears flowed down his chubby smiling cheeks, and with his last few words, his trembling lips broke into deep, gasping sobs. "I'm sorry; I've been through a lot. But I feel better just being here."

Bob had accepted a disc jockey offer from Carroll, a gay friend, who managed a small radio station in Boise, Idaho. That was about a year and a half earlier, when he looked good and felt confident. He was convinced he would succeed. After all, it wasn't acting, his boss was a good friend and everyone thought he had a great radio voice. How could he miss? Easy—he didn't know his boss was on the verge of losing his job. He didn't know it was a western music station, or that he was moving to a land of "red necks."

Bob blew his nose vigorously, wiped his tearing eyes and continued. A few months after his Boise arrival, Bob's gay friend was replaced by a new station manager. He was a local "good ole boy" who had no tolerance for "queers." Despite growing suspicions, no one in Boise knew Carroll was gay. Only Bob knew. When Carroll left for California, Bob realized no one else could ever know.

Bob had never actually been so alone and reluctant to trust anyone. That was an alien environment where he had no friends and a surplus of potential enemies, starting with the station manager. Bob's strategy was straightforward. Act "butch," no flirting with men, keep a low social profile and become an outstanding disc jockey.

Bob's size facilitated his "straight" masculine role and withdrawing from relationships was fairly easy. No one was particularly friendly. One relatively minor problem was the women who flirted with Bob. They found him handsome and very eligible. He realized that his response to them was critical. Rebuffing them would certainly arouse suspicions about his sexuality. Yet dating them would invite a whole new dimension of problems. Bob managed to eliminate the dilemma by being ineligible. He was engaged to a woman in Los Angeles. That ploy not only reduced gay suspicions, it reduced the resentment of local men. They didn't want this hunk's competition for their women.

Within a few months, most of Bob's strategy was working pretty well, except for the loneliness, his sexual charade and the radio station. Other than some superficial banter with neighbors and some co-workers, he had no one in whom to confide.

His cherished interest in discussing current events and the arts had shrunk to reading the paper and watching television. Portraying a John Wayne macho man was artistically easy, but emotionally crippling. He simply wasn't a straight, rugged male. To make matters worse, he hated acting. The least tolerable of all those irritants was his job.

As he further explained the Boise saga, Bob's tears had dried. His voice toughened into a huskier expression of anger. "I really wanted the disc jockey job to work, but they didn't let me," he grumbled. Bob had initially tried interspersing jazz and rock and roll with the western music. The station was reportedly flooded with complaints from country and western fans. The new station manager was enraged. He threatened to fire Bob.

Reminiscent of his acting days, Bob was repeatedly under attack by his new boss. His clothes weren't western enough, his commercials weren't read with sufficient enthusiasm, his between-record monologues were boring and his selection of western music was terrible.

Practically broke and embarrassed to return to San Francisco too soon, Bob struggled to hang on for another four months. During that time, his anger and frustration were barely in control. He withdrew from any social contacts. He played consecutive western selections from lists provided by the station. He spent most of his free time eating fast foods in his apartment.

When Bob did fly back to San Francisco eight months later, he was in full retreat, 85 pounds overweight and absorbed in anger and self-pity. His occasional suicidal thoughts, however, always yielded to his angry conviction that the defeat wasn't really his fault. Again he was thrust into a situation in life that aborted his efforts to succeed. Again his blaming was justified. Also, once again, his reasoning was pathology-ically flawed. Similar to his experiences with his parents and acting, now he must avoid anything associated with radio broadcasting.

Bob's emotional accounting of the Boise, Idaho odyssey lasted most of the hour. Then, as if he just remembered he had won the lottery, his cheeks flushed into a deeply dimpled smile.

"Oh goodness, Dr. Wonderling, you haven't met the man I'm living with. He's in the waiting room. May I bring him in for just a moment?"

When Jerry ducked through my door, I didn't know whether to gasp in awe or convulse with laughter. He was at least 6'7", with long, clean blond hair, a ruddy complexion, rugged square face, tidy sports clothes and massive shoulders. He also had a massive belly that only slightly detracted from an otherwise well-proportioned physique.

If you include me, there must have been 1,000 pounds of raw flesh in my office. I wondered if my floors could handle the load. As we all stood smiling at each other, I couldn't help but notice how the office had changed from "small" with only Bob, to "minuscule" with both of them. Bob and Jerry barely managed to share the couch. It seemed to groan and then disappear under the bulk of these giants.

Another surprise was when Jerry spoke. I must have expected a deep, clear bass from a man larger than Bob. That may be why I practically bit my tongue when I first heard his voice.

"I'm Jerwy, and I'm so gwateful for your kindneth in helping with Bob'th pwoblemth."

The sounds coming from this intimidating-looking hulk were soft, high-pitched and lispy. Once Jerry spoke, his size seemed to shrink. As we became acquainted, both Jerry's appearance and voice faded well behind a more gentle patience and compassion. Bob was indeed fortunate to have such a person for his partner.

This time I was optimistic about Bob's treatment progress. He had the perfect return profile—a disastrous experience following termination, an overwhelming weight gain after a satisfying treatment weight loss, a positive relationship with his therapist and a caring relationship with a stable partner. Once again, we were off to a good start.

Doubling the sessions the first month enabled Bob to repeat every traumatic reaction to the Boise experience. It was a period of catharsis to help him mentally get back on that horse. Bob eventually did get tired of talking about Boise's external stressors.

When he began focusing on himself, his one persistent concern was his obesity. Physically, he was constantly tired for obvious reasons. He was packing around about 200 pounds of excess weight. Even getting in and out of seats required exhausting effort, especially car seats. Another serious weight related problem was his rapidly developing agoraphobia. He was so ashamed of his size and gait, he was afraid to walk outside without being seized with anxiety. He believed he waddled, and he was right.

Jerry was an extraordinary companion with a monumental commitment he never shirked. Even though he held a full time job demonstrating pianos, he was always prepared to assist Bob in any way. They lived in an apartment on Hyde Street at the outer perimeter of the Tenderloin. Bob was comfortable with the Tenderloin area, where he had spent so many earlier years. Now, however, he would go nowhere without his partner. Jerry drove Bob to every appointment, managed all their shopping and called me constantly for advice on helping Bob.

The only suggestions difficult for Jerry were those discouraging too much help. As I repeatedly explained to Jerry, Bob needed to diet, exercise and maintain some responsible activities. Doing everything for him would debilitate Bob even further.

Jerry listened attentively with an apologetic reply. "Oh I know, Dr. Wonderling, I just want him to be happy. I'll twy harder."

During the next several months, I was surprised and delighted with Bob's gradual improvement. He lost over 50 pounds, and also agreed to brief walks with me during the therapy hour. Sometimes the three of us walked together. In the shadow of those two timid giants, I was reminded that appearance tells nothing about the kind of person we really are.

Those men never intentionally hurt any one. As two gay men, their relationship was enviably stable and warmly loving by any standards. Bob often talked of his trusting bond with Jerry. When they met, both were well beyond the usual gay lover physical relationship that is so shallow and frustrating in too many gay communities. Bob and Jerry had developed a genuine friendship. They were loyal companions, prepared to care for each other for the rest of their lives.

There was little doubt about their relationship contributing to Bob's gradual therapeutic gains. I was still very concerned, however, about some serious treatment obstacles. He told me of a seemingly innocuous "voice-over" offer that nearly triggered a panic reaction. While having coffee at Tommy's Joynt at Van Ness and Geary, a woman had presented her movie agency card to Bob. She assured him his voice was perfect for movie and commercial voice-overs.

"It was awful, Dr. Wonderling. When we went to her office, she wanted me to read a few lines dramatically before signing a contract. I started hyperventilating and I could feel my heart pounding. Jerry and I left."

He was convinced acting was the problem. Of course, I knew better. So when he threw up his arms, shook his head and looked at me for sympathy, I didn't have any. Nor did I have the skill to change his mind.

Bob's physical health was another concern to Jerry and me. He still weighed in at over 370 pounds. Even struggling out of my poor sagging couch was, to him, like climbing the Matterhorn. Halfway out, his grunts and groans grew more alarming. He broke into a gasping, heavily labored breathing until he achieved his freestanding summit. I was always ready for the 911 call. Bob, however, kept managing to get up, as I kept expecting him to collapse over the couch.

Bob repeatedly resisted a medical examination. He angrily argued he was ashamed of his "grotesque fat," and didn't "want some slender, straight male laughing at me."

When Bob later agreed, I was delighted. That's when I also learned that Bob was sure he had some dreaded disease he didn't want to know about.

I had known Dr. Milney for several years. She was a rare, gentle, caring physician, who was both female and fat. She was ideal for Bob. He agreed. To my absolute astonishment, Dr. Milney informed me a few weeks later that Bob was actually in excellent health, with no suspicious laboratory findings.

"He'll probably outlive us both." She laughed.

Jerry and I were relieved about Bob's health and satisfaction with his new physician. I was also glad she had reconfirmed the importance of his current exercise program. Bob also tried a practical, nutritious diet that could quell his ravenous appetite.

Seven weeks after his medical examination, Bob's weight was down to 355 pounds. That provided positive feedback that his efforts were really working. He even started driving to appointments alone.

"Where's Jerry?" I asked during his first solo visit.

Bob grinned and silently looked out the window toward their car. "I've put Jerry through so much. He has lost too much work and business because of me. I'm sorry. You know, it's about time I carry my own weight."

That comment sparked a hearty chuckle from both of us.

The next six months of summer and fall were unforgettably promising. Bob continued his gradual loss of weight, while spending increasing amounts of time helping Jerry. He was actually house-cleaning, cooking and shopping. Jerry had been promoted to manager of a large music store.

Bob also had a solid relationship with Dr. Milney. She was still warmly jolly, compassionate and fat. Bob seemed to be doing well, and he looked forward to our sessions. This time, he didn't confuse his progress with a cure. He assured me he had no intention of terminating therapy. Those were indeed memorable months for Bob.

Then the crisp air and cheerful colors of fall slipped beneath the cold and dreary days of winter. Bob had been complaining of occasional deep blunted pains around the kidney and bladder. He hadn't told Jerry and he was hesitant to tell Dr. Milney.

"God, Dr. Wonderling, Jerry's been through enough, I don't want to worry him and if I tell Dr. Milney, I'll be hospitalized and die."

There were no histrionics in his clear resounding words. He was telling me something I needed to know. His head was drooped forward, hiding his face, and I wouldn't have even known he was crying until I noticed tears dripping onto his old raincoat.

At first I gently challenged his reasoning. As his pain worsened, however, I pleaded with him to just see Dr. Milney.

"I'm sorry, Dr. Wonderling, I know I'll die in the hospital. Please accept what I know." His reply was always with a very calm, grim resolve.

I felt powerless in persuading him to obtain the medical help he needed. I even considered calling Dr. Milney. I quickly dismissed that idea. She would also be powerless to coax him into her office. Even worse, Bob might lose trust in us.

This isn't a prophecy, I thought, *it's an irrational belief that I have to help him overcome.*

Jerry and Dr. Milney both called me on a cloudy January Sunday. Bob had been hospitalized and Jerry was devastated. Dr. Milney had assured him Bob had only a few kidney stones. I felt better talking with her because she was always thorough and honest with her medical findings. Dr. Milney was also reassuringly cheerful over the phone.

"It can be painful, but stones are common and not that serious. With treatment, he'll be home in several days."

When I went to see Bob that Sunday evening, he still looked huge, even though he was down to about 320 pounds. He was lying back on two pillows. I thought he was asleep until he opened his eyes.

Although Bob looked vulnerable without his old raincoat, there was something peaceful about him. Then it hit me. He seemed untroubled.

Trying to be upbeat, I offered a few get-well clichés. "Hey Bob, I know it's painful, but Dr. Milney said it's not that serious. You'll be out of the hospital soon."

Bob slowly reached out his big chubby hand. We held hands silently for a while. Then he looked at me with an unusually relaxed smile. "Thanks for every-thing, Dr. Wonderling. I won't need you anymore. Take good care of yourself."

Bob died in the hospital that Sunday night of reasons unknown. Even an autopsy failed to determine the cause of his death. Medicine had to acknowledge one of its many uncertainties. Bob just died—of something. Medicine may remain a science of uncertainty, as long as it overlooks the power of the mind. However, there is one certainty I learned from Bob, anything is possible—especially prophecies.

After all these years I'm not quite sure why I have such vivid memories of Bob. Maybe it's because he was so huge. He was also my first known homosexual client with complex problems that had little if anything to do with his sexuality. So, maybe it's really because Bob unwittingly taught me that those righteous stereotypes about *gays* are as pathetically naïve, narrow-minded and flawed as any attempt to stereotype *straights*.

13

MARILYN

The Best Match

The physical sciences remind us that man's genetics are both male and female. Man is bathed in mother's vital fluids during gestation; and after reluctantly leaving the security of mother's womb, he must depend on her for sustenance. During his most vulnerable early months on earth, it is mother who protects him with loyal nurturing love. Recorded history, however, too often belies this gentle blending of the human genders. Perhaps we men keep forgetting that masculine and feminine are in all of us. Believing he must be "all male" in order to be male at all, man may become less than whole.

The social sciences suggest that man has forsaken his beginnings by treating women as a separate, subordinate species. It's as if man misconstrued mother's nurturance as lifelong servitude, or possibly man's physical strength and unbridled sexual avarice demanded he identify only with the male in him. Whatever the reasons, man's denial of his own femininity has contributed to his bigoted view of women—as his chattel.

Arguably men's relentless domination, ridicule and abuse of women relates to most males' own fragmented identity. Throughout history, women have been bullied or bluffed into submission and conned into thinking that their absolute purpose in life was to serve man. Fortunately, women in the United States have been challenging man's self-imposed authority. Yet, even in liberal San Francisco, especially in areas like the Tenderloin, there are women who are still struggling with their subservience to men.

Despite my conviction that the Tenderloin is a relatively safe place to live, it can be very cruel to some women. Tragically, many Tenderloin women haven't the self-esteem or confidence to defy male control. Even worse, too many Tenderloin men are alcoholics. That translates into abusive control. In fact, of all my Tenderloin clients, those women who succumbed to such primitive abuse have been some of the most frustrating to treat and pathetic to know.

＼＼ ＼＼ ＼＼

Marilyn had been a Tenderloin resident for several years when referred to me by the Department of Social Services. Her diagnosis was Alcohol Dependence and Borderline Personality Disorder. Those were common psychiatric labels for most of my clients who were emotionally unstable heavy drinkers.

The minute Marilyn entered my office for the initial interview, I realized it would be very easy to feel sorry for her. If she had worn a sign, it would have clearly read, "Please Control Me and Even Use Me Because

I'm Only a Woman." She resembled a Keane painting of the inimitable saucer-eyed children, but older, more fragile and vulnerable.

When I offered Marilyn a seat, her big, sad, moon eyes looked at me mournfully as she stumbled into the side of my desk. She hit really hard, yet her only reactions were an apologetic glance and a frail smile.

"Are you all right?" I asked.

Sprawling against the side of the desk, she forced another faint smile. "I'm sorry. I'm fine, thank you."

Helping her sit, I could smell the residuals of spilled alcohol and cigarette smoke, masked by cheap, sweet perfume. Those were the pervasive odors that drifted through the doors of any Tenderloin tavern—unmistakable and sad. Her thick make-up also seemed especially sad. It only barely disguised the bruises and scars on her face, while distorting the few remaining hints of a once natural beauty. Her long, well-brushed hair, manicured nails and clean, nicely fitting blouse and skirt were more encouraging signs she hadn't completely given up on herself or her femininity.

Marilyn's petite body couldn't have weighed over 100 pounds, and her womanly figure looked much younger than her 45 years. As I sat opposite her, I had to acknowledge the pitiful irony of her appearance and her predicament. Living in the Tenderloin, her passivity, clean feminine appearance and small shapely body, marked her as easy prey to the local predators.

Those macho bullies might fight over her, but never for her. I also knew from her file that, like so many others, Marilyn had moved to the Tenderloin alone, troubled and an easy victim. It apparently didn't take long either—about a month, before she chose one of the predators to shield her from the others. Looking beneath her heavy make-up, I wondered how I might eventually shield her from him, as well as the others.

Although her alcoholic diagnosis seemed accurate, it was more of a symptom than the problem. Heavy drinking is too often a defensive solution that simply doesn't work. What generally happens is that the original problem is effectively buried under a layer of drunken binges. That is a major obstacle in treating alcoholics.

Her other diagnosis of Borderline Personality Disorder wasn't much help either. I would gradually learn that Marilyn fit many diagnostic labels without being clearly described by any of them. As usual, labels were solely for classifying, not understanding a client. Treatment, without trying to understand the individual, should be reserved for clinical advice columns and talk shows—not psychotherapy.

During our first session together, I avoided inquiries about those bruises beneath her make-up. For that matter, I avoided asking about anything hidden beneath the superficial surface of our initial contact. I didn't want to frighten her off with embarrassing questions. I didn't and probably couldn't.

Marilyn wanted help and wouldn't be embarrassed into retreating easily. She was exceptionally receptive and cooperative, and the interview was surprisingly productive. She had never been in any kind of clinical treatment program, and she wanted to learn all about therapy. As Marilyn learned from me, I began to learn more about her than I had expected in a first session.

An only child, she was raised in San Francisco by alcoholic parents who were more interested in indulging themselves than caring for her. Her mother was a submissive housewife, constantly intimidated by a husband who needed a sex mate and maid more than a companion. As a father, he was cold and distant when sober and abusively strict when drunk. Her mother

never tried to protect her when Marilyn was occasionally beaten. At sixteen, she finally left home when her
drunken father sexually propositioned her.

Marilyn managed to graduate from high school,
while working part time and living with a boyfriend's
parents. That living arrangement, however, ended abruptly when Marilyn discovered she was pregnant. A
botched abortion left her sterile, alone and very
unhappy. She was eighteen. Having nowhere else to go,
she returned to her unsympathetic parents long enough
to find a job and a hotel room south of Market Street.

Later she had enjoyed office work where she could
practice typing and sharpen her filing skills. Marilyn
wanted passionately to become a private secretary,
while too many of her bosses passionately wanted her
body. That led to lots of affairs with married men, a bad
reputation and terminations, despite excellent job
performance.

To Marilyn, beginning with her father, she was
surrounded by men she couldn't please for very long. In
attempting to resist office romances, Marilyn began
hitting neighborhood bars, where she started dating
neighborhood drunks. They proved to be worse than her
office bosses.

During the second session, Marilyn didn't need the
slightest encouragement to continue where she left off.
It was apparent she never had an opportunity to openly
reveal her past to anyone. Each new disclosure evoked a
flood of sobs, deep sighs and gentle smiles. At last, she
seemed able to share those memories with someone who
only demanded a MediCal sticker.

She arrived early with much less make-up; which
accentuated those underlying bruises. I was hoping she
wanted me to notice them, or maybe she just didn't want
her make-up to run all over her face while crying.

Marilyn peeked at me coyly, quickly dropped her big eyes and inhaled with short gasping breaths. Grabbing a tissue, she peeked at me again. "I'm sorry, Dr. Wonderling, I must have looked funny last time with smeared make-up all over my face."

Then I thought I knew why she lessened her make-up. "You did look kind of funny, but your tears seemed very real and sad."

"Thank you, they were," she replied with more tears.

She recounted an endless succession of relationships with men whose faces were never in focus. They were generally the bar room drunks whose roguish charm and generous supply of drinks were the lures that tempted her. Half drunk and longing to be cared for, Marilyn was easy, too easy. Rough, clumsy sex usually followed, along with promises of the love and protection she needed to hear.

The next phase, which she called the "honeymoon," lasted for a few days to nearly a year before boredom, suspicions, possessiveness or just plain ugliness began to unfold.

"I could feel it coming," she said, as she rinsed the make-up from her face with more tears. Her lovers would become irritable, unreasonable, demanding and physically abusive. That was a period when each man abandoned all pretense and revealed his true character.

"They were all beasts," she said, "but all different kinds of beasts." Some just slapped her around when they were drunk and apologized when they were sober. Others punched her with clenched fists, drunk or sober. There were some who seemed to practice boxing on her, as if pretending they were fighting a man.

"This type would knock me down and then dance around pounding clenched fists, like he was waiting for the ten count. I'd always try to stay down," she added.

Marilyn furtively looked around the office, as if afraid of being overheard. "I get sick when I think of the sadistic ones, some who would tie me up. I thought I'd be killed. One guy used to choke me unconscious, and another stuck kitchen spoons and stuff up my vagina."

As I listened carefully, I had to ask one clinically critical question. "How long did you stay with these guys during the physical phase?"

"I'm ashamed to tell you," she said. "It could be weeks, months, sometimes years."

Good God, I thought. "I see," I said.

Marilyn's owl eyes narrowed as her face wrinkled into a frown. "Dr. Wonderling, you don't think...I didn't stay with them because I liked to be hurt. I hated it!"

She was unusually open and insightful, especially for a second session client. Then after a brief, reflective pause, she added, with some of her refreshing candor, "You know, I guess I was afraid I might get someone worse, or end up alone. I even thought that maybe it's a woman's role to endure man's abuse."

Marilyn was a client that psychotherapists long for. She was bright, amenable and both open and eager to understand herself. Marilyn was not only highly motivated; she had the physical and intellectual potential to facilitate positive change. Even her subordinate role to men was being shelved during our therapy sessions. She was treating me more as an equal than a dominant male. She freely challenged some of my opinions and never hesitated to ask incisive questions. Marilyn's bruises were fading along with her excessive make-up, and the smell of alcohol was missing from the odor of her cheap perfume.

Patiently helping a client learn through their own discoveries is an important aspect of therapy. However, when Marilyn still hadn't brought up the man she was living with, I was concerned. I knew he was the same guy she was with when I first met her and those terrible bruises. Maybe he was gone I hoped, but I knew better. She had made remarkable progress, at least in exploring the past.

What about the present, I thought. I not only didn't know her mate, I knew nothing about her daily activeities. I wondered if she could handle this guy any better than the others. Frustrated, I concluded she just wasn't ready to confront my own impatience. I wasn't going to rush her.

When Marilyn missed her fifth session, I had an ominous hunch. It had something to do with trouble in her present life. Clients frequently drop out of therapy without warning during their early months. Some drop out if they feel rushed into facing their long-repressed inner pain. Then there are those who simply can't afford it, or those who don't like their therapist. None of those possibilities seemed to fit Marilyn. She was well motivated, MediCal was paying for the sessions and I certainly wasn't pushing her too hard. I thought we were getting along fine.

As her paid therapist, I was reluctant to call. Therapists are neither parent nor guardian and it's not their job to manage their clients' lives. They are simply available when needed. So, I just had to wait for that time—when needed.

Marilyn called the following week, and it was sadly obvious she was in serious need. There were no wails or small talk, just a few halting mumbled words, "Can I see you soon?"

The next day, I actually felt sick when she entered my office. Marilyn was barely recognizable. Her huge moon eyes were buried under swollen, discolored flesh that she could hardly see through. There was a large red knot on her nose and wires through her jaw. Both had been broken. Her head was so swollen on the left side, it looked like some terrible goiter. Nothing above her shoulders seemed to have been missed. Even her neck revealed hideous finger bruises.

When I eased her carefully into a chair, I dropped to one knee in front of her. I tried to look directly through those awful swellings over her eyes. I had to bite my lip to keep from sobbing with deeply felt sorrow and frustration. Then I thought, *Marilyn is a client in desperate need of my help—not my tears.*

Swallowing the warm salty blood in my mouth, I searched for the right combination of strength and compassion she needed from her therapist. "Has your physician taken good care of you?"

She nodded slowly.

"Anything I need to know about injuries I can't see?"

"No, it's all in my head and neck," she replied slowly, without moving her crusted lips.

She must ache terribly, I thought. That's when I noticed a few tears seeping through the corners of her swollen eyelids.

Still kneeling in front of her, I very softly grasped her hands and tried a warm, calm smile. "I'm sure glad you came back. Now we can get back to work. You know your physical injuries are going to heal nicely; it's the other pain we'll handle together. Okay?"

She answered, without the slightest hesitation, and I could hear the determination in her mumbled words. "Oh God, yes!"

Marilyn did heal nicely in about six weeks; and as her pain diminished, she was able to talk more.

I sat quietly, as I finally learned about her present

life. She explained that after years of enduring abusive relationships, she had become more fearful of living with a man than living alone.

She continued to frequent her local Tenderloin hangouts, where she made enough money as a "B" girl, hustling drinks, to supplement her SSI checks. Drunk, she would struggle back to her apartment every night and collapse across her bed in a dizzying haze of self-contempt.

Sometimes she brought a man home, which usually resulted in sloppy, unsatisfying sex and a quick clumsy exit once the guy "got his rocks off." There were others who angrily complained that she wasn't sexy enough, when they "couldn't get it up."

"It really didn't matter what happened," she added, "I kept ending up alone, lonely, drunk and unhappy."

Marilyn even started drinking with the street thugs and winos during the day. Then, about six months before her first therapy appointment, she was gang-raped in some Tenderloin apartment, while sharing a bottle with five men she barely knew. It was hard to complain when she looked back through her adult years.

She had been infected with syphilis once, gonorrhea half a dozen times and crab lice about every other week. Being gang raped was disgusting, but not an over-whelming trauma.

After her forced sex with five men, Marilyn felt she couldn't sink any lower. In order to survive with any semblance of self-respect, she would have to find a way of life beyond corrosive liaisons with men.

For a week, Marilyn was free of all the indignities associated with her bondage to men. Sex even repulsed her. That is, until she met Ron, a new tenant who moved into a room on her floor just down the hall. He was over six feet tall, muscular and outrageously handsome, with a deep pleasant voice and an exceptionally attractive shyness.

Whenever they met in the hall, he would smile rather bashfully with lowered eyes. He never initiated small talk of any kind; and after he had politely opened the hallway door for her a few times, it was Marilyn who introduced herself.

The relationship developed swiftly from that brief introduction: friendly chats in the lobby, strolls together on Market Street, long conversations over coffee in her room, a gentle kiss goodnight at her door and then passionate sex in her bed.

All of that occurred within a week, yet curiously Marilyn hadn't seen the inside of his room. It didn't really matter to her. She had learned from him that he was a freelance writer from New York and he was looking for a job. Whenever he wasn't working, he intended to complete his novel and write poetry. She was impressed with the few poems he gave her, and she was eager to read some of his novel. She never did, and that didn't matter either.

Marilyn knew this was genuine love. She was ready to excuse any of his questionable behavior, and there were many behaviors to question. Ron moved into her room with a small overnight bag containing not much more than a few articles of clothing, so typical of transients. He usually sat around her room all day watching television. He never found a job and Marilyn never saw him write. He did, however, help her spend her meager SSI checks, and it took only a month before he began purchasing alcohol with her money.

Marilyn was still hopelessly in love with him. She was also so ashamed of her previous fiascoes with other men; she kept denying the glaring warnings that the "honeymoon" was nearing an end.

Yet her denials were bolstered by the absence of any violence. That reprieve lasted for their first five weeks, when Ron was getting all he wanted and Marilyn was giving all she had. Then, a week before her first appointment with me, Marilyn caught Ron removing the last few dollars from her purse.

"If you need money, just ask me, Honey," was her response.

Those words were barely out of her mouth before he punched her in the face several times shouting, "You don't trust me? Do you trust me now?"

As she lie bleeding on the floor, Marilyn automatically reverted to her well-ingrained submissive role. "I'm sorry, Honey, I trust you completely."

Marilyn further acknowledged that, during her early sessions with me, she was afraid to discuss Ron, or her bruises. She believed I might scold her or try to talk her out of a relationship she desperately wanted. She even childishly thought they had resolved their problems and were doing fine together. She had become his slave and as long as Marilyn complied with his demands, they would keep doing fine together—for a while.

Then he nearly killed her, and the bizarre irony prompting his assault was Marilyn's refusal to give up therapy. While Ron was drinking in her room, Marilyn made the near fatal mistake of bringing up the value of therapy and its importance in her life. Of course, all Ron wanted to know was the gender of the therapist. When she told him, Ron demanded she drop therapy. Another irony is that she might have. Instead, Marilyn naively laughed in surprise.

Enraged, he punched her until she fell, then he kicked her in the face, screaming, "Do you think it's funny? Is this funny?"

That's the last she heard as she lost consciousness.

She learned in the hospital that two female tenants on her floor probably saved her life. They called the police, who arrived in minutes. When they broke open the door, Ron was choking Marilyn as he eased her out an open window.

"You know, Dr. Wonderling," she paused with her mouth slightly opened as if silently debating her next comment. Then she closed her eyes and sighed, "I'm glad the cops saw the assault. They didn't need me to press charges. I don't know if I would've testified against him in court." Marilyn opened her eyes and looked at me. "How can you love a man you hate?" she asked.

"That's easy," I said. "Having some of your fantasies of a handsome prince satisfied, until he tries to beat you to death."

She grabbed another tissue and tore it in half. "I guess I loved the dream."

Ron was convicted of assault with intent to do bodily harm. He received the outrageously lenient sentence of one year in the county jail. At least Marilyn never saw him again, nor did she attempt to contact him. Her days of confusing dreams with reality were unceremoniously concluding. She was ready to deal with life "as is," not as it should be.

In the two years after her recovery from the assault, Marilyn never missed a therapy session. She became thoroughly acquainted with her weaknesses and the self-defeating aspects of her fantasies. She was learning to rely solely on herself.

Perhaps one of her most useful insights was her frequent reply when I would ask, "What are you going to do about it?"

That was when she sat up straight and cleared her throat with an air of confidence. "Try something else.

Nothing changes unless you change your own behavior."

Marilyn was constantly trying something else. She finally realized that falling is an indispensable part of learning, provided you take a good look at how and why you stumbled. For Marilyn, those were productive years of experiential learning.

Her premature enrollment in a community college lasted only a couple of months, when she fell flat on her face. She wisely discovered, however, that she wasn't ready for academic life until she could manage her personal life.

Marilyn then decided to try Alcoholics Anonymous, which she found much more rewarding. For someone who had been struggling with loneliness and depression by drinking in Tenderloin bars, sobriety was tough. Once she tried substituting taverns for nightly AA meetings, she found support and companionship along with gallons of coffee. AA offered a social structure she needed. She confined her activities to studying and discussing the "AA Twelve Steps." She soon realized she could easily resist those lecherous males whose primary AA goal was seducing female members.

Marilyn was also developing solid relationships with some women at the AA meetings who had been beaten by their men. Discussing their awful experiences together after AA meetings was so gratifying, Marilyn organized one of the earliest battered women groups in the Tenderloin. The first group started with three women, meeting in her small hotel room. Within six months, it expanded to ten women meeting in a large Tenderloin conference room.

Marilyn's changes in her lifestyle generated a sense of self-reliance she had never before experienced. One of her early accomplishments was the AA pin she proudly received as a recovering alcoholic with one year's sobriety.

Celibacy, however, was still an illusive goal primarily because, for her, the goal was unreasonable. She had a healthy libido with enjoyable sex and easy orgasms since puberty. In fact, she was beginning to recognize that sex had never been her problem. The problem through most of her adult life was cruel, abusive treatment by men, along with her obedience to their selfish sexual demands.

Marilyn tried a few more sexual encounters during those two productive years. Each time the initially attractive man turned ugly and the relationship soured. By then, however, she was perfecting the skill of falling on her face more softly, recovering more quickly and profiting by the experience.

I can remember asking her once if her many relationships with men had taught her anything. I'll never forget how she leaned forward in her chair, looked me directly in the eyes and offered a profoundly reflective mini-lecture in a calm, articulate fashion.

"Who needs 'em!"

Marilyn certainly didn't need them; she hadn't needed men in many years. But old habits are hard to break, especially when there's nothing better to replace them. Like too many abused, insecure women, she had assumed that being alone was the only alternative to being with men. Marilyn was unaware that her groups were providing a gratifying replacement.

Toward the end of her second year of therapy, several members of the battered women's group had become good friends with Marilyn. Their weekly sessions had expanded to dinners at one of the many fine, inexpensive San Francisco restaurants, attending movies, lectures or just sightseeing together.

Marilyn had never had a girlfriend or woman companion. Most of her adult life, she believed a woman's station was at the side of—and slightly behind—her man. She had long thought all women were male-dominated.

"No wonder I was so lonely," she regularly said. "I thought all women were worthless like me."

It took most of the second year for her to figure out that women make wonderful companions. She learned they could express both male and female characteristics. Another of Marilyn's revelations was that women were much better off than men. They didn't need to act "macho" and hang onto a pair of balls they never had in the first place.

At the beginning of her third year in therapy, Marilyn introduced me to Nancy—a tall, willowy, attractive woman in her early thirties. Her warm, engaging smile complimented her natural friendliness and delightful sense of humor. As we chatted, they kept looking at each other endearingly, and it was obvious that Marilyn and Nancy had become great pals. They had visited just about every district in San Francisco at least once. It was a joy to see both women's enthusiasm as they described their adventures together.

I learned during the next few months that their companionship had blossomed into a loyal, enduring friendship that seemed to enrich both of their lives. They could share each other's deepest secrets and vulnerable weaknesses with confidence in their trust and loyalty. Openly laughing or crying together was another refreshing experience for both Marilyn and Nancy. They had learned long ago to fear such feelings with their men. Their relationship was encouraging, considerate, supportive and very caring. Quite naturally, affection was soon to follow.

During one of our usual bi-weekly sessions, Marilyn wasted no time asking me a question that had been bothering her. "Can two women love each other?"

I had a good hunch she wanted my approval, and I was ready to give her my blessings. "Can two persons fall in love?" I asked back.

"Of course," she said with a big grin.

"I don't think you have to be a prescribed height, weight, color or gender to fall in love," I added. "Doesn't it have just about everything to do with how we treat each other?"

Her grin changed to a teary smile. She knew I approved.

After most of her forty-nine years of distasteful, frightening or even terrifying relationships with men, she had found the best match. It just happened to be another woman. In Marilyn's case, to wait for the "right man" would have been absurd. She finally had the right person, and to leave Nancy in search of another man, would have bordered on the insane.

Sadly, some of the moral majority, with their righteous need for labels, will call Marilyn a lesbian; which, of course, fails miserably to describe her or her story.

I was best man at her symbolic wedding; and since that marriage of love and trust many years ago, Marilyn and Nancy have continued to live happily and without their earlier years of loneliness, fears and broken bones.

Do they have sex together? Why should anyone care? They found the best match in their lives, and what they do or don't do in their bedroom is no one's business but their own.

Marilyn and Nancy have been inseparable for over ten years now. Their daily gratitude, trust and loyalty to each other are probably unrivaled by spouses in the best of traditional marriages. They even "rescued" a three-year-old boy, whom they adopted as their own. In 2007 he was a healthy, happy age six.

14

ROMEO

Book Covers

Tenderloin newcomers, outsiders and visitors too often expect danger to lurk on every corner. They typically envision a big, black, ugly, tattooed, Neanderthal, whose sole mission in life is to rip their heart out after he's ripped them off.

Romeo fit that physical description right down to the tattoos and Neanderthal ugly. His arms were as big as most people's waists and his waist was as small as most people's arms. Regardless of the weather, he characteristically wore a tight tank top that spotlighted his bulging muscles, while equally tight jeans emphasized his bulging genitals. His walk was a cocky swagger of muscle rippling shuffles like a black panther stalking prey. To add to his menacing appearance were skull and cross-bone earrings, headband and leather driving gloves that seemed more for punching than driving.

Those who fit the physical description of mean nasty

predator usually exude mean nasty sounds. Again, Romeo was no exception. If the predator resonates clear articulation, he doesn't seem very menacing. Also a broad vocabulary and grammatically correct sentences are much too refined to qualify as mean. The sounds that came from Romeo thoroughly complimented his appearance, suggesting that he was extra mean—a world-class predator.

He had a breathy, raspy mumble that bullied and brutalized the English language. His speech, what there was of it, was without syllables—just a meshing of guttural sounds that always ended with one clear word—"man." Everybody was "man," including any woman, race or age group. Romeo also had a nasty, almost devilish laugh of the "gottcha" variety—a slow wheezy barely audible "hee, hee, hee." Whenever his throaty mumbles turned into a laugh, strangers were tempted to check their valuables, or run for it.

Romeo lived deep in the Tenderloin on Ellis off Taylor Street where he was king of his mountain. Virtually all the residents of the project were afraid of him. They avoided anything that might be construed as a challenging criticism, such as prolonged eye contact or even walking too close to him. The men in the project were even hesitant to offer a friendly greeting to Romeo's flirtatious woman for fear of arousing her and annoying him—or rejecting her and arousing him. Consequently, no one bothered him. He was just too big and mean-looking.

📖 📖 📖

That physically intimidating appearance was the Romeo I met, but not the Romeo I eventually learned to know. A San Quentin Prison parolee, Romeo was referred to me by the Department of Corrections and the Department of Social Services. They were in the process of reinstating his disability benefits, provided he accepted treatment for alcohol and drug substance abuse.

He had been in prison for about three years as the result of a felony conviction associated with the possession and sale of heroine. He was 36 then, and he was well-acquainted with most California penal institutions. He had served various periods of time in juvenile detention facilities, county jails, psychiatric hospitals and more recently, Soledad and San Quentin State Prisons.

Despite a moderately successful professional boxing career and his mean, pugilistic appearance, none of his periods of confinement were violence-related. There were no assaults, muggings, armed robberies or threats of violence. Even his drug convictions were more symptomatic of ghetto efforts to solve his emotional problems with drugs.

Unfortunately for him, it was very early in his life that acute anxiety reactions were too hastily treated with Valium rather than psychotherapy. That legal drug made him feel better without dealing with the underlying problems that were triggering his distress. Like so many others, he discovered the sinister side of Valium, as he became a treatment victim.

He was hooked. So when physicians began recognizing his drug dependency, they cut him off with the admonishment that he was becoming an addict. Romeo wasn't becoming an addict; he was an addict. When he lost his legal suppliers, he understandably took to the streets where he quickly learned how to score illegal drugs.

📖   📖   📖

Those were the experiences and exposures that accompanied that big, menacing-looking man to my office for the first time. His flirtatious wife was on his arm; and when I asked if she would mind waiting in the adjoining room, their separation was like a mini-melodrama. He gently took her hand, looked at her comfortingly and mumbled something with a whispered rasp.

She offered a strained, martyred smile and said, "Yes, I'll be all right." After an embrace, she turned to me with a somewhat pained expression. "I'm ready," she said, as if prepared to run the gauntlet or face the guillotine. That's when I led her into the next room.

When I returned, there was Romeo slumped low in his chair with a huge sheepish grin, as if he had just gone through my desk drawers. He was also pounding his right fist into his open-palmed left hand, which rippled the muscles from his lower arm all the way up to his neck. Although certainly intimidating, I later realized it was just a habit, not a threat, especially not to me.

To conceal any hint of uneasiness, I walked directly toward Romeo, stuck out my much smaller arm and mustered a big voice, "I'm glad you found my office with no problem."

He replied with a surprisingly soft, puny handshake and an equally surprising, somewhat warm, uneasy smile that erased his grin.

Romeo spent most of the first session talking in his whispered, rasping mumble, and as I listened carefully, I could only understand the word "man." His comments sounded something like, "shiryowheehardinsuobroman."

I quickly learned to reply with an "uh-huh" after the word "man." By the end of the first session, the only thing I knew about Romeo was that he didn't like to go anywhere without his wife, that he had a warm smile, a dainty handshake and that his language was just about incomprehensible to me.

By the third session, I still didn't know what Romeo was talking about, and my "uh-huhs" were just that, a frustrated gesture. I was still listening, even though I didn't understand anything. *Maybe I'm just a slow learner,* I thought, or maybe that was another way Romeo manages to block relationships. Either way, I knew that I had to candidly confront him with my problem and his alternatives, including finding a therapist who understood his language.

I even asked flirtatious wife to join the session as interpreter. I was surprised to learn, through his wife, that Romeo wanted to stick with me, that his verbal expressiveness was the only way he knew how to talk and that he felt very insecure alone, talking with some "official" who probably didn't understand him.

The strategy was clear, flirtatious wife was to become my translator until I could learn some of his slang and communication style. Typically, they would sit next to each other hand in hand while I managed to sit close enough to Romeo to hear each breath and see each lip movement before any translations.

I soon discovered that I not only wanted to understand him, he really wanted to be understood. Within a few more weeks I learned some of his favorite expressions. That gave me a baseline of familiar sounds on which to build communication.

"Hyodo-he-man," meant, "How are you doing (devilish laugh) man?" "Ibesalsna-man" meant, "I was sick last night, man" and "Aanobulsibro" decoded to, "That's no bullshit, brother."

Another of his repeated phrases was, "Yagotta-cumsamapa-man," meaning, "You have to come see my house, man." That was a relentless request by Romeo that always sounded like a demand.

Toward the end of the third month, I was beginning to grasp some of his jargon and throaty whispers, and flirtatious wife was back in the adjoining room. Despite his incomprehensible mumbles, Romeo was very persuasive. I finally gave up and visited his house.

Their Tenderloin apartment was exceptionally clean and well-furnished, with nothing that even hinted of "mean" or "macho" man. It was a place of white rugs, dainty boutique-like objects and furnishings that encouraged shoe-removal at the door. Romeo was obviously proud of his apartment. It was his private castle, where he could kick back and be himself. That was the beauty within the beast.

Later that day Romeo and I walked around his Tenderloin neighborhood, where he was greeted in a friendly, albeit subservient, manner. He was "the Man" and every thug, prostitute, junky, ex-convict and pensioner knew it. He looked bigger and meaner on the Tenderloin streets, like a snarling alpha dog, the leader of the pack. His casual amble became a more purposeful strut with bobbing head, swinging arms trailing palms cupped inward and amplified throatier jive responses that I couldn't begin to decipher. That was Romeo's territory.

Three years after our first session, Romeo was still honoring his appointments even though he rarely discussed his weaknesses or anything else of a reflective nature. He knew his SSI benefits were contingent upon psychotherapy. Actually, his strategy was quite pragmatic and responsible. He was willing to go to therapy, but not *do* therapy.

At least he thought he wasn't doing therapy. Romeo occasionally mentioned the social pressures contributing to the "anxiety attacks" that he never mentioned by name.

"Being top gun is tough. There's always somebody challenging you," was a loose translation of one of his frequent mumbles and grunts. His wife was more open in revealing his morning "shakes," that he denied. However, his denials were usually weak, followed by a casual description of periodic sweaty palms, shortened breaths and dry mouth.

Romeo also worshipped possessions. He dwelled on the things they would buy or acquire for the house, the stuff that was stolen from his house and the stuff he wanted. He was especially proud of his cars. Once a year, he'd drag me out of my office to show me his new, second-hand Cadillac.

He also liked just chatting with someone who was predictably trustworthy and friendly—me. During those three years, he even had fewer anxiety attacks and he was staying out of serious trouble. Therapy actually seemed to be working—even though he didn't *do* therapy.

📖 📖 📖

During the fourth year, Romeo displayed his full range of behaviors to my delight and chagrin. When ill, I prefer solitude and distant sympathy. So, while in the hospital recovering from an operation, I told friends to stay away and clients, including Romeo, that I'd be gone for a few weeks.

Everybody stayed away but Romeo. How he found out about the operation and which hospital to visit remain mysteries. The biggest mystery, however, is how he managed to communicate with hospital staff to find my room.

On the evening following my surgery, I was into a mild snooze when I heard that unmistakable raspy mumble. I thought I might be dreaming, until I opened an eye. There was Romeo, towering over my bed like some nightmarish creature. Anyone else in the hospital probably would have screamed for help. I just asked, "How did you find me and how did you know I was to have an operation?"

"Hee, hee, hee," he answered. "Heyendo? (How are you doing?)" he asked.

Romeo never told me how he knew about my operation and I really didn't care. I was moved by his show of compassion, especially when he gave me a get-well card with his personal scrawl, "You be well, bro."

Not long after my recovery, Romeo missed his appointment with me. Ordinarily when someone doesn't show up, it's a good time to catch up on my endless paperwork. Romeo's absence was different. He rarely missed an appointment, and if he couldn't make it, for whatever reason, he or flirtatious wife would call to cancel. As Romeo's empty appointment hour ticked by, I became increasingly worried, and for good reason.

I learned later that day from his parole agent that Romeo caught his wife having sex with a recently paroled giant of a man. Romeo had apparently returned unexpectedly to their clean, delicate apartment where he found his wife kissing and masturbating the giant.

The explosive force of his wrath was so thunderous, practically the entire apartment complex heard the devastation. While some neighbors watched in horror through the open door, Romeo used many of his dainty furnishings, especially chairs and vases on both his wife and the giant. The white rugs were red. And when it was over, Romeo reportedly dropped to his knees sobbing. In violation of his parole, Romeo was quickly returned to San Quentin Prison, and both wife and the giant were hospitalized with concussions and broken bones. They both survived, and I never saw flirtatious wife again.

Although I didn't hear from Romeo for years, the ubiquitous "grapevine" of ex-convicts supplied me with a variety of Romeo prison stories. He'd boxed his way to a heavyweight prison championship, he was no trouble to any prison officials and, of course, he was the indisputable leader of his cellblock toughies.

Years later, a phone call renewed an old memorable relationship. Like in the hospital, I was glad to hear from him even though how he got my new unlisted telephone number was another one of those mysteries.

"Dewogimenamin-bro," the voice protested.

I barely understood a word and knew immediately it was Romeo! I finally figured out that they, the prison authorities, wouldn't give him the money he had saved in the four and a half additional years he had spent at San Quentin. He was being paroled once again in a week and he desperately needed $50 until his SSI kicked in. He even explained where to send the money and gave me his account number. I couldn't possibly have refused. Besides, he wanted me to be his therapist again.

Several weeks later, Romeo was slouched in one of my chairs, mumbling all sorts of comments, complaints, apologies and expressions of gratitude, much of which I couldn't understand. By that point in our relationship, clearly understanding him didn't matter.

He also had a new, very pretty wife whose eyes and hands were always exploring a part of him. Romeo was indeed still a "Romeo," and as expected, she looked as if condemned to exile when asked to wait in the adjoining room.

Romeo never missed another appointment, and he

paid me the $50 he owed in less than a month after his first visit. During the next two years, however, he kept trying to repay me, and had I let him, I would have made over $500. He remained the Tenderloin terror and no one ever challenged his reign.

The last time I saw Romeo was the day I retired. During that last appointment he and his wife proudly showed me his shiny new car, another Cadillac, and we hugged a deep-felt goodbye.

As I walked back to my office, I had to smile. Romeo, that fierce-looking man, had gently taken a tiny little girl by the hand as she began to walk out into the street. He escorted the little girl to her apparent mother standing on the sidewalk and mumbled something to the terrified woman about watching the girl more closely.

As Grandma used to say, "See you just can't tell a book by its cover."

Where is Romeo now after seven years? No one in the Tenderloin seems to know. But, if alive, he no doubt has a pretty lady on his arm, a shiny "Caddy" and a menacing look that intimidates anyone who didn't notice what is really, really beneath his "cover."

15

RANDY

Another Book Cover

"What you see is *rarely* what you get," are echoes from those "Book Cover" metaphors of life's endless surprises. Whether it's book covers or packages, they all come in a wide variety of sizes and shapes. Some are wrapped in discarded newspaper, some gift wrapped in pretty colors, while others are sealed in bloodied butcher paper. Yet, beneath the wrappings, they all hide the real message, who they really are.

I learned about the deceptive wrappings early in life through happy surprises and sad disappointments. Later, in my practice, I discovered that a professional grasp of human behavior wasn't much help. Who's really in there? I kept wondering. Finally I realized that I just had to observe carefully, wait and hope for the best.

We have all met many grotesque-looking *Romeos* in our lives, cloaked in thick, coarse, scary butcher paper. Yet, when eventually unwrapped, there may be pleasant surprises of sensitivity, friendship and even an inner beauty.

Sometimes it takes a while before wrappings give way to the hidden real message. For me, it was always worth it. Well, not always.

☐ ☐ ☐

As conditions of his parole from the medium security Soledad State Correctional Facility, twenty-one-year-old Randy was ordered to find a residence, a job and undergo psychotherapy biweekly. He found a Tenderloin apartment, a bank clerk's job, and with three choices by his parole office, he chose me as his therapist. After reviewing all his court records, I felt I knew enough to accept him as a client.

The actual crime had occurred when Randy was nineteen. Witnesses saw him and his twenty-two-year-old girlfriend, Eloise, entering her single unit rental "shouting and staggering like they were drunk." It was approximately 9:30 p.m. At about 11:00 p.m. Randy was again seen by other witnesses staggering from the house as smoke bellowed from front windows.

When fire trucks arrived shortly thereafter, Randy lay sprawled on the front lawn screaming. Once the fire was under control, Eloise's partially charred body was discovered in the kitchen under a pile of scorched and broken plates, bottles, skillets, pieces of chairs, part of a utensil drawer and other kitchen items.

Cause of Eloise's death was inconclusive. The coroner's examination revealed suffocation, probably by smoke inhalation; however, her head and neck were so badly burned it was difficult to rule out strangulation. Her more preserved torso had several cuts and impact wounds, with none sufficiently severe to contribute to her death. Her blood alcohol was .09 along with evidence of Methamphetamine ingestion.

Randy was arrested at the scene babbling incoherently. Lab reports later indicated blood alcohol of .10 and Methamphetamine usage. Other than a few second degree burns, he had no noteworthy injuries at the fire scene.

Randy remembered nothing about how the fire started, Eloise's death, the trashing of the kitchen or how he managed to end up screaming on the lawn in front of her house. He vaguely recalled a "big party" somewhere with lots of alcohol and drugs, but he couldn't remember anyone at the party or its location. He did vaguely remember dating Eloise for a few months, that he stayed at her house at least on weekends, and that they had a passionate relationship with lots of drugs and alcohol.

Initially he was charged with second-degree murder. Then the cause of the fire was determined as "probably" due to a faulty stove pilot light. There was also no convincing evidence that Randy intended to murder Eloise. There was, however, plenty of evidence that his carelessness and intoxication contributed to both the fire and his total disregard for her safety.

Other than drug and trauma-induced retrograde amnesia, psychiatric examinations revealed "no significant mental or emotional impairment." At the advice of his attorney, he pled guilty to the "lesser included offense" of Involuntary Manslaughter, with a sentence of four years. His exemplary conduct earned him a parole during his first Adult Authority hearing following eighteen months' confinement. He was described as a "model inmate."

☐ ☐ ☐

While waiting for a new client to show up, I never quite knew what to expect, and as usual, I really didn't expect what entered my office with a light knock on the door.

Randy was blond, curly-haired and more pretty than handsome—kind of an older Mouseketeer, or a young Brad Pitt. A powder-blue V-neck sweater over a contrasting turtleneck, white trousers and loafers, along with a slender body, provided a collegiate look of bright, youthful innocence. I couldn't help wondering how he survived those inevitable prison sexual predators. *Then again*, I thought, *maybe he didn't.*

His mannerisms easily complimented his physical characteristics. He had a broad smile, direct eye contact, a shy boyish grin and a spontaneity suggesting uncensored openness. His gait had a childlike quality of fragile unsteady lightness, like tiptoeing through a flowerbed. *Nothing slick or ruthless about this kid*, I thought. *Even his out-stretched arm and firmly delicate handshake signaled a guileless desire to befriend.*

I had to smile to myself when out of his mouth came a soft, contralto voice that blended seamlessly with the rest of him. "I'm sorry. Dr Wonderling?"

I nodded with a more visible smile. "You're a little early but that's okay."

Still looking a bit awkward, he added, "Is it all right if I go to the bathroom first?"

"Certainly, it's in the waiting room at the foot of the stairs where you came in." As he left the room, thanking me twice, I figured Randy was probably very nervous about seeing a therapist, and I wondered if he was always so submissive toward authority. By the end of the first session, I had a pretty good hunch he thrived on acceptance, especially from authority.

After thanking me profusely for permitting him to use the bathroom, he openly acknowledged his uneasiness, explaining that he had never been with a *real* psychologist. He said he didn't quite know what was expected of him, and it became increasingly apparent he just wanted to do it right, whatever that meant.

Asking about his background seemed to provide a comfortable structure for Randy. Wrapped in an inviting array of pleasant smiles, Randy's monologue was non-stop.

An only child, he had *wonderful* parents who divorced when it dawned on them that they disliked each other. When they went their separate ways, he went to live with his devoutly religious grandparents who have "ignored" him since his arrest.

"As long as I can remember," he explained, "I admired my parents for their intelligence and guidance, but no matter how hard I tried, they kind of ignored me too." His mother wrote to him once while he was incarcerated.

"Did you ever write to any of them while in prison?" I asked.

He briefly hesitated with a pensive smile. "All of them, at least once a week."

School was *wonderful*, he recalled. He had difficulty learning to read but his teachers were "very helpful and patient." By grade ten, he was an avid reader with a "B" average and well-liked by his teachers and other students. He further remembered the joy of being with girls, and although they were "very nice" to him, he became "real shy and uneasy" when they flirted with him.

His after-school activities were apparently limited to regular part-time jobs. Starting with a paper route in grammar school, he always managed to find work, including busboy, stock boy and finally pizza delivery.

With sagging smile and eyes drooping toward the floor, Randy's monologue shifted to more sober reflections. He had no close friends in high school, and sexual fantasies made him "nervous." He was "fairly good" at many things but not great at anything. He wasn't particularly interested in sports, as participant or spectator. Neither did he fit in with the school nerds—he wasn't that bright or into scholarly pursuits.

Socially, he explored school clubs, with drama his first choice. After receiving minimal recognition and obscure acting parts in school plays, he left the drama club for enrollment in the school dance club. "I loved dancing. Tango and ballroom were my favorites," he explained. Realizing he was really pretty good at something, Randy danced his way through his last year of high school.

Following graduation, he was hired by Bank of America where he was promoted to teller after a year. Working at a Mission Street branch, he met Eloise, his first girlfriend. She introduced him to sex, discos, alcohol and street drugs. "Gosh, she was *wonderful,*" he reminisced.

When asked about the night Eloise died, for the first time during the interview Randy sat quietly gazing up at the ceiling for more than a minute. Along with his reply were reddened eyes glistening with single tears. He volunteered that he was responsible for Eloise's death even though he still couldn't remember anything related to that "terrible" night. Those fleeting thoughts seemed to tug at his wrappings and hinted that whatever he didn't remember, he clearly felt.

By the end of the first session Randy was again well gift-wrapped with friendly grins and smiling apologies for "rambling too much."

Poor kid, I thought, *there must be a lot of pain somewhere beneath those smiles.*

During the next seven months, Randy never missed a session. It had become obvious he wanted to tell me *everything*, as long as *everything* didn't include painful memories. He was always early for his appointments and neatly wrapped in smiles. There were no more painful reflections or tears that were evident in the first session. Well-insulated from troubles of the past, Randy rarely needed any encouragement to free associate— psychoanalytic style—about what he'd been up to during the last weeks.

As if he had a homework assignment, he smilingly greeted me with a warm "it's really nice to see you, Doctor." After a vigorous handshake, he would quickly sit, take a deep breath and describe his life since the last session. Although I reassured Randy that it wasn't necessary to tell me *everything*, he told me *everything* anyway—while his perpetual happy face said *not quite everything*.

Randy had a very pleasing sense of humor. His favorite stories were related to his work. "I'm sure glad people don't see what we do with their money. They'd probably hide it under their bed instead of in the bank."

"Oh?" I asked.

"Like last week before closing. There's this pretty girl teller. She's sometimes stationed next to me. On my way to the restroom with a big cup of orange juice, I reached out to offer her a sip the same time our big fat manager bumped me. The whole cup of juice ended up in Sherry's open cash drawer. Have you ever seen hundreds of dollars floating in orange juice?"

We both had a hearty laugh.

Apparently, Randy was rarely alone or idle. When he had lived in the Tenderloin for less than a month, he probably knew most of the Tenderloin junkies, alcoholics and counselors. By the second month he was attending three Tenderloin Alcoholics Anonymous (AA) meetings, two Narcotics Anonymous (NA) meetings and several Tenderloin church group meetings every week. He also called or dropped by to see his parole agent at least once a week, even though he was required to see him just once a month. When asked why, Randy offered his usual positive reply. "He's really a great guy, and we get along fine. I don't think he minds."

Randy was right, his parole agent liked him, as did his church pastors—all three of them—and the AA and NA secretaries. He was always cheerful with unhesitating replies that seemed to cheerfully dodge painful experiences. To Randy everybody was *wonderful*. He seemed almost too good to be true.

Despite his constant smiles and defensive suppression of any negatives, I really had no serious reservations about Randy. I figured seven months of consistently positive behavior was a compelling testimonial, especially since most law-abiding persons finish their entire lives without ever confronting suppressed demons. *Maybe he's just a real Pollyanna*, I thought.

During our second session, I had also routinely administered a comprehensive battery of psychological tests. The results had been reassuring. There was no evidence of disordered thinking, emotional control problems, high violence potential or other indications of deviant personality characteristics.

The haunting loose ends shrouding the fiery death of Eloise, however, left nagging questions about what really happened that night. Had Randy been the usual low-life junky with a record of violence, the grizzly crime scene would have been a less mysterious, more routine murder scene. Even the criminal justice system had given Randy the benefit of their doubts. All had agreed the death of Eloise made more sense as a grue-some accident involving negligence and irresponsibility.

So, in the final analysis, there was clearly nothing sinister or clinically suspicious about this friendly, easygoing client. And in the absence of any gnawing concerns, I agreed with his parole agent's plan to recommend his early release from parole in a couple of months. *You are what you do*, I thought, *and he's been doing fine for seven months.*

📖 📖 📖

During his eighth month in therapy, Randy spent most of the session happily talking about his new girlfriend, Cindy. He met her at a church social. "Gosh, Dr. Wonderling, she's really beautiful and she goes to college. She's nineteen and wants to be a social worker, kind of like your job. We take long walks, talk about everything—we're in love."

Typical of him, there was nothing blasé or matter of fact about his comments.

Randy's last three sessions teemed with childlike enthusiasm and openness. He discussed their "great sex" while quickly assuring me they planned to marry when he completed his parole. He described her parents as *wonderful*, and he asked me for a favor, his only request during his eight months of therapy.

"Would it be all right if I brought Cindy to meet you?"

"Sure."

A week later his parole agent called me. As I listened, my whole body shook in protest against his message. At a social gathering in the home of Cindy's parents, Randy entered the kitchen where he discovered Cindy kissing a former boyfriend, who was also the family's next door neighbor.

At that time Cindy's parents were sitting in the living room. Grabbing a butcher knife, Randy stabbed and slashed both Cindy and the former boyfriend multiple times. He then dragged their bodies to a back room.

As Randy tried to wipe the blood from the floor, Cindy's father entered the kitchen. Randy stabbed the father over thirty times. The father's screams probably saved the life of his wife. She wisely called 911 and ran from the house.

📖 📖 📖

Randy's temporary insanity plea didn't work. He was convicted of three counts of second-degree murder with fifteen years to life consecutive sentences. Before his transfer to maximum security San Quentin Prison, Randy requested I visit him in the city jail. Rewrapped in warm, colorful smiles, the shear glare of Randy's boyish exuberance blurred any hint he was at all troubled.

"Hi, Dr. Wonderling! It's really good to see you... They've been very nice to me here... My attorney was *wonderful* in court..."

Randy only remembered seeing Cindy in the kitchen. The rest was lost to amnesia.

As I left Randy, I was somewhat lost in my own deep thoughts. *Should I have known—broken through the defensive barriers? Could I have prevented the tragedy?* The answers had to be "no." Sometimes, no matter how carefully we look, what we see just isn't what we get. I'm pretty certain Randy will again be a "model inmate"—this time for the rest of his life—or until something else shreds his wrappings.

16

JAKE

Popeye the Sailor Man

During forty years of clinical practice, I could never quite understand why most psychotherapists seemed to spend more time studying mental classifications than the uniqueness of their clients. As I may have mentioned in other chapters, the *Diagnostic and Statistical Manual of Mental Disorders (DSM)* is supposed to provide scientific definitions of mental disorders. What I didn't mention was the incessant revisions to the original *DSM I*, published in 1948. *DSM IV* emerged with its many changes in the 90's, and since scientists never seem to get it right, a *DSM V* is probably on its way.

One of its fickle mental classifications is the term psychosis, aka schizophrenia, lunacy, insanity or craziness. Psychosis may keep resisting scientific classifications because mental "symptoms" are "behaviors" which vary with the unique behaving individual.

There is another more controversial reason why

mental classifications don't seem to work. The famous psychiatrist, R. D. Laing, and other clinicians, have argued that societies may be crazy, while adjusting to societies is the first sign of lunacy. Such conclusions are clear to anyone living in the Tenderloin, where the term psychosis may not be taken too seriously.

As a micro-society, the Tenderloin is a peculiar host that often demands peculiar behaviors from its residents. Crazy behavior sometimes becomes a way of adapting to a crazy environment. That adaptive form of craziness in the Tenderloin is accepted by many of its residents. It is even respected by some. Most Tenderloin residents are keenly aware that behavioral differences and peculiarities are essential to their survival. If you're too straight, you may be considered a mark. If you're too dependent—a victim. If you're too confident—a cop, if too slick—a hustler and if you're too agreeable—a snitch. But if too crazy—you're either humored or left alone.

📖　📖　📖

Jake was one of the Tenderloin's journeyman crazies, by just about anybody's definition. That may indicate he was really crazy. On the other hand, maybe he was the proverbial "crazy like a fox," a hard-core survivor, whose personality peculiarities blended well with his Tenderloin street savvy. Again, different from other San Francisco areas, the Tenderloin fosters a special brand of craziness, a unique blend of the peculiar that Jake personified exceptionally well.

Jake's qualifications were impressive. For over twenty-five years, he had lived everywhere on, as well as in the Tenderloin. His home was his van. Parking all over the Tenderloin, he became familiar with every street and was known to just about every Tenderloin regular. He had been a Tenderloin part-time everything, including bartender, bouncer, dishwasher, hustler, swamper and, of course, a crazy.

Understanding some of Jake's more spectacular displays of craziness begins with understanding his cherished pastime. The San Francisco waterfront is a historical montage of contrasting old piers and new shopping areas that keep changing the original shoreline. The old piers creak and groan beneath their memories of moored sailing ships and freighters with exotic cargoes, as well as seamen from around the world. There were legendary longshoremen struggling, dragging and pulling with steel grappling hooks, like extensions of their huge muscular arms and calloused hands.

Even in those early rugged days, the waterfront was sprinkled with fishermen who claimed special places on the piers. Maybe they couldn't afford a boat or market prices of fish. Or maybe they just needed a relaxing place to pass the time.

By the middle of the 20th century, Jake was one of those fishermen. He loved the sport and his favorite spot much more than the fish he rarely caught. At least four or five days a week he would drive the van from his Tenderloin parking place to his little piece of territory on an old dilapidated San Francisco pier. That was his special fishing hole. He would sit all day sipping coffee and scanning the Bay. He often dozed and sometimes indifferently pulled in a terrified fish. It was Jake's territory and everyone knew it. At least everyone in the Tenderloin knew it.

On one warm, balmy September Monday, Jake left the Tenderloin a bit later than usual. He had his full pot of coffee, plenty of fishing gear and pleasant thoughts of a lazy day at his personal fishing spot. He drove down Taylor Street by the Golden Gate Theater, across Market onto Sixth Street, the area known as South of Market. He then turned left on Mission, past Third Street, where, in those days, most of the old stumble bums hung out. Mission ends at the Embarcadero, where Jake turned left toward his private pier.

Jake had resented Asians for a long time, primarily because they were swarming all over the piers, taking over all of the best fishing areas. So far they hadn't bothered him. He took care of the possible "Asian invasion" by blocking off his little territory. He would attach a rope from the rear door handle on his van to an old rotted piling loosely protruding about three feet above the pier. He attached more rope from his front hood ornament to another piling. That was Jake's own space, the length of the van and about four feet wide. On that day, however, everything would be different.

To start with, his reserved space was occupied. Worse, the intruders were Asians. There were about ten of them, all merrily fishing and chatting in some Asian language. Infuriated, Jake could feel that surge of adrenaline and quickening heart rate. It was the invasion he had dreaded. The showdown—like Pearl Harbor.

"You have five minutes to get out of my private spot," he shouted in his loudest and meanest voice.

The Asians looked up and smiled. Some even waved before resuming their chats and fishing. They hadn't the slightest idea what he was saying.

Jake had no other choice. Slamming his van into reverse, he backed up around fifty feet. There he paused, with a wave of nausea, cotton-dry mouth and a racing heart thumping in his chest. He shifted into neutral, revved the engine and began the countdown.

"Four minutes," he screamed. "Three minutes and

counting. I'm serious, leave now!" Jake's foot was nervously slamming the gas pedal, causing an explosive engine roar that nearly drowned out his booming threats.

"Two minutes, Goddamn it!" Jake was hysterical, almost pleading by the one minute count. He shoved the lever into drive. As the rear wheels burst into swirling smoke and squeals, the van began its wild skidding charge. "Get out of the waaaaayyyy!!!"

That front-page incident occurred long before I knew Jake. According to all accounts, miraculously, no one was injured. Once the smiling, chatting and fishing Asians noticed the crazy van careening in their direction, they stopped smiling, chatting and fishing. They ran for their lives.

Scattering in stark terror, one Asian jumped or fell off the pier just as the van soared well over the flailing body. The Asian's fall ended in a belly-flop splash.

That was followed by the van's headfirst crash into the water about twenty feet beyond the floundering and terrified Asian. Some bystanders reported that the fallen man and the flying van looked like some choreographed circus act with perfect timing.

Inside the van, Jake had both hands frozen to the steering wheel and feet crushing the gas pedal. He screamed his way off the pier, through the air and into the water. It was a surreal experience that lasted between twenty seconds and two hours, depending on the observer.

Upon impact, the van did a momentary headstand, which offered Jake a glass-bottom-boat view of the Bay's murky water. As the van settled back on its still spinning wheels, Jake could have been watching through a power boat's windshield.

A wonderful view, he thought. He cruised another few feet until the engine died. It reminded him that this wasn't an amphibian or a dream, it was his van and they were really in the water.

. Uninjured and shocked into a sense of calm, Jake opened his door and casually stepped into the Bay. He was a bit surprised when he sank up to his neck, while his van floated beside him. Swimming around his van several times, Jake thought of getting back in and trying to start the engine. He finally dismissed that idea when the van sank beneath him to the Bay's muddy bottom.

Jake actually floated on his back along and under the old waterfront piers for nearly a half hour before he was picked up by a San Francisco fireboat. According to the newspapers, Jake was rescued. According to Jake, he was caught. Either way he was taken to a locked psychiatric institution where he stayed for seven months.

Several years after his release from the psychiatric institution, Jake had another van, a new coffee pot, plenty of fishing gear and a permanent Tenderloin parking place in a friend's alley parking lot. The old San Francisco pier territorial disputes were history, hardly worth mentioning. His newest preference was for public pier fishing, especially at Aquatic Park, where there was plenty of room, all day. Since his hospital release, he even liked Asians and couldn't remember why he ever disliked them.

Jake was financially secure with his SSI, and he was free to live wherever he pleased. There was, however, one small annoyance he had to handle. He had been awarded SSI as a "Bipolar Disorder, Manic Type with Paranoid Features." Like so many of my other clients, he needed a therapist to insure his continued SSI and MediCal benefits. That's when I met Jake's voice, a phone call not easily forgotten.

☐   ☐   ☐

"Hello, this is Dr. Wonderling."

"Can you use a few extra bucks?" The voice was clear, cheerful and melodious—perhaps an old friend.

"Come again?" I asked.

"Do you need a new patient?" The voice was a tinge more serious, yet still soft, casual and chatty.

"No, not really," I replied, more formally.

"Come on, Doc, I need a shrink and I was told you're OK." The voice's cheerful melody switched to all serious.

In those early days I could always use an extra client, even though my first analysis of the message within that pleasant voice was "trouble." I reluctantly agreed to see Jake, who was perceptive enough to sense my reluctance.

"Gee thanks, Doc. I'm looking forward to seeing you and I apologize for wasting your phone time with my stupid humor." His final phone comments were courteous, gentle and businesslike.

Two weeks later, I met the rest of Jake. As he entered my office, my expectations about his physical appearance were totally shattered. I'll never learn that a person's voice has no relation to what he/she looks like. Jake's appearance seemed like one massive contradiction. He was a presence impossible to ignore, including his gigantic container filled with coffee. Gripping it in his right hand like a trophy, it could have been an old artillery casing with a handle.

About 5′ 7″ tall, Jake was built like a huge fireplug. Below his broad shoulders were big, flaccid arms, a barrel chest and an even bigger bulging stomach. On top of his round body was long wavy clean black hair, a creamy smooth face with dark flashing eyes and a delicate prettiness that remarkably resembled the old screen idle, Tyrone Power. Jake was proud of that facial similarity and he mentioned it frequently. He also saw to it, however, that his near-cherubic appearance was offset by ruggedly masculine, intimidating embellishments.

He pony-tailed his otherwise curly locks and his dimpled cheeks were partially concealed beneath a shabby growth of whiskers that never seemed to become a beard. A dagger earring dangled menacingly from his left ear and a narrow leather headband crossing the middle of his forehead gave him a warrior look. Jake also wore tank tops or old sweatshirts with the arms ripped out, emphasizing his big, albeit fat, arms. Topping off this mean look was a huge occult medallion resting on his belly by a thick chain. It resembled a pit bull's collar.

It was all too clear from the start that this enigma of a man could be a bully and an overbearing pain, who wanted to take charge, while quickly backing down if challenged. Yet, he had dramatically shown in San Francisco that, if he felt cornered, get out of his way.   .

"You must be Jake." I grinned.

"You must be Doc.," He chuckled.

Before I could offer him a seat, Jake was down on the more comfortable of the two chairs—mine. At that point I knew I'd better define and structure this relationship immediately, or he might end up charging me for his services.

"If you really want to be my client, the first thing you've gotta know is that's my chair you flopped in."

Jake leaped to his feet with surprising agility and unleashed a hardy laugh. "I almost blew it again, Doc. I'm sorry. I need you for all kinds of reasons, one of which is to keep me on SSI."

"I don't think that'll be a problem."

Jake knew what I meant and unloaded another whole body laugh. "You're the boss."

During our long therapeutic relationship, Jake turned out to be one of my least troublesome and most interesting clients. He was exceptionally bright, perhaps too bright for his lifestyle. His tested IQ was well above the 99th percentile, the genius range. Such an IQ, combined with his hyper-vigilance and marked sensitivity to others, entitled him to some unusual gifts.

He could frequently grasp what others, including me, were thinking. He could also out-reason most people in a discussion. Unfortunately, Jake couldn't modulate these skills. In other words, he couldn't control his mouth, and since he was brighter than over 99% of adults, his assets were his liabilities. People are easily threatened by others who are smarter and bigger than they. Jake was both. His "in your face" tendency to jamb his brilliance down your throat made him an annoying threat.

Jake was well-acquainted with his assets, but resisted knowing why they didn't work too well. He proudly described himself as hustler, manipulator and con man. Those were talents he could have easily mastered, except for his mouth. Like many Tenderloin regulars, he cherished the "I gottcha" game. It was the passion for "one-upping" people that made him a terrible con man. He knew, of course, con men don't act like con men, and certainly don't flaunt the tricks of their trade. He did anyway.

Perhaps that analysis of Jake was too harsh or even inaccurate. Maybe Jake was just interested in survival, with no particular concern for normalcy or professional success. It might have been a big game to Jake, and with his huge coffee mug, fishing pole and mouth, he had a lot of fun.

He often told me that the "crazy house" was a great vacation. He enjoyed teasing the nurses, and he felt especially proud of acting crazy for the doctors. Then he could stay there through the winter. He even admitted preferring to live in his van to an apartment.

"On SSI," he explained, "my income lasts a lot longer rent free in the van."

Such comments had elements of craziness and clear thinking. After a few years, analyzing those observations ceased to be important. Jake and I both knew he couldn't hold a regular job. He needed his SSI to survive. I also knew that permanently residing in an institution was a clinical alternative costing at least four times as much.

So, as Jake continued to survive in his own special way, I stopped puzzling over the crazy and sane parts of his special way. I finally figured out it didn't matter. Jake's behavior was a fluid concoction of psychiatric-crazy and Tenderloin-normal. There were no definable parts, just a very unique Jake. So, all I could do for Jake was heighten his awareness of his weaknesses, help him survive more effectively without hurting anyone, keep him on SSI and enjoy our sessions.

Jake and I probably got along well because he never considered me his therapist, and I never treated him as a "patient." He viewed me as a friend, yet he always called me Doc, an apparent metaphor of respect. Jake was an experienced patient with numerous therapists in the past, both psychiatrists and psychologists. He used to describe them as "shrinks" who "played therapists to hide their own puny personalities. They thought they were superior to their lowly patients," he used to grumble.

Thankfully, I never played therapist with Jake. Maybe because I knew he'd see through any facade, or maybe because I never really knew how a therapist was supposed to act. In those days, playing therapist meant calling your client a "patient," which I never did. So, I just played the only self I ever knew, with loyalty to my "client" and a deep concern for his welfare.

Jake was one of the few clients who somehow knew my birthday, and as his friend, he needed to give me gifts. During our bi-weekly sessions, many subjects came up, including Popeye, which became my birthday present. Jake happened to mention once that he enjoyed Popeye cartoons as a kid. He said Popeye had the "courage to protect Olive from Bluto, a loyalty to Wimpy" and self-confidence in his "I yam what I yam."

I guess I was reminded of my childhood memories and Popeye's impact on my early life. I told him that, as an anemic kid, one of the only vegetables I'd ever eat was spinach, because of Popeye.

Jake never forgot that conversation and seven months later I got a Popeye can of spinach in the mail. For my next birthday, I received a Popeye poster, then a Popeye funny book, and later, Olive and Sweet Pea dolls. One of his last and most special gifts was a Popeye music box. The music always triggers old memories mixed with smiles and tears.

Although the effectiveness of psychological treatment is difficult to measure, Jake was showing some kind of therapeutic progress. He seemed to enjoy our sessions, as did I. He managed to avoid legal trouble and even use his psychiatric craziness wisely. He couldn't wait to tell me when some of his craziness had actually enhanced his ability to cope with reality. One of the many examples was the portable radio episode.

📖 📖 📖

Overlooking the three blocks of Market Street that border the Tenderloin are rows of old buildings. Those are historical remnants of a once bustling, colorful downtown San Francisco. Before the onslaught of shopping malls, Market Street literally teemed with an endless variety of classy shops and restaurants, filled with scurrying patrons, all excessively well-dressed by today's standards. It is a deeply nostalgic area for the old-timers and a fleeting curiosity for the newcomers. Other than a few ornate vestiges of another era, the charm of those old buildings was abandoned long ago, together with their rich assortment of elegant goods and services.

Today, like old weathered letters from the past, too many of the storefronts that embellish the buildings' ground floors have aged badly into stark, dreary discount houses. The almost sadly unpretentious stores deal in "seconds" merchandise and cater to many poor Tenderloin patrons who believe in the perpetual "close-out" sales. There are no window displays or artfully decorated departments. There are just piles of naked merchandise, unsellable in the bigger stores, slightly damaged, older models or just outdated styles.

When Jake decided he needed a new AM/FM portable radio, that's where he headed. As far as Jake was concerned, the Market Street discount stores had the best prices in town.

A short walk south on Taylor Street to Market put Jake right in the heart of those stores. He found one called Discount Appliances, with cameras, small TVs and radios perched on upside-down cardboard boxes inside the storefront window. Each of the displayed items contained an "On Sale Today" tag, which included one for a portable radio.

It was the place Jake was looking for. There were hundreds of items on tables all over the room and as he hit the door, Jake was immediately greeted by one of several tall, dark middle eastern salesmen.

"Can I help you?"

As a self-styled con man, Jake wasn't going to be hustled by any of those salesmen. "I know exactly what I want. An AM/FM portable radio and I have $20 on me, no more." he said a bit defensively.

The salesman quickly moved to one of the tables, returning in seconds with a portable radio about the size of a paperback book. "Here's exactly what you want, sir. There's plenty of volume, great little speakers and the radio is impact-proof. It's only $19.99 plus tax, but we'll give it to you for twenty dollars, including the batteries. We'll pay the tax."

The salesman turned on the portable radio, and after quickly sampling a couple of stations, turned it off. "Can I wrap it for you?"

Jake quickly gave the man his $20, self-assured he had beaten the store out of batteries and tax. *I probably intimidated the guy*, he thought.

That night, after eating his take-out Chinese dinner and pouring a fresh pot of coffee into his canister, Jake was ready to sit outside his van and listen to some of his favorite FM country western music. He grabbed his lawn chair, big coffee mug and new radio in preparation for a relaxing evening with some of his old Tenderloin pals.

Once he turned on the radio, however, he knew he'd been out-hustled. The portable radio had no FM switch; it was just a little AM radio. A closer look revealed it was probably worth about $7.

Jake's relaxing country western evening with his buddies was over before it started. Suddenly he felt a mixture of humiliation, rage and business failure. He was even too ashamed to tell his friends. He had to handle this defeat by himself, and he stayed up most of the night rehearsing possible strategies.

When the Discount Appliance store opened at 10 a.m. the following day, Jake was standing there, clutching the radio, the receipt and flashing a fixed smile through clenched-teeth. Not to be out-flashed, the first salesman to greet Jake beamed an even broader, toothy smile.

Just as quickly, the salesman's eyes narrowed as he noticed the radio and receipt. "Can I help you?" he asked dryly.

Jake had his lines well-prepared. "You certainly can. You must have given me the wrong radio by mistake. I guess the AM/FM radio I actually purchased is still here, somewhere."

Still holding his scripted smile, Jake pointed to yesterday's salesman. "That's the guy who gave me the wrong radio by mistake."

The salesman with Jake had changed from cheerful to serious. "Rasiq," he gently called with a snap of his fingers.

Rasiq approached, forcing a tentative smile. Before Jake could repeat his monologue, Rasiq and the other salesman were in a foreign language dialog that Jake couldn't understand. In less than a minute, a third man, obviously their boss, joined in the foreign language discussion.

When the talk stopped, Rasiq stepped toward Jake. "I'm so sorry, you must have misunderstood yesterday. I definitely told you that only the AM radio could be sold for $20. All of our AM/FM radios are $35 and up. If you re-read your receipt, there's no return on electronic merchandise."

As Rasiq completed his hastily prepared disclaimer, with apologetic overtones, Jake knew he had been "rat-packed." There was nothing he could do about it.

Feeling the rumblings of inner frustration and rage, he reconsidered—well, almost nothing.

Although Jake hadn't rehearsed the "almost nothing," he'd had plenty of practice in the past. As Rasiq, his boss and the other two salesmen grinned triumphantly, Jake conjured a trembling in his lower lip, followed by uncontrollable teeth gnashing, tense eye squinting, heavy grunting and a face-filling grimace. Jake had their attention and they stopped grinning. Alternately clenching his fists and flailing his arms, Jake began to mumble, "I can't stand it. I can't stand it. I have nothing now, you're making me crazy."

With gaping mouths and wide eyes, the stunned salesmen tried to recover enough to ask Jake to calm down and leave. That was Jake's signal to amplify his crazy, volatile display. Climbing on one of the sturdier tables, 245 pound Jake began beating his chest and screaming, "Help, help!! My money's gone. Too much pressure, I've been robbed. I'm going crazzzyyy."

Pedestrians were peering through the doorway with varying expressions of disbelief, fright, sadistic amusement and pity.

"Give him the $20!" the boss shouted. He'd had enough.

"Then what happened?" I asked.

Jake turned his head away from me for a moment, and when he turned back, his eyes were noticeably teary. "I beat 'em, Doc. They ganged up on me and I beat 'em." He dried his eyes and smiled. "I remember taking the money from Rasiq and walking straight out the door, through a bunch of gawking people. I didn't say another word to anyone. Back on Market Street, I walked fast to my van. I was really happy, Doc. You see I had the twenty and the AM radio!"

We both sat quietly for a few minutes, patiently

sharing the silence. I knew Jake needed to say something else and he finally did.

"How'd I handle it, Doc? Not bad, huh?"

I smiled into Jake's inquiring eyes, "You did fine,
Jake. Real fine."

📖 📖 📖

As our relationship grew stronger, so did Jake's need for
my encouragement and approval. He wanted me to tell
him he was making progress, and most of the time, with
a few clinical compromises, I could. Once in awhile,
however, condoning an activity of his was a difficult
stretch—even for me.

Jake's old friend, "Weird Carl," was back in the
Tenderloin after serving six months in the county jail for
an assortment of unpaid traffic fines. They had met
years earlier, during a seventy-two-hour psychiatric
lock-up. They had so much in common, a lasting
friendship was inevitable. When together, their large
size intimidated others, and they had both lived in the
Tenderloin before with similar reputations as weird or
crazy. Beneath their menacing facades of headbands,
tank tops, chains and tattoos, they were highly sensitive
and secretly insecure. They needed someone to trust,
which they found in each other. Weird Carl, with his flat
scarred face and smashed nose, looked meaner than
Jake. But neither were tough street fighters.

One of their hobbies was planning hustles. None of
them ever materialized until they saw a gangster movie
on TV, depicting a bunko artist faking pedestrian
injuries.

Their plan was simple and "foolproof." Jake would
cross the street against a stop signal. As an awaiting car
began to move, Jake would hit the side of the car with

his palm, sit down in the street and hold his arm, whimpering. Weird Carl would be an indignant by-stander, accusing the bewildered driver of moving by Jake too soon. Then, for some money, he'd forget the whole thing.

Their criminal career lasted two days, three cars and no money. The first was a big, late model Cadillac, driven by an old lady who insisted they call the police and her insurance company. They declined.

The second car was a small Honda, with an astonishingly gigantic driver. He growled, "Get lost assholes, or I'll put you both in the hospital."

They complied and quickly got lost. Those two attempts occurred in the Tenderloin—the first at the O'Farrell and Ellis intersection, and the second at Turk and Taylor.

Their last try was at a traffic signal at the corner of Geary and Van Ness. Jake waited until the green light had turned yellow; as he walked across the intersection past a white Ford sedan, he stopped. When the car began to accelerate, the driver's side view mirror hit Jake's poised arm, knocking him flat on his back. That wasn't part of the plan. Immediately Weird Carl was running his pitch to the driver, not yet noticing Jake, like a wounded elephant, holding his bruised arm. He was in real pain.

The driver and the three passengers were police detectives on their way to a meeting. When Weird Carl saw their badges and Jake flat on the pavement, he quickly helped Jake struggle to his feet. Weird Carl confessed that his friend shouldn't have stopped in the middle of the intersection.

"Can we take your friend to the hospital?" the driver shouted.

Moving away from the car, they both looked back

with feeble smiles. "No thanks, there's no problem."

"Well, Doc, I guess we screwed up, but I really learned a lesson."

I looked at Jake with a show of surprise. "What's that?" I asked.

"Weird Carl should have done the falling and me the talking. What do ya think, Doc?"

I shook my head slowly, with my best show of exasperation, "At least you weren't seriously injured or jailed."

During the next few years, Jake's behavior kept improving. He still loved fishing, drinking coffee from his huge mug and looking tough. Remarkably absent were boastful scams, the hustler image or crazy antics. His new hobbies were cooking and reading, both of which he attacked with his characteristic zeal. He couldn't wait to tell me about new recipes he'd created and the books he had read.

About a year before I closed my office in San Francisco, Jake moved from the Tenderloin to Sacramento with his still good friend, Weird Carl. I haven't seen him since, yet he's certainly not easy to forget. Every time I bump against the old Popeye music box he gave me, it plays a few notes before sadly groaning to a halt. "I'm Popeye the saaiillloorrr…ma…."

Jake's affection for Popeye also taught me something about personal pride and the uniqueness of individuals that I'll always remember. *I yam what I yam. I'm Popeye the sailor man.*

After all these years, I still have the Popeye music box reminding me that "I *yam* what I *yam*" and Jake *is* what he *is*, no matter where he *is*.

17

BILLY

The Secret

What do alcoholics have in common? Ironically, despite modern day medicine, the answer is still from old vaudeville slapstick: "They're all drunks." Seems like that punch line continues to have more merit than the genetic predisposition theory.

Drunks, especially street drunks, get little sympathy from self-righteous, temperate adults. That's because such indignant persons seldom look beyond an alcoholic's first layer trademark stagger and stench, to notice the unique differences in each of them.

$$\square \quad \square \quad \square$$

Billy was the perfect example of a hard core Tenderloin drunk. His appearance and first layer of behaviors were stereotypically freefalling alcoholic with a defective parachute.

His second layer of behaviors was a bit less obvious—until you got to know him better. Billy wasn't just a drunk. He was receiving SSI benefits while always broke, which wasn't unusual for alcoholics. In his early thirties, he was a tad younger than most Tenderloin boozers, which wasn't that unusual except for his alcoholic related brain dysfunctions. He was a young man, yet his brain was very old.

Billy was also a thief, or perhaps more clinically, a kleptomaniac. That was one of his more subtle second layer characteristics unless, of course, you found something missing when he was around.

"I really didn't mean it," was a frequent apology to those he knew.

Another of his second layer signatures was his HIV, related to homosexuality rather than street drugs. Characteristic of many Tenderloin gays, Billy didn't confine himself to other gays. He comfortably hung around anyone with a bottle or readiness to drink—preferably another drunk like himself.

It required no great psychodiagnostic skills to figure out his first couple of layers. All that was needed was to pay attention for a while and Billy would unabashedly or clumsily show you.

The third, deepest layer, however, is never easy to figure out, even for seasoned clinicians. Those are the behaviors well-hidden from everyone, sometimes including the person behaving—kind of like "book covers" in previous chapters.

Third layers are tough to penetrate by the closest of friends and the sharpest of professionals. Remember that nice guy across the street, your neighbor for five years? He was finally arrested for molesting forty kids—or was he a serial killer? It doesn't matter. No one, except the victims, actually knew until he was finally caught. Then suddenly the crimes were reduced to the second layer and he's the evil guy that lived across the street. Curious how we're positive we know someone until we learn something else about them.

📖   📖   📖

Like so many other Tenderloin residents, Billy needed a psychotherapist to preserve his SSI checks. I was the chosen one for the usual reasons. I was conveniently located in the Tenderloin, and had a reputation for not interfering with their lives unless they asked.

A half-hour before his appointment, Billy practically flung himself into my office with a slurred apology for being late. Tripping over the rug he barely managed to prevent a fall by grabbing the edge of my desk. He was drunk, which wasn't a surprising first appearance by new alcoholic clients.

I could easily overlook his early intrusion into my private time. Brain-damaged alcoholics often confused appointment times. On the other hand, I don't like alcoholics who come to my office drunk. So I couldn't come up with my initially friendly greeting.

Precariously easing himself into a nearby chair, Billy smelled like he had been awash in a pool of booze, laced with B.O. Looking at Billy, I sighed with a thinly veiled frown. That changed, however, into a restrained smile when I noticed that Billy resembled a scruffy puppy, leaning forward, panting with eyes wide as if awaiting my command. It was time for the lecture on session ground rules. As I came around to the front of my desk, Billy reached up and handed me a crumpled wad of something. It was his referral from the Department of Social Services.

"Billy," I said a little sternly, "do you really want to see me every two weeks as your counselor?"

"Yes, Sir," he shouted, still with a wide-eyed stare.

At that moment I felt like a drill sergeant as I fought back a grin. "Are there any days you don't drink at all?"

Billy paused. "Sometimes, Sir."

"That's good, Billy, because I have one strict rule. You can't have even one drink on the day you see me. Not one. Can you do that?"

"What, Sir?"

"Can you stop drinking on your appointment day before you see me? In other words, I won't see you if you've been drinking. Got it?"

"I won't drink next time. No, Sir."

"Okay. Here's my card with my name. You don't have to call me sir."

After a brief explanation of my role, another carefully explained appointment date and a reminder to bring his MediCal card—which he forgot—Billy left, and I grabbed my air freshener.

📖 📖 📖

Billy showed up for all subsequent appointments either too early or a little late, but never drunk or even smelling of booze.

He did have one convulsing seizure in my office, which he didn't remember. Epilepsy with frequent seizures was another of his second layer behaviors. Since he was just about always drunk or drinking, except on appointment days, like so many alcoholics, seizure medications didn't work.

Regaining full consciousness after his seizure, Billy looked around, with a sheepish grin. "I'm sorry, Sir."

"Do you want to go to emergency?" I asked while knowing his answer.

"No, Sir."

I let him leave early that day, also knowing he needed a drink. He hesitated at first. "What's the matter, Billy, you broke?"

He answered softly with lowered eyes. "Yes, Sir." He had never stolen from me, even though his record was replete with shoplifting arrests. I gave him five dollars that day.

📖 📖 📖

Penetrating Billy's third layer was neither necessary nor relevant to me. I knew enough about him to develop a noninvasive, supportive treatment strategy. He was a gay, brain-damaged alcoholic who was always broke, stole when he could and was in need of SSI for basic survival shelter and food.

Billy was comfortably oblivious to behavioral change while any counseling efforts were received as friendly "blah blah." For him, remaining sober before an interview was major progress, and helping Billy stay out of jail, keep his shelter and survive another week were my therapeutic goals. His seizure activity, along with his passive resistance to HIV medical appointments, kept reminding me that basic survival treatment was all that really mattered. I had arranged numerous medical appointments for HIV medications, together with discussions of their importance.

Billy would smile, thank me and never show at the clinic.

I'm always troubled by a client like Billy that I feel sorry for, while knowing he's killing himself. At least he seemed to look forward to our sessions, and he never displayed the slightest mean streak.

During one session he even mentioned feeling a bit guilty about his SSI checks. Under questioning, he meandered into some other topic; which wasn't unusual for a guy with sever attention, concentration and abstract reasoning problems. I figured he recognized that a lot of his SSI checks were spent on booze, so maybe that's what prompted the guilts. He never told me and I never pursued it.

I saw Billy every two weeks for nearly a year. He never got any better, nor did he seem to deteriorate beyond his original referral condition. *That's a real accomplishment*, I thought. Yet, I used to wonder if his one open expression of guilt had been about his drinking or something else. Perhaps there was something else he wanted me to explore. Maybe I should have, but what would we have accomplished?

Probing his innermost *third layer* of naked secrets could crack his fragile defenses and expose the cold chills of conflict and torment. So I figured that was a bad idea. I finally realized, since he didn't have much of a life left, there wasn't much point in stirring up therapeutic insights. It probably wouldn't have made him feel better, and why run the risk of making him feel worse.

📖 📖 📖

Billy died instantly when hit by a bus on Market Street during one of his seizures. Witnesses saw him shaking violently before collapsing in front of the on-coming bus.

Like so many Tenderloin residents, there was no known next of kin, no apparent insurance and dim prospects for a funeral.

I did, however, get the hotel manager's permission to check Billy's room for possible phone numbers. What I found in the barren little room with a few empty bottles and a tiny portable radio will drift around in my mind forever.

On top of an old wooden dresser was a stack of papers with several letters from a Christian organization thanking Billy for his monthly donation of $60 to support two orphan children in Africa. There were also a couple pictures of little black girls with big smiles. Papers indicated he had been sending money for over a year.

I wondered, was that the reason for his one comment about guilt? Was that his secret? If so, I was actually relieved. It was a reminder of other Tenderloin winos who secretly donated a sizable portion of their meager SSI check to less fortunate third-world kids.

So, in the final analysis, even though Billy had no family, close friends or a funeral, he did indeed have two little girls in Africa. He also had a therapist who would share Billy's secret with others, especially those more fortunate, not as generous and less tolerant of Tenderloin winos.

※   ※   ※

After all these years, I'm still grateful for all I learned from so many of my Tenderloin clients. In fact, such lessons may have prompted this Second Edition story. Thanks to Billy, I'm now helping two little girls and their families in third-world countries.

18

JODY

A Special Letter

How parents can best shape their children's developing behavior has invited hundreds of scholarly texts, with nearly as many theories. Those pop child-rearing volumes jamb today's bookstores. Yet most of those "books" have, at best, just a few sound principles that could have been clearly presented in a small pamphlet. The rest of the book, like the formulas in your medicine cabinet, contains inert ingredients. Ironically, even the basic principles cannot insure success in life—just survival.

Perhaps the most important and fundamental principle for families to acknowledge is that parents cannot *not* contribute to the shaping of their children's behavior; and children cannot resist a parent's influence, no matter how hard they try. Regardless of what a parent does or doesn't do, the child will somehow be affected.

That wouldn't be a developmental concern if parents really knew what they were doing. Unfortunately, they don't; and even if they were dedicated and bright enough to strive for perfection, no one would know how to teach them.

There is simply no perfect way to raise a child, because there are no perfect parents, no perfect environments and no way to define perfection. There are, however, some clearly defined pragmatic principles vital to a child's welfare and relevant to this chapter.

In order to survive with the best chance of achieving one's potential, a child must have nurturing love from its parents. Without it, children can die. On the other hand, if a parent crosses that critical boundary with too much of the wrong kind of love, a child may live with a curse worse than death. That's when a parent's love becomes entangled in lust.

     📖   📖   📖

Drip, drip, drip. . drip . . . . . drip . . . . drip . . . .
Then silence, except for labored breathing.

"Oh, my God," she gasped when she opened her eyes. *What a terrible mess, and I'm not dead.* She could see both hands dangling over the arms of her chair. *They look like scarlet gloves*, she thought. Below each hand was a large pool of coagulating blood. Her inner wrists were throbbing where she had cut quarter inch deep transverse gashes.

The bleeding had stopped along with any peaceful dying. She'd have to find the razor blade and cut deeper into both wrists, but that would hurt too much.

"Oh shit!" she cried, "I can't do anything right." Whimpering, she picked up the phone and dialed a bloodied 911.

An hour before her call, a faceless, bald-headed man, with an enormous belly and tiny penis was between her spread legs. His terrible breath and crude, clumsy movements made it difficult for her to even fake passion. She shut her eyes, turned her head away from his breath and tried to ignore his complaints that she wasn't doing anything.

Jody wasn't the problem. The big-bellied man had ejaculated when she was fondling his penis to check for venereal diseases. It would be hours before he could have another erection, and he angrily knew he was out of time. Crushed under his weight, and sickened by the smell of his body and breath, Jody couldn't bear him any longer.

"I'm sorry, that's all for tonight," she whispered. She braced herself for the impact, knowing he wouldn't leave easily. He didn't.

After slapping her a few times, he bit her hard on her right nipple, slapped her again and rolled off the bed. Grabbing her coat, he removed the $25 he had given her on the street, plus $15 of her own—all the money she had. Jody lay there holding her bleeding breast as she impassively watched him. After putting on his clothes, he tore apart her coat, skirt and blouse before leaving.

Jody pulled a soiled blanket up around her shivering body and looked at her image in the old stained mirror over the bed. She felt as empty and ugly as her barren Tenderloin studio apartment. Everything seemed dark gray, just dreary shades of hopelessness. The wooden floors needed varnishing, the walls were pleading for new wallpaper and the dilapidated bed, dresser and armchair needed replacing. She tearfully sneered into the mirror, "So do I."

It was just a few months earlier, now light years away, that she had discovered her lover, a generous, caring older man, fondling a prostitute in a Tenderloin restaurant. She was more confused than actually hurt, which prompted thoughts about her future. *Why do men flirt with you adoringly, lavish gifts and loving attention until they have you sexually, which is all they wanted in the first place. Then their attention is invariably distracted by new sex objects and you become less than you were. The courting and romance are over.*

That's when Jody decided to sell sex and skip the charade. *That's all men want anyway*, she thought. Her apprenticeship was an unexpected downhill plunge into humiliation and abuse. She really wasn't in control. The "Johns" were.

Without a pimp, she was brutalized and sometimes forced into disgusting sex play with a repulsive man or men. With a pimp, she would experience similar abuse, less money and no freedom. Jody was trapped without a future. She had wept bitterly and agonized over the only way out.

A week before she slashed her wrists, Jody walked toward the center of the Golden Gate Bridge, where, like thousands in the past, she contemplated suicide. It was a clear, crisp morning and looking out over the eastern railing, she could see Alcatraz, Angel Island and a breathtaking panorama of San Francisco and the East Bay cities.

"I'll try a few more tricks," she concluded. "It's a nice day."

Ⅲ   Ⅲ   Ⅲ

The ambulance arrived in a few minutes. When Jody opened the door, she was sobbing uncontrollably. The paramedics looked at the pools of blood on the floor and the open wounds on her outstretched wrists, before gently leading her to the ambulance. No interview was necessary. She was immediately driven to the General Hospital. After a few stitches, she was admitted to the psychiatric wing for seventy-two hour observation. In San Francisco, it's standard procedure when anyone is suspected of harming themselves or others.

📖 📖 📖

Two weeks later, I met Jody for the first time. Referred by the Department of Social Services, she had agreed to undergo psychotherapy when released from the psychiatric ward. On the day of her appointment, her knock on my office door was barely audible.

I figured it was a knock of hesitation or maybe pre-interview nervousness. Either would be understandable. Even I was always a little anxious waiting for the arrival of a new client.

"Come on in." As the door opened, my jaw began to slacken along with my widening eyes. Framed in the doorway was an extraordinarily gorgeous eighteen-year-old. I quickly summoned my best professional composure and leaped from my seat.

"Hi, I have a sneaking hunch you're Jody. I'm, Dr. Wonderling. Here, have a seat."

Jody smiled tentatively and moved with a slightly clumsy uneasiness to the chair.

Poor kid is nervous, I thought—*me too.*

It was easy to forget that Jody was an un-sophisticated, high school dropout, still struggling through her awkward and naive teenage years. Just sitting in my office, her physical appearance practically glowed like a sparkling golden-haired Cinderella, with smooth creamy skin and soft delicate features, cradled on a slender neck—a rare crystal wine glass.

In alluring contrast, Jody displayed a strikingly natural voluptuous quality, guaranteed to tilt the heads of women, as well as men. Full, sensuous lips, firmly prominent up-turned breasts, narrow waist flowing into well-contoured hips clearly highlighted her womanly beauty. Reading over the hospital's brief referral, I couldn't help but wonder why she failed as a prostitute. It took only a few sessions to discover why.

Trying to put her at ease, I explained all about confidentiality, my sole role to help her and that she wasn't expected to tell me anything she didn't want to.

Jody sat silently with bright, discerning eye contact as I talked to her about my background and long interest in working with people. I also brought up the issue of trust, which I've always believed is essential to a positive therapeutic relationship.

"At this point, Jody, you have no reason to trust me. After all, you don't even know me. I'm going to have to earn your trust and respect, and I'll sure try."

She smiled with a deep sigh and looked pensively out the window.

Silence can be rather thunderously unnerving during a therapeutic session, and despite its possible value, I've never been comfortable with it when silence lasts over a few minutes.

"Would you like to tell me a little about yourself?" I asked.

She continued to look out the window while the steady stream of tears gliding down her cheeks was already telling me about her sadness. After several minutes of total silence, Jody turned her head toward me. Her reddened eyes were glistening with a few remaining tears and her thin smile seemed steeped in both anger and melancholy.

"Dr. Wonderling." She paused, grabbed the nearby

box of Kleenex and wiped away new tears. "I don't know what to do, I can't manage my life and I can't even commit suicide."

It was obvious this fragile woman desperately needed a lot of support and encouragement. *Otherwise,* I thought, *she might manage to kill herself next time.* "I guess that's why you're here. Together we'll learn how to best manage your life."

Those were probably very superficial assurances from a stranger, but they needed to be said anyway.

Jody burst into deep sobs. "You don't understand what's happened all my life."

I handed her a few more Kleenex and waited quietly until her cries slowed to a muffled sniffing.

"You're absolutely right," I said. "I don't so then help me understand."

Wiping her face again, she blew her nose and grinned almost leeringly, as if to say—"You asked for it."

"My father really loved me and he used to take me everywhere, read to me and bounce me on his knee."

That's when Jody was about three years old. At around age five, the bounces were more of a slow rubbing up and down motion further back on his thigh. During that time, she noticed a huge bulge beneath the fly on his trousers. He was also holding her much closer and caressing, rather than patting, her buttocks.

At her age, that was close affectionate contact with a devoted father. It always made her feel warm and loved. At that stage of paternal fondling, her father, like too many others, enjoyed the feelings while ignoring the implications.

Each year his affectionate overtures became a little more openly sexual, and when she was nine years of age, her father unzipped his pants and placed her hand on his erect penis. By then, he was kissing her on the lips and lightly stroking her vagina through her clothing, while trying a little distraction with a vigorous rubbing of her back. Even at nine, Jody was enjoying this light affectionate sex play with a father she loved and obeyed.

Through those years, Jody's seduction by her father had been so subtly gradual, seemingly natural and paternalistic; she assumed it was acceptable family behavior. That was until the evening she playfully approached her father while her mother was in the living room. When she started to climb on his lap, he sternly whispered, "Not when mother's here."

Her girlfriends were also beginning to talk about sex, while sharing sexually arousing secrets. Although Jody liked to listen to her friends, she never mentioned the only sexual experiences she ever had—with her father.

One of her girlfriends wasn't as cautious. Jody remembered clearly how the girl tearfully bragged about sex with her father. It wasn't long before everyone in school knew about the girl's terrible sex problems. When she was later placed in a foster home, Jody recalled feeling sorry for her, while relieved that her own home situation was different.

"By the time I was ten years old, there was no way out for either of us." She paused for a moment with a prolonged glance. She seemed to be awaiting a sage comment from me.

I didn't have any. My only comment was one obvious question. "What about your mother?"

Jody grinned approvingly, "You've been listening, Dr. Wonderling. Looking back, I'm sure she knew. She just never admitted it to me. Mom even called me a liar when I finally told her."

Jody's mother was rather plain, passive and not

particularly talented. That may be why she was willing to overlook just about anything to keep her husband a satisfied family provider. Her mother also had that late thirties "housewife syndrome," which sadly included a chronic fear of being alone and unwanted. Unfortunately for Jody, her mother was emotionally cold, a mediocre parent and useless as a protector. As an only child, Jody had no one to closely relate to except her eagerly affectionate father.

That was the family dynamics when Jody was swept away by her father's more blatantly perverse sexual strategy. Removing her under panties, he began applying Vaseline finger massages to her vagina while whispering he loved her. He used to tell her that when you're in love, you take care of each other "all the way."

Since vulnerable ten-year-old girls tend to worship their fathers, becoming the lover of a father, who is also a pedophile, is both tragic and tragically understandable. He had convinced her they were in love and that making love was all right.

Following several months of gifts and "loving" attention, her father was able to penetrate her vagina. Those early fatherly hugs had finally erupted into textbook incest, and Jody was a classic victim. Her symptoms were also classic.

She experienced chronic guilt, depression, sleeplessness and ambivalence. They had sexual intercourse at least once a week and, of course, Jody was assured by her father that he had no other sex partner, not even his wife.

Then one early evening, when she was supposed to be studying in her room, Jody peeked through the slightly ajar door of her parents' bedroom. Her mother was orally copulating his penis. She felt betrayed and disgusted until her father explained that it was just a stress reliever. He assured her it wasn't love and that he didn't want to burden her with the need to relieve his stress. Inevitably oral sex, as well as sexual intercourse, became part of their incestual routine.

📖   📖   📖

It was two years later that the active incestuous relationship finally ended between Jody and her father. It was over for none of the right reasons. Jody was still eager to sexually pay for her father's affection. Despite his sex crimes, her father wasn't exposed, jailed or psychologically treated. He simply left his boring wife and troubled kid for another woman.

"The dirty bastard. How could I love him so much and hate him even more?" Jody sent me another prolonged glance.

"Come on, Jody, you knew. You've been telling me how for the last half hour. He is a dirty bastard. He conned you, a child, into loving him so he could satisfy his own lust. You know, he would have probably caused you less psychological trauma if he had skipped the love and just plain raped you."

Jody smiled. "You're probably right."

Incredibly, that was the first time in Jody's life she was able to openly disclose and discharge her tormented feelings. At that point, it was essential that I simply listen and accept what I heard. There's a noteworthy similarity between psychological catharsis and vomiting away food-poisoned toxins. Both are necessary before healing. By the second session, Jody was still retching, so I kept listening.

When her father abandoned them, her mother had some sort of "nervous breakdown," and Jody, at age twelve, was left confused and angry. To the rescue was

Jody's maternal uncle, Bill, who cared for his sister and shortly after moving in with them, began caring for himself by showering voluptuous little Jody with sympathy and affection.

Like deja vu, Uncle Bill's warm tender hugs evolved into hot sensual fondling, which, of course, resulted in passionate sexual intercourse. With the help of court-mandated support payments from the father, Jody's mother quickly recovered, resumed her mediocre maternal duties and remained defensively oblivious to her daughter's sexual abuse.

Uncle Bill begrudgingly moved away when his sister remarried a fifty-year-old alcoholic. Jody, who had just turned fourteen, again felt abandoned; and within a few months, she was responding with coy smiles to stepdad's lecherous peeks at her breasts and inner thighs. It no longer seemed to matter if mother was in the same room. Jody had long realized that her mother was blind to such sexual displays and her stepdad didn't care either way.

"He wanted me, Dr. Wonderling. I knew it and he knew I knew it. So I let him have me. There was no affection and embracing first. He just fucked me and I let him."

That time, I met her prolonged pausing glance with my own pause. I really had nothing to add, except my clinical curiosity. "What would have happened if you had said no to him from the first time he looked at you that way?"

There was no grin when Jody turned her head to stare silently out the window. It was her reflective mode. After a minute, I began to think she had forgotten or rejected my question.

Then she turned toward me with a rather cold crisp reply. "Even if I wanted to, I couldn't."

The reply was a clear reminder to me that Jody wasn't ready to think beyond her well-established role with men. She had learned since childhood that she was only permitted to relate to men sexually.

"I'm sorry, Jody, I guess that was a stupid question."

She smiled.

During the following two months, I learned a great deal about Jody; and as it became easier for her to tell me, she learned a lot more about herself. She had discovered that, no matter what she told me, I neither flinched nor dozed, which encouraged her to dredge up more.

In the middle of one intense session, she stopped abruptly and looked at me with childlike exuberance. "God, I'm telling you stuff I'd forgotten even happened."

Psychotherapy seemed to be working.

The two and a half years with her mother and stepfather were frightening, as well as humiliating. Jody's stepfather frequently slapped her mother around during his drunken rages, and he became increasingly rough and sexually demanding with Jody.

It was no doubt fortunate for Jody and her mother that the stepfather was arrested for passing bad checks. He was sentenced to one year in the county jail and five years probation, with the condition he refrain from drinking and not return to their home as long as Jody still lived there. The pre-sentencing probation investigation revealed the wife beating and strong possibility of child sexual abuse. Ironically, it was the stepfather who caused the suspicions by unwittingly talking too much during the interviews. Jody was well beyond the point of telling anyone, and her mother, hopelessly dependent, wanted her husband back.

About a year earlier, Jody had quit school at the age

of fifteen. After a succession of brief, unskilled jobs, her major lesson wasn't too surprising; sexual currency was just about all she had to offer. Each employer was especially attentive and supportive until she adamantly refused sexual advances. Pathetically, her work efforts would become unacceptable and she was terminated. It even occurred once with a female boss, who, after persuading her to try lesbian sex, fired Jody as too young and "inexperienced."

When her stepfather went to jail, it became painfully obvious that Jody's mother wanted her out of the house before his release. Mother even provided her with some start-up money. Reluctantly, Jody moved from the only home she'd ever known to a nearby studio apartment in the Tenderloin.

Predictably, this lonely, beautiful teenager, from a sexually perverse, thoroughly dysfunctional home, was willing prey to just about everything that's Tenderloin. It seems as if everyone in the Tenderloin wanted to turn her "on" to drugs, "out" to sex, or both. She tried it all and miraculously Jody managed to survive the Tenderloin's worst predators.

She hated street drugs, including booze, and she couldn't stand the slick, abusive pimps who tried to control her. So, by age seventeen, after a life-long apprenticeship, Jody was an independent professional prostitute. It was the disastrous career that had nearly ended her young, troubled life.

📖 📖 📖

Jody's first four months of therapy ended gratifyingly for both of us. She had replaced agonizing over the past with efforts to understand it. She was no longer pre-occupied with suicide solutions. Lifestyle alternatives had become her central concern, and she had even enrolled in a vocational training program as a machinist.

I was delighted with her progress, yet not all that surprised when Jody started treating me differently. Initially she had been so preoccupied with her own pain, she desperately relied on me as her "doctor." However, as she improved and the therapeutic relationship strengthened, Jody began to see me more as an older man, more attentive, supportive and trustworthy than any man she had ever known.

All mental health practitioners in private practice will undoubtedly agree that psychotherapy is an intensely intimate relationship that is never socially or physically intimate. Jody began trying, in unintentional ways, to entice her therapist beyond that delicate professional threshold. Psychoanalytic jargon may define it as "transference" for the client, and "counter transference" for the too vulnerable therapist.

No matter what you call it or how defined, the client wants her therapist as a lover, and the beautiful client makes it even more difficult for the best of therapists to resist the seduction. After all, a male therapist is a man, whose libido accompanies him wherever he goes, even to therapy sessions.

Non-verbal communication can be much more powerful than words, yet often easily denied or misread. When Jody started wearing make-up to sessions, I was glad she was beginning to take an interest in her appearance. Then came the low cut blouses and mid-thigh skirts.

"Hey, are you meeting somebody tonight? Have you got yourself a boyfriend?" I laughingly asked during the beginning of the session.

"Oh, no. Do you like it?"

"Jody you look just stunning," and I meant it—I just

didn't get it. Then I started to wonder if this might be her sexually seductive stage. It took only a couple more sessions to find out. All sexual subtleties were gone. Jody would idly rub her breasts while adjusting her low cut blouse, or inadvertently spread her legs just enough to provide a hint of panties.

It was one of those times in a psychotherapist's professional life when clinically you don't know quite what to say, but you're certain you have to say something.

"Are you practicing your trolling skills?" I glanced quickly and as casually as possible at her fingers teasing her nipples.

Jody smiled.

"As your therapist, I'm a lousy subject because any turn-on would end before it started."

I had mistakenly assumed Jody understood my comment. After her late afternoon phone call the following day, it dawned on me she probably understood it—the wrong way.

"Dr. Wonderling, I'm so upset. I have to see you. Please, please come by soon." Jody hung up before I could reply.

I spent the next ten minutes dialing her number to no avail. I was becoming increasingly concerned; especially when I received repeated busy signals. Jody's history of suicide attempts was a grim reminder. I knew that the possibility of another suicide try should always be taken seriously. Then again I wondered, was the call some sort of naïve, impulsive set-up, a come-on?

Ten minutes later, I was in the Tenderloin, leaning on her outside apartment bell. I was relieved when the buzzer unlocked the front door. I had no trouble finding her apartment door, because Jody was peering out her door waiting for me.

"Are you okay, Jody?"

"I am now. I'm so grateful you came. Please come into my little home."

As I entered, Jody, who had been shielded behind her door, closed it behind me. Before I turned completely around, I was experiencing a nervous stomach, and in seconds it was evident why.

This firm, fully-breasted, gorgeous young woman was standing in front of me wearing bikini panties, nothing else.

"I'm sorry, Dr. Wonderling, I was just about to take a shower. Would you like to join me?"

Flabbergasted, and perhaps too angry to be sexually aroused, I walked to her only chair and sat down. "Sit down, Jody, let's talk." I felt compelled to stare directly into her eyes and nowhere else.

Jody sat on the edge of the bed, anticipating my next question. "No, I'm okay now. I just wanted to know if you'd come over when I really needed you." She looked around her room. "I also thought you'd see me differently in my own home, away from your office and MediCal stickers."

"You set me up, Jody, and that angers me, but it's my fault as well. I knew better than anyone how men have sexually used you, and I should have clearly defined my professional role months ago. If I had sex with you, we'd both fail."

Jody put a towel over her shoulders, covering her breasts, as she continued to listen. Her eyes were filling with tears. For an instant all I wanted was to sit next to her on the bed, hold her comfortingly and show her another lecherous old man—so much for professional principles and her progress.

Instead, I tried to soften my anger by giving her a few supportive compliments. "You have to know that practically all female clients have romantic notions about their therapists, and of all the flirtations I've experienced, you're by far the most arousing. Now, can we get back to work?"

Wiping a few remaining tears, she smiled. "Okay."

Jody remained in therapy with me for two more years, during which time she usually wore high neck shirts and baggy pants. "I'll try not to frustrate you anymore." Then she would laugh.

She was a hard-working, responsive client, who finally understood what therapy was all about. Jody had met a guy her age in the machine shop where they both worked. She fell in love, and after their marriage, we agreed she was ready to terminate therapy on other than an "as needed" basis.

It was nearly three years before I heard from Jody again. She sent me a short letter from Hawaii where she was vacationing with her husband. The letter was so gratifying; I read it several times, while wiping away a few of my own joyful tears.

Dear Dr. Wonderling,

...When I first started seeing you, you told me trust and respect was important, and that you would try to earn my trust and respect. Well, you did. You're the first man in my life I ever trusted and respected.

I'm doing well with my life and husband. How long it'll last I don't know, but I do know I'll never need to please a man just with sex. Thank you for so gently refusing my stupid sexual advances....

Wow, I thought, *the most important part of therapy for Jody was what I didn't do.*

❄　❄　❄

Not all favorable therapies have happy endings. A few years after the first edition of this book, an old friend and colleague told me Jody was divorced, back to prostitution and approaching obesity. It reminded me that old habits are tough to break.

19

HERMAN

The Obnoxious

Watching a wheel-chaired amputee struggling up a steep curb cut or a blind person tapping cautiously into a treacherous intersection releases in most of us a surge of compassion. Our feelings are drenched with understanding, sympathy and an urge to help.

Watching the irrational rantings of an arm-flailing schizophrenic or the gibberish of a manic-phased Bipolar triggers in most of us a flood of repugnance. Our feelings are charged with alarm, annoyance and an urge to run.

By just about any definition, they are all disabled, crippled and not responsible for their handicap. But ironically, it's infinitely more humane to judge behavior, than the behaving body—until the person being judged happens to be clinically crazy. Then our noble human response deteriorates into a nasty intolerance.

Of course, competent psychotherapists have learned through years of professional training, to treat all mentally disabled non-judgmentally, with benevolence and tolerance. Well—most of the time. Even the most competent psychotherapist is irrevocably human, which often translates into experiencing biases and annoyances. Take me for example—maybe not the most competent psychotherapist, but certainly human.

Many of my mentally disabled clients were witty, bright, courageous or just downright likable. Others were barely tolerable bores. And a *few* were plainly insufferable to be around. Trying to work with those few was never worth the money, especially at the MediCal rate of $27 a session. It was also apparent that I really couldn't help them, because I actually felt like strangling them.

So once I overcame the visionary, save humanity passions of a newly licensed psychologist, the decision was easy, get rid of the obnoxious ones; if not by strangulation, by referral to someone else. Practicing that decision, however, was another matter.

📖   📖   📖

I first met Herman, one of the *few*, before I even knew there was a Herman. I was soon to find out. He was like that electrically charged piece of scrap paper that sticks stubbornly to your hand, no matter what you do.

Often after visiting an ailing client, I used to walk through the Tenderloin for a rewarding dinner at one of the many fine restaurants that bordered the area. Polo's Restaurant was my destination on that particular late afternoon. As I weaved my way down Turk Street, dodging more drunks than usual, it dawned on me. It was the first week of the new month, which is always an auspicious period in the Tenderloin.

It was "payday" when SSI, welfare and pension checks were eagerly received. It was that very special day when bills were paid, groceries were replenished and the secondhand stores were bustling with customers. Even pawnshops were unusually busy with clients retrieving their possessions. It was also the day of the prey and the predators. An ominous time when the drunks get drunker, richer, more vulnerable and more tempting to the predators.

Dodging a staggering drunk or stepping over a fallen body is not uncommon in the Tenderloin, especially on payday when there are more of both. On payday, however, that crumpled body resting on the pavement might be suffering from wounds inflicted by one of those payday predators.

Usually I tended to side step the fallen drunks. Sometimes I'd call MAP (the Mobile Assistance Patrol), who would take them to a detoxification shelter where they'd be treated for a few days and released. But it was payday, so I checked them more carefully to make sure they weren't wounded or dead.

About three blocks from an anticipated pleasant dinner at Polo's, I tried to ignore a large man sprawled face down across the pavement directly in front of me. He didn't seem wounded or dead. He was half crawling and half slithering on his belly like a huge bug or slug.

Trying to casually step over him was my first mistake. Just as my right foot began to slide over his torso, he rolled onto his side, which entangled my foot in his jacket. Hopping on my left foot while trying to untangle the other foot, I lost my balance, sending me sprawling over his big carcass with my knees buried in his bulging belly. Rolling sideways across his belly, I finally managed to unwind his jacket from my foot; and as I got up, my pant legs were wet with that familiar smell of urine—his. At that point, I just wanted to walk away, but pausing for a moment was my next big mistake.

Typical Tenderloin, no one seemed to pay attention to me or the big undulating lump lying on the pavement.

Then I heard a foghorn groan that terminated in a harsh, whiny plea, "Help, help, help, I neees help!"

That's when I looked at him closely for the first time. I gasped as I followed the foghorn voice to his mouth. *No wonder his voice is so loud*, I thought. Most of his lower face was mouth, practically from ear to ear, with thick lips and giant false teeth, *a piano keyboard* I mused.

The rest of his soft fleshy face wasn't startling, but definitely distinctive. His puffy eyelids almost concealed his squinty eyes, reminding me of old Mr. Magoo cartoons, or maybe a guppy. His face could have looked pleasantly amusing, except for his sharp, stingy little nose. That might have been the warning I never regarded.

Beneath an old dirty baseball cap were matted strands of grayish white hair, covering his ears and dangling above a wrinkled mass of wet clothing. Everything he wore seemed wine or urine soiled, including his one remaining shoe that was covered with something resembling vomit. I avoided a closer look.

My biggest mistake was my next move. "Can you get home okay?" I naively asked.

"No," was the surprisingly quick decisive reply. "Booye, I woont to go hoome." He pointed to the old apartment building across the street.

Looking him over again, I realized he wasn't as big as I thought, just a big belly. Otherwise, he was rather short, maybe five feet four inches.

It's not too far and he's not too big, I stupidly reasoned. "Sure, I'll help you to your room. Come on, up now."

His hands grabbed my extended arms, and I was

again surprised. He had a vice-like grip. I'd also forgotten to consider that dead drunks are dead weight; and as I tried to pull him up, everything—except his fierce grip on my arms—went limp.

After I pulled and tugged for several exhausting minutes, he had slid only a few feet closer to the curb. At that rate, across the street might as well have been across the city.

"Come on now, I'm going to leave you," which would have been difficult with his hands virtually handcuffed to my arms. "I can't help you if you don't help yourself."

As drunk as he appeared, he again surprised me with a quick response to my comment. Relaxing his grip, he somehow seemed to wiggle around to a sitting position as he began clawing his way up my arms to my shoulders. "Less gooo, booye," he bellowed.

Crossing Turk Street, the first leg of our journey, was a particularly dangerous obstacle. I sure didn't want to get smashed by some car while trying to pull a drunk across the street. Curiously, that drunk's body language clearly announced he didn't either.

Tugging, lifting and pulling him was a tedious, backbreaking process until a car approached. Then, magically, he seemed lighter and more cooperative with my efforts to avoid the oncoming vehicle. Once on the opposite curb, I gave him my first irritated look, while trying to catch my breath.

"Too bad there weren't more cars. We would have crossed in record time."

Ignoring my panting dash of sarcasm, the drunk looked up at the old apartment building—way up. "Pleeash help, help. I wanna go hoome."

Not surprisingly, once safely away from the street's traffic perils, the drunk lost interest in cooperating and I was losing interest in being a Good Samaritan. The first climb was up half a dozen well-worn marble steps leading to the lobby. At the second step, he was limp again and I was out of breath.

"Move. Help me get you home or I'm out of here." Immediately I could feel his muscles once again tighten as he resumed gripping me with his arms and the stairs with his knees. While I strained to lift, he pulled at my shoulders and shoved his knees up the stairs.

My God, he must have steel plated knees, I thought. He also had a breath that could probably strip varnish; and whenever his gaping mouth neared my cringing nose, I had to fight off gagging.

When we reached the top marble stair, I was so thrilled that the front door was open, I almost forgot I was aching, and soaked in my sweat and his urine. When we both crawled into the lobby of this five-story apartment building, I must have smelled as bad as he did. Instantly, I noticed the big sign on the elevator, "Out of Order;" which prompted another question I shouldn't have asked.

"Which floor?"

"Take me to the fifth floooor, boooy," was the dreaded reply.

The ascent must have taken an hour as I pushed, shoved, dragged, pleaded and threatened him up those stairs.

He moaned, groaned and bellowed at my urgings; and at the top of every floor, we just slumped face down on the worn carpet for a ten-minute rest break. When we finally reached the fifth floor, *the summit*, I thought I was a goner. There was no flag to proudly fly, no pictures or panoramic views. Just two near delirious, foul-smelling, exhausted bodies on the verge of collapse. Had I been stronger, I might have strangled him.

Face down on the carpet, and breathing heavily, I didn't notice a man looking down at me.

"What the hell are you two doing here?" he shouted.

As I tried to lift my head, I discovered a man in coveralls towering over the drunk and me. Still too out of breath to even speak, I feebly pointed to the drunk and to the rooms.

"I...heh...helped...him...to...his...room here," I managed to gasp.

"Get out of here—both of you. He's always hanging around outside bumming cigarettes and wine. He never lived here. One of his old wino buddies used to. Now get out—both of you."

My first impulse was to throw the drunk down the elevator shaft, followed by me. My second thought was to argue with the man standing over me. I couldn't do either, because I was still too weak and exhausted.

Even the drunk kept his big mouth shut as we literally rolled, bounced, skidded and slammed our way down the five flights of stairs.

The descent brutalized my battered body, but at least gave my suffering lungs a rest. When we finally made it back down to the marble stairs, it was hard to enjoy my easier breathing because of the bruises and aches. I hurt all over.

Looking down at the drunk, it would have been impossible to enjoy anything. Sprawling almost too comfortably across the bottom marble stair, the drunk was happily snoring. I crawled over him, struggled to my feet and limped back up the street toward my car. I wasn't hungry any more and Polo's probably wouldn't have let me in anyway.

A few weeks later, my memories of the incident began to fade, along with my multiple bruises and aching limbs. Within a couple of months even the rich, blue/black bruises had lost their luster to pale yellow/browns. The Good Samaritan ordeal was forgotten. Then one Monday morning I was abruptly reminded that chance or destiny could be terribly cruel.

📖　📖　📖

Sitting in my tiny, cozy Geary Street office, I was awaiting the first appointment at 9 o'clock. The referral was from an attorney. All it said was that Herman, an SSI recipient, had been in "non-compliance" for nearly a year, and unless he saw a therapist regularly, he would have to forfeit his benefits. His court appointed attorney would also lose his percentage of the retroactive benefits if Herman didn't comply. Protecting his investment, the attorney was escorting him to the first session.

I was growing accustomed to recalcitrant alcoholics who, in need of SSI benefits, resisted anything associated with treatment. At that time in my very early career, I never declined a referral. I needed the business and figured I could handle any client. I even naively assumed that, once they came regularly, I could help them. I had so much to learn about the real everyday practice of psychotherapy, about Tenderloin drunks and the endless exceptions to textbook theories.

By 9:30, I was just about to write them off as another of many no-shows, when I heard a firm knock at my door. Anticipating first sessions was always a bit unnerving, so it wasn't too unusual, when I leaped startled from my chair. This time I spilled my half-filled coffee cup on the floor.

"Dr. Wonderling," a high-pitched voice chirped through the door.

"Just a moment," I shouted, grabbing some napkins to clean up the mess.

When I finally opened the door, a well-dressed, attractive, middle-aged woman extended her leather-gloved hand.

"Dr. Wonderling? I'm Mrs. Brookins, Herman's attorney. I'm sorry we're late. He had agreed to meet me in front of his south of Market hotel, and when he wasn't there, the hotel clerk was kind enough to escort me to Herman's room. He was still in bed." Mrs. Brookins offered me one of those quick, mechanical smiles, which I automatically returned.

"I understand, Mrs. Brookins. Aah…where is Herman now?" I asked, looking over her shoulder.

Mrs. Brookins turned and glared impatiently at the empty hallway. "He was right behind me. Herman!" she screamed.

"Yeaass, boooy."

Suddenly, my tight-lipped smile became a dangling-jawed grimace. "That voice sounds familiar," I yelped.

"Oh?" replied Mrs. Brookins.

Just then a little potbellied, moon-face man with a huge mouth came trudging down the hallway.

Mrs. Brookins flashed another pretentious smile.

At the same time, my drooping jaw tensed into grinding, gnashing teeth. ***"That's Herman?"***

Without the slightest acknowledgment or show of concern, she speedily opened her briefcase and whipped out several papers. "I'm very late, please sign these documents and I'll be off." Then she turned to Herman with a searing glare, "Now sit there, Herman, and don't move."

As she shoved a pen into my hand, Herman obediently sat down. Just as obediently, I signed the papers.

Grabbing the papers, Mrs. Brookins seemed to vanish in an instant; and I was left looking down at

Herman.

In flashback clarity, I was back on Turk Street re-experiencing that ordeal. Then I started weighing the options. I had to conclude that I couldn't possibly help someone I couldn't stand.

His booming W.C. Fields whine, his distinctively nauseous odor and even his big mouth were additional compelling reasons for the only prudent decision. **Throw him out!**

Of course, I didn't, which represents one of my most egregious clinical blunders. My next mistake was another decision. At the time, it made a lot of sense. Herman was going to be trouble—a real management problem; and the only effective treatment was a direct, stern, reality-oriented approach. He needed a parole agent, not a psychologist.

As I sat on the edge of my desk, still looking him over, I felt good about my decision to be straightforward and tough, yet fair.

"Do you remember me from a few months ago in the Tenderloin?" I should have known he wouldn't give me a straight answer, or even a prompt one.

He just impassively gazed at objects in my office, which included me. His indifference, or perhaps passive resistance, reconfirmed my strategy. As long as he complied with my demands, it didn't matter anymore if he remembered me.

That was the time to clearly and directly structure the relationship before the first interview ended. Mrs. Brookins had finally gotten his attention I reasoned, why couldn't I?

Displaying my severest expression and most commanding voice, I stared directly between his puffy eyelids into his squinty eyes. "Listen very carefully, Herman, you've been ordered by the court to see me twice a month. If you don't show up, you will lose your benefits and you must come here sober."

When Herman adjusted his old baseball cap and looked up at me, I thought I might have gotten through to him. Then his mouth began to move. "Boooy, I gotta go now. Come on, come on, can I go?"

"No!" I shouted.

I was furious and spent the remaining ten minutes lecturing him. That's when my fury turned to downright frustration. As I handed him his appointment card, I heard that unmistakable dripping. He had peed his pants, my chair, my floor and my rug.

He looked down at the wet floor, then up at me. "Seee, boooy, it ain't my fault, I needed to gooo."

I couldn't tell if the expression on his face was a rueful smile of embarrassment or a mocking sneer of contempt. I'm still not sure. All I knew then and now is that, every time I was with Herman, somehow he seemed to urinate on me.

"Just get out," I said in exasperation, "and don't miss your next appointment two weeks from now."

Herman was never on time. I used to rationalize that perhaps it was all brain damage. Tests had revealed attention and concentration problems, short-term memory loss and other deficits associated with chronic alcoholism. On the other hand I reasoned, passive aggression was much more likely. He managed to avoid missing appointments that he knew could have resulted in a non-compliant loss of benefits. He was just reliably late. That created other suspicions.

Sometimes, when he appeared in the waiting room ten minutes before the end of his appointment, I would stand in the doorway smoldering and muttering to myself, "He's crazy all right, crazy like a fox."

Invariably, as he entered my office, his excuses were

as beguiling as his unfathomable smile. "You need to call MUNI, they were late again," was one of his ploys. "I got lost and I forget things, you knooow," was another. Both of those excuses had just enough accuracy to be possible. They were reasons he probably figured I wouldn't challenge. He was right. There's no doubt, he was also aware of the disruptive affects his tardiness had on my schedule.

In fact, once when I let a client come in ten minutes earlier, Herman was pounding on my door a minute later, charging that I was using his time for somebody else.

"Boooy, that ain't nice, I pay you my MediCal," he would argue when I finally let him in.

After a month and a half of five to ten minute sessions with him, I found myself dreading his next appointment day. My authoritative approach wasn't really working, and I still didn't have the slightest idea what "Boooy" meant.

At least he no longer urinated in my office. I figured he knew better than to anger me again. As usual, when speculating about Herman, I was wrong. I soon learned he was urinating everywhere but my office.

My Geary Street office was a psychologist's dream, it was near most of my Tenderloin clients, and it had good public transportation—practically to the door. It was very inexpensive and the building was owned by Roger, a retired Highway Patrolman. He was a real nice guy.

The building was newly renovated, charming and spotless, and I was pleased that my little office was nearest the shared waiting room. The only possible drawback was the other tenants' unfamiliarity with mentally-troubled clients, especially drunks. Those ten-ants were not clinicians; they were attorneys, investors, insurance agents and one chiropractor.

Not long after my first session with Herman, an anonymous note was slipped under my door. "The strange man who left your office is doing nasty things. He urinated in the doorway. He looked at me and mumbled something about a boy."

"God, it's Herman," I grumbled.

Roger was also being deluged with complaints. "A dirty-looking little man with a big mouth was begging for cigarettes… the waiting room smells like urine…all the towels and toilet paper were in a mess on the bathroom floor. It smells terrible…customers are afraid of the derelicts hanging around," were some of the comments.

I guess I must have been expecting Roger when he knocked on my door. He entered without his usual broad, generous smile and direct friendly eye contact. He silently stood in the middle of the floor for a few moments, with somber eyes shifting from me to the floor.

"Larry, I think we get along fine, but…I don't know how to say this. My other tenants just can't cope with your patients. Some are going to move if I don't do something."

That had to be one of the most amiable, courteous evictions on record.

He gave me all the time I needed. Three weeks later I moved to my second, even smaller office within a more tolerant Tenderloin clinic. In a way, I felt genuinely relieved being in a new work setting, where everyone seemed to belong, even me. Looking back, Roger had no choice and the other tenants were understandably frightened by clients that just didn't fit. I couldn't even totally blame Herman; I had too many other clients who would have eventually insured my eviction.

Herman blended less conspicuously in the Tender-loin, yet managed to become a nuisance to most of the Tenderloin clinic staff and their clients. He rambled louder, smelled worse and begged more than anyone else near the clinic.

I continued to dread our appointments and was increasingly glad he showed up late. Ten minutes of Herman was about as much as I could stand at one time. It seemed easy for Herman to worsen any situation with either unwitting innocence or intentional malice. I was never quite certain which was the case. All I knew for sure was that he was effortlessly obnoxious.

Herman also constantly lost his MediCal card, meaning I rarely got paid for his appointments unless I helped him through mountains of bureaucratic forms, for a duplicate card. I never did. The MediCal bureau-cracy was nearly as intolerable as Herman.

Surprisingly, during the next three months, inter-actions with Herman were less hectic. They were almost too uneventful and curiously tolerable. As Grandma used to say, I started waiting for the other shoe to drop, and it did—with a bang.

📖 📖 📖

I loved my new answering machine. It enabled me to listen directly to a client's call, rather than through an operator's message from some answering service. After the initial investment, an answering machine was much cheaper than an answering service. The operators, like Mrs. Murphy at my last answering service, were never fully able to translate all of the fine nuances of an actual call. With this new technology, I could just hit the mes-sage button and instantly hear the voices of clients, friends and colleagues, who called hours earlier. *What a great invention*, I thought. Apparently, so did Herman.

Less than two weeks after I wired the new answering machine to my telephone, I received the first message from Herman. As I was soon to learn, his calls weren't really messages. They were just a rambling assortment of words, like the psychiatric "word salad" of a crazy person, or a more calculating communication jam, designed to make me crazy.

His first call was kind of an innocuous, incomprehensible greeting. It was innocuous because at the time it was his first and only call.

"Boooy, here's a messagge…You said leave onne…Why not then…What are you doooing anywaaay…come onn, come onn…Boooy, hallloo…I wanna a cigarette…make it go way…"

The entire call lasted three minutes and when I pressed the rewind button, I wistfully thought, *if only I could get rid of him as easily as erasing this tape.*

Herman's first call became a one-a-day call, which was annoying, but still tolerable when I learned how to limit the calls to thirty seconds. Unfortunately, for me, that seemingly effective solution turned into another catastrophe. Restricting all other calls to thirty seconds resulted in many "half calls" from colleagues, friends or clients who didn't bother calling back with the rest of their message.

Herman, on the other hand, was delighted to call back, even though he never had a discernible message. His daily calls escalated at an astonishing rate—two-a-day, five-a-day, then eight, ten to fifteen-a-day. Two weeks after my time limit solution, Herman was really trying to finish me off. Thirty calls per day.

One well-meaning, unthinking colleague, rather absently listened to my dilemma. "Don't pay any attention to him, he's not worth it. Erase his messages," he suggested.

Then I quickly realized that such a simplistic comment could only come from someone who didn't know Herman. "What's the guarantee that all the calls were consecutive?" I asked. I knew, and no doubt so did Herman that I had to listen to all of his calls to get that occasional in-between, possibly important call.

"Yeah, you've got a problem," replied my astute colleague.

Many of Herman's calls were bathed in alcoholic nonsense, others were testy demands and some were laced with downright rage. "Boooy, whatcha want to do?...What's out there anywaaay?...So, you wanna plaaay?...Where's my MediCaaal?...I should be on SS, you gotts me on SSI...You stole my MediCaaal...You rat, scum, you, I gotcha nooow, dog."

He had me all right, and, once again, it didn't matter why. Crazy psychotic, menacing sociopath, or brain-damaged alcoholic are meaningless clinical labels when trying to explain how to deal with an obnoxious client.

Herman simply wasn't crazy or dangerous enough to be institutionalized. Yet, for years he had apparently been cunning enough to derail all treatment efforts. He had managed to survive with full SSI benefits, a variety of diagnostic labels and an assortment of frustrated, baffled clinicians.

A year had slowly passed since I met Herman and I cringed. I had become one of those frustrated clinicians. I still didn't know how to help him, I didn't know how to protect myself from him and I remained bullied by the same nagging question. What do you do with a client who resists treatment while driving his therapist to the brink of lunacy?

Most clinicians will agree that you can't be in a

hurry to assist your clients. Trying to rush a client will yield unproductive or negative results. Positive change will, however, gradually occur as long as therapy includes: rapport between the client and therapist, an equitable fee for services and a client sufficiently discontented to be well-motivated to change. In Herman's case, there was no rapport, no equitable fee for service, no motivation to change and I was always in a hurry—probably to somehow get rid of him.

As a clinical psychologist, supposedly well-trained in the use of behavioral modification techniques, I was stunned when I couldn't even extinguish one simple, non-addictive behavior. Herman's thirty calls a day stubbornly defied all of my strategies. I tried positive and negative reinforcers, pleas, indifference, commands and threats. I even tried reasoning with him.

"It must cost you plenty to call me," I casually commented during one of our ten-minute sessions.

Herman was equally casual and more convincing, "Noooo, my friend's got a phoonne. We drink together and have fun making caallls."

In desperation, I impulsively had my number changed to an unlisted one. That, of course, was a bad solution that inconvenienced just about everyone, but Herman. After I spent hours writing agencies and calling clients, a few never got the message. Worse, others seemed to receive the wrong message—that I was trying to get rid of them.

Not Herman, of course. Nothing I could have said would have bothered him out of my life.

There were two tranquil days with no calls from Herman. Then, like the resurrection of some slain dragon or a renewed outbreak of the bubonic plague, Herman was back. He left five messages, the first of which said it all.

"Boooy, you forgot to give me your new number. Whoo do you think you aarre, huhhh? I got friends."

Herman had beaten me again and I unconditionally surrendered. Not to Herman, but to Mrs. Murphy and her answering service. They were perhaps the only real winners.

📖   📖   📖

In believing that I had lost each battle with Herman, I had lost sight of the equal possibility that he was never aware there was a battle. Maybe, like Don Quixote, I had been fighting non-existent dragons while fearing defeat. Perhaps my only real defeat was in failing to help a client.

I was finally beginning to realize that the year and a half with Herman was worth the frustration. After all, hadn't I at least learned there are some people you can't help or even tolerate? When that happens, you can best serve them and yourself by letting go.

Inspired by this new insight, my treatment strategy was finally clear and uncomplicated. I even felt good about myself and sorry for Herman. My own negative feelings had interfered with Herman's treatment. I should have referred him to someone else long ago. I had avoided the clinical obvious that simply because I couldn't help Herman, didn't mean no one else could. What arrogance!

For the first time since I met Herman, I was professionally concerned with his welfare; and as he entered my office for the last time, I experienced a near saintly sense of calm and relief. I even offered him a genuine smile.

Scratching and twitching, Herman replied with a grin that curved his mouth up to his ears.

"Well, Herman," I began, "this is our last session together. I've referred you to the Center for Special Problems. I'm sorry I couldn't help you. Let's hope they can."

Herman seemed to listen impassively as he looked around the office, scratching, twitching and smelling unusually bad. I assured him his SSI and MediCal wouldn't be affected, and I wished him well.

"Do you have any questions?" I asked, handing him his new appointment slip.

"Noooo, you're right thoouugh. Thank you, boooy."

My final gesture was also my final mistake. I shook his hand and patted him on the shoulder with my other hand. That's when I noticed the reasons for his odor and scratching. He had diarrhea, which dripped over his shoes onto my floor, carpet and somehow on his hand, the one that was shaking my hand. He was also infested with lice that were scurrying all over his head, neck, shoulders and my other hand.

The rest of that day was spent cleaning carpet, fumigating the office, the outside hall and myself. Yet, after a week, I was again relieved and consoled, realizing that it really wasn't Herman's fault. Besides, he had another treatment opportunity.

Then, that night as I slipped between my warm, clean bed sheets, I felt an aggravating, relentless itch and saw the unmistakable red line on my skin. Herman had beaten me again, this time with a dose of scabies.

Christ, I thought, *he's the most obnoxious guy I've ever met. I pity anyone who ever tries to help him! I should have strangled him when I had the chance!*

Herman is no longer frustrating his therapists. Early in 2004 he died alone in his Eddy Street room. Oddly when I found out, I had a fleeting sense of sadness. Like too many other Tenderloin residents, without caring friends or relatives, he had apparently been dead a week before finally being discovered.

20

HARRY

Redemption

As an undisputed safe haven for the socially estranged, the Tenderloin has never gone out of its way to invite social progress. Prostitutes, pimps, alcoholics, the mentally ill, the physically vulnerable and even predators co-exist in the Tenderloin with few incentives to change or look elsewhere.

When one of its residents transforms into a responsible something else, it's a *so what* event that's hardly noticed and rarely acknowledged by those who will never move beyond where or what they are. Some may even wonder why any resident would give up the invisible safety of belonging in the Tenderloin where there's a listless tolerance and anonymity for all.

Harry, however, was one of those rare abusive residents who suddenly disappeared, and when he reappeared he was so astonishingly different, he was beyond recognition. From a street bully and low-life

junky seething with rage, he switched virtually overnight to a defender of those vulnerable to other street
predators.

But this story isn't just about Harry's incredible
change. It is about a nameless man, the essence of love
and the ingredients of miracles.

       📖   📖   📖

I first met pony-tailed, 6′4″, tank-topped, bulging
muscled Harry in the early 1980's. He was difficult to
forget. His big ugly, hairy face growled and snarled its
way around the Tenderloin, intimidating anyone in his
way—including me.

Stomping down the middle of the sidewalk, Harry
was even harder to ignore. You couldn't miss him
especially since his size alone occupied most of the
sidewalk. So just about everyone walked around him—
including me.

Side-stepping my way off the curb, I would give
Harry a broad smile along with a cheerful "How are you
today?"

His reply was always the same, "fuck you."

According to many of my Tenderloin clients, Harry
knew me as the resident "shrink," which afforded me an
unspoken safe passage. Although I felt fairly secure
with this dismissive protection, I dropped the greeting
but kept smiling—while stepping off the curb.

       📖   📖   📖

By the middle 80's, I had just about lost track of Harry.
Moving to a new Tenderloin location, he was no longer
around to intimidate me off the sidewalk. Harry was still
bad news though, and when I occasionally heard about

him, it always had something to do with drugs or violence. Admittedly I was glad there weren't many Harrys roaming the Tenderloin.

Then about a year before I retired my Tenderloin practice, I had an experience so astonishing it can only be described as *cognitive dissonance* or something you see but you don't believe what you're seeing.

After many years, I finally got around to visiting an old friend at an off-Market Street Tenderloin clinic. During our chat about old times, I noticed an oddly familiar guy, seated at a desk apparently interviewing a sickly-looking client. "Where have I seen that big guy over there at the desk?" I asked.

My old friend unleashed one of his wry smiles. "Yeah you know him, but you'll never place him. Take a closer look."

After a few minutes of staring and impatient head shaking, I gave up and my old friend gave in. "It's Harry."

Searching for clues in disbelief, I kept silently shaking my head.

That's when my friend nudged me. "Come on, you remember Harry—the Tenderloin terror!"

The change was so incredible, I thought my friend was kidding, or maybe Harry had a twin brother.

No, it was a well-groomed, shorthaired, clean-shaven Harry with slacks, long sleeved shirt and polished shoes. It was obvious his demeanor had changed as well. He had a warm friendly smile, a light easy gait and a soft engaging voice. When I introduced myself that day, Harry didn't remember me, but why should he? I had been one of his life's many irritants, a socially responsible nothing.

During the next few months, I had lunch with Harry once a week. His change was so fascinating I just had to known why. I even took notes, and as his story of metamorphosis unfolded, my goose pimples, my teary eyes and my humanity believed every word. I still do.

📖 📖 📖

October 18, 1989 loomed pleasant, bright and windless above a Tenderloin that Harry then saw as ugly shadows embedded in misery. It was World Series day in San Francisco and Loma Prieta day in history.

That morning he left the second floor room of his tired old Tenderloin hotel, thumped down the rickety staircase and sneered at a smiling neighbor walking upstairs. He had seen the old man many times, yet their only communication was a smile and a sneer. Harry couldn't even describe the neighbor's appearance. "Just an old man," he said.

That same day, as usual, Harry was fuming with anger at his dirty little room, his self-imposed captivity in the wretched Tenderloin, the scum wandering the streets and rousts by the police. There wasn't much he didn't hate or distrust. He had no friends, a few sycophants who ran his errands and plenty of frightened victims who learned to hide from him.

Harry did have a real appetite for food, which became the restaurant owners' curse. He enjoyed eating out, and through trial and error he managed to bully several local cafés into free or half price meals for protection services—against himself.

Following his two-hour breakfast at a local café down the block, he left the owner with an earth-shaking belch. The owner snickered with relief. This time Harry had actually paid most of his bill.

In his 30's, Harry spent the rest of the day at a Tenderloin Senior Center playing pool with tremulous seniors. He even grabbed several of their "Meals on Wheels" lunches while intruding into their card games; which he regularly won by cheating.

It was almost 5:00 p.m. when Harry finally left the senior center to silently cheering seniors. Approaching his hotel, Harry confronted the last person he would ever intimidate. As he passed an attractive middle-aged woman who typically tried to avoid him, he patted her firmly on her posterior.

She murmured a "please, no," while Harry leered his way to the front door of his hotel.

Inside the hotel, he shot his usual sneer at the smiling old man coming down the stairs carrying a paper bag. At that instant, Harry's bully power, his anger and his mistrust of others succumbed to the fury of a distant rumble.

Terrified, Harry was seized with an overwhelming sense of helplessness. He felt the old rickety staircase groan beneath his unsteady feet. Losing balance on the undulating stairs, he frantically clawed at the groaning banister that was parting from the crumbling wall. Harry cringed at the deafening pops, cracking and snaps of splintering boards. The entire staircase was collapsing, and entangled in the falling rubble, he had nowhere to go but down. The velocity of the crash sent the shattered stairs through the stairwell, ripping apart the sub-flooring, and finally crashing in a heap of ruins and billowing dust on the basement floor. Then a deadly silence and darkness.

Harry lay motionless for several minutes, not knowing if he were unconscious, buried alive or dead. The answer soon came when he began to feel the intense pain of broken bones, deep lacerations and gasps for air.

Part of the supporting staircase beam was resting mercilessly across his crushed chest, and for the first time in his life, Harry knew the fear of dying.

On the thin threshold of unconsciousness, Harry heard movement twisting through the shattered fragments. Barely able to turn his head toward the sounds, he managed a glimpse at a small beam of light coming closer.

"Help," Harry gasped. "Is that you old man? Help!"

As the sound grew clearer, Harry felt a gentle stroke across his bloodied forehead. The light beam seemed to glow more brightly, and Harry saw the old man's smile.

"You're going to be just fine." The voice was as warm and comforting as a mother's soft, loving caresses.

"My mouth," Harry pleaded, "the dust. It's so dry, so dry ..."

Then there was another gentle stroke across his forehead. "Isn't it strange? When the stairs fell apart, I grabbed an orange from my bag. I've still got it." The old man laid his little pen light on the debris, peeled back a small piece of the orange skin, and squeezed the juice into Harry's mouth.

To Harry, the sweet flowing liquid was like some heavenly elixir, freeing his throat of choking dust.

Both men lie in silence for over an hour, and as the pin light died out, the only sound Harry could hear was from the old man. It was like a faint whistle of air rushing through a nearby body cavity.

"We gonna die here?" Harry asked.

In a few minutes, the answer was another gentle stroke and some fading words Harry has never forgotten.

"You'll die someday and it will only take a moment. Then you'll find peace. But not now, not now. You're going to live."

It took rescuers five hours to find Harry, who was nearly buried in rubble. He was in a coma for seven days, and during his long recovery from a variety of life threatening injuries, Harry learned that there was another, older man found near him. The man had died from a jagged wooden splinter through his right lung.

Like many rickety Tenderloin hotels, Harry's hotel was demolished after the Loma Prieta earthquake. He still doesn't know the old man's name. Harry does, however, profoundly understand that for the remainder of his life he will keep helping others find the peace he knows will come to him in due time.

Three thousand seven hundred fifty-seven people were injured in the earthquake. Harry was one of them. Sixty-three were reported killed. Harry still mourns for one of them who he only knew as a smiling old man.

✳   ✳   ✳

Seems as though every time I've wandered the Tenderloin since the first edition of this book, it has awakened another story. This time was as much about an old man I never met, as it was about Harry's redemption following one of San Francisco's most terrifying earthquakes.

21

THE THERAPIST

Personal Demons

Many years ago I explained in my first private practice brochure the fundamentals of psychotherapy and the differences between psychiatrists, social workers and psychologists. What I didn't mention were their professional similarities. They are all "therapists" and fallible humans with their private demons. Those similarities may be why the three professions have a strikingly similar sacred oath to at least "do no harm." It's well over forty years later and the similarities still haven't changed—nor have I.

Wandering the Tenderloin late in 2006 triggered butterflies fluttering around in my stomach, then a sickly feeling. I had just witnessed a big, burly cop knock an old unruly drunk to the ground.

Why was I so upset? Did I identify with the drunk or the cop? Maybe neither. Was it my resentment of authority, my mixed feelings about drunks, protecting the underdog? How about all or none of the above.

Admittedly, I've never been a fan of cops, especially those who seem to enjoy bullying the little guy. And drunks? Since I gave up heavy drinking years ago, I've experienced mixed feelings of anger and sympathy for drunks, which probably has something to do with my beloved, alcoholic mother. Or maybe, like a dream, the cop and drunk scenario had nothing to do with that knot in my stomach.

Most likely my butterflies just reawakened a well-decayed gut-wrenching fragment of a past I thought I had forgotten for good. Those initial symptoms simply signaled my vaguely defined, uncontrollable dread of certain individuals. It's one of my most regrettable hang-ups as a therapist. Fortunately I've experienced this curse only about four times in my life, including the one intrusion into therapy.

If I seem to be rambling, it's because I still haven't resolved this introspective quagmire. I probably never will, and after forty years of clinical practice it's about time I realized that pursuing our personal demons frequently leads to a psychological dead end.

So, why I have inexplicably despised several persons in my life may be one of those rare questions without an answer. Then again, neutralizing an illusive demon may not need an answer after all.

📖 📖 📖

In retrospect, I wasted too much clinical time as a professional trying to answer a client's initial *whys*.

"Why do I drink… beat me wife… kick my dog… torch houses… cry a lot?"

I could invariably provide several psychologically convincing answers. That's because I'm the psychologist, the proclaimed authority in possession of all those clinical reasons for faulty behaviors. The only problem was that I never knew which answer was correct, if any, nor did it really matter, since it was a "so what" therapeutic issue. Learning from me *why* they did weird, self-defeating things never seemed to result in positive change for any of my clients.

So, in trying to practice what I used to preach, I'll try to avoid the pitfall of pursuing my personal *whys*. I could rationalize that I'm only human, and that those unanswerable demons showed up only four times in my life. Regretfully though, as I mentioned earlier, one of those times was with a "patient" I was sworn to help as a therapist.

📖 📖 📖

It didn't take long to discover that Tenderloin clients were demographically different from those in more upscale, conventional neighborhoods. Most of my clients were court or Department of Social Service referrals, living in a neighborhood that more or less condoned or at least expected weird behaviors.

How many therapists have a caseload of pre-dominantly mandated referrals who love their SSI checks and resent their therapist? How many times during my Tenderloin practice did a client openly call our sessions "a bunch of bullshit?" Those obstacles rarely bothered me, nor did the assortment of crazies, druggies, hustlers and street thugs.

Some, of course, were really obnoxious, intimidating or just plain frightening. But I managed to tolerate them all—even Herman from an earlier chapter. That's because, in the Tenderloin, I expected such behaviors. If you don't like the heat, stay out of the

kitchen was one of grandma's oldies, and I pretty well
adapted to the "heat."

□□   □□   □□

Then Vinny entered my professional life and the heat
became a scorcher. Looking back, I should have known
he was the fourth of the dreaded three—another
repugnant phenomenon that sucked all the good
intentions out of me. The first three had been seared into
my memory as personal disasters to avoid. Yet, when
those intuitive alarms in my stomach began warning me
about this new arrival, I didn't listen. I must have been a
slow learner.

While buried in medical billing, I heard a knock on
my office door, quickly followed by the sound of my
door opening.

"Gee, I'm sorry, you look busy. I'm Vinny Wagner,
a good friend of Harry Morgan, one of your patients.
Can I talk to you for only a minute?"

Glancing up from my paper work, I was mildly
annoyed by this unremarkable, average-looking guy.

"What's up?"

"Well, I'm on SSI, and my social worker says I need
a counselor to stay on SSI."

My practice was a bit scrawny in those early
Tenderloin days which prompted a premature acceptance of Vinny, even though there was something about
this guy that didn't *feel* right.

His appearance certainly wasn't threatening. In his
20's he was about 5'9", white, sober and flabby, with no
visible signs of a weapon. The real persuader, however,
was his MediCal card.

"Here's a sticker for your trouble."

"Well, sit down then, we might as well make this your first interview."

The first couple of sessions were fairly typical. On that first day came the ground rules. A MediCal sticker a session, two sessions per month, no intoxication from drugs or alcohol during sessions, periodic evaluations to Department of Social Services, the limits of confidentiality, etc.

Aside from calling me Larry during our second session, there wasn't much to objectively dislike about Vinny, except for those visceral warnings. He played the therapy game well by showing up on time, exploring all kinds of innocuous problems, peeling off two stickers on the first of the month before sitting down. He also managed to selectively avoid any issues associated with his history of drug substance abuse, alcoholism, pimping, burglaries and informant activities.

Clinically, Vinny was the classic sociopath, aka psychopath. Actually sociopaths are usually easy to work with so long as the therapist is prepared to have friendly chats in lieu of therapy.

Vinny and I had a clear chatty relationship. His major goal was to better manipulate others, while mine was to keep him from manipulating me. He had no interest in positive behavioral change, and I had no interest in trying to change him. He was exceptionally comfortable with his errant behaviors, and my most realistic therapeutic goals were to try to keep him out of jail, control that increasingly obvious, insufferable knot in my stomach during our sessions, and prevent him from conning his therapist.

My earlier experiences as prison guard and parole agent were invaluable in "working" with ex-cons like Vinny, who cleverly search for ways to seduce authority into a friendship to exploit. I remember San Quentin

Prison inmates befriending guards with down-home innocence and small gifts, followed by subtle requests until the guard became their "mark" as the roles were reversed.

"Hi, Larry. Is that your Mercedes parked in front?"

"No it isn't. How are things going for you?"

"Afternoon, Larry. Boy, you're in good shape. What kind of exercises do you do?"

"I stay active. So, what have you been up to these days?"

"Good morning, Larry. You know I've notice all those sailboat pictures on the wall. Here's another for your collection, I picked it up at Goodwill."

"Vinny, thanks for the offer but you know better than that. Put it on your wall. Now, what's up?"

"Hi ya, Larry; this ain't a bribe. Your waiting room coffee sucks so here's some good stuff."

"You just don't give up do you? Anyway thanks."

"Hi, Lar. Are you married?"

Vinny's low-keyed hustle, along with his endless chitchat was not my main concern. It was that gnawing knot in my stomach every time he entered my office. It may sound strange, especially coming from a psychologist, that his behavior was tolerable, while he wasn't. I couldn't stand being around him. I felt trapped in a therapeutic relationship that was unwholesome, at least for me.

📖 📖 📖

Ironically, it took an ugly showdown to finally get rid of those butterflies that, by then, seemed like woodpeckers tapping away at my stomach. Vinny showed up staggering drunk for his appointment.

"Hey, Dr. Larry. You think you're so fuckin' smart."

"You're drunk, Vinny. Get out of here and call me when you're sober."

"Hey, I'm not leaving. You got both my MediCal stickers."

"You've got five seconds to get your ass out of here. If you're still here I'm calling the cops."

"Fuck you, Wonderjerk."

That's when I stopped Vinny's forward motion and pushed him toward the door. During a brief tussle, he ended up flailing and bouncing down several stairs onto the sidewalk.

Vinny was taken to General Hospital where his scrapes and bruises weren't considered serious. However, his nasty mouth and efforts to belt a para-medic resulted in a 72-hour psychiatric evaluation.

That was the last time I saw Vinny, and I felt blessed. He never filed charges against me, and I had finally lost that knot in my stomach.

Why was I so emotionally overwhelmed by Vinny or his three predecessors during my life? All four clearly displayed dissimilar behaviors. Even their ethnicity, appearances and ages were markedly different. One of the four, who had effortlessly tied my stomach in knots, was a young female.

📖 📖 📖

That episode with Vinny happened at least twenty years before I retired, and it didn't require consultation with a group of colleagues to figure out how to effectively cope with any further episodes.

I've never figured out *why* I fall apart with some individuals and it no longer matters. I simply listen to my gut, and when it begins to knot, I run for it.

22

JUNE

Family Memories

The Tenderloin represents infinitely more to me than a place in San Francisco with a bad reputation. Since that first time I lived in the Tenderloin as a youth, my experiences there have sometimes been intensely dramatic or ponderously educational, yet always memorable. It's a phenomenon that must be related to the people I've met there. Providence may lead us unerringly through life, but it's our relationships that relentlessly shape our destinies.

For me, enjoying that burst of colors splashed across the sky as the sun sets is so much more spectacular when gasping in awe—together. Eating alone at the finest restaurant pales to the savor of a fast food dinner with a close friend. The final chapter of many good books I've read easily provoked brief tears of joy and sadness, while the tears and laughter I've known with friends have provided profound lessons I'll never forget.

Relationships may be the core of our existence, a catalyst that shapes and reshapes our behaviors. Like some fathomless driving force, it compels us to keep moving, learning and changing. Without relationships, there probably wouldn't be too much to strive for, to emulate or, for that matter, to fret about. There's no doubt that relationships have unwittingly designed many of my biases, attitudes and my passions.

As a youngster, before I ever knew about puberty and self-confidence, I was vulnerable to anything unfamiliar, new or challenging. That was just about everything. At that time in my life, I was especially influenced by family, a relationship that was my life. Maybe that is why one of my earlier Tenderloin encounters as a young adult is so unforgettable.

Childhood Innocence

My sister, June, and I were born into a fairly typical family that turned out to be a dysfunctional mess by the time I reached my teens. My father managed to escape from family responsibilities before I managed my first month of life. That wasn't unusual in those days. It was 1930. I was one of those Depression babies, trying to survive in a period when fathers frequently abandoned families they couldn't support.

My mother, a willowy, rosy-cheeked, clear bright-eyed beauty, had just turned 20. She was stuck with a 4 year old, June, and an infant, me. Many single parents were desperately poor and insecure in those days. It wasn't unusual for their children to be placed in the many available orphanages.

My mother, desperately poor, insecure and a single parent didn't subscribe to the usual. She was determined to keep her remaining family together, and she did—

despite her desperation.

Providing us with the basic necessities of food and shelter was our mother's sole purpose in life. There were no easy ways to ensure our survival. Her options were limited to marrying one of several willing suitors she didn't particularly like, selling sex to horny married men she liked even less, or a job with the Works Progress Administration (WPA). She chose the WPA, which just barely kept us alive and sheltered. We lived in a one-room apartment on a steep Jackson Street hill above San Francisco's North Beach. Although small, it was near a school and streetcar lines. The apartment was also large enough for my mother to work for the WPA at home. She sewed there ten to twelve hours a day.

My first five years of life were apparently spent playing barefooted on the Jackson Street sidewalk. I used to enjoy watching my mother sew, helping her prepare our meals and waiting for my sister to come home from school. I could always spot June and her Chinese girlfriend walking backwards up the steep streets. Sometimes they would wildly stray to play tag or hop scotch. Her girlfriend went to a Chinese school later in the day. That's when June watched after me.

All families like ours had adult responsibilities for everyone. Surviving on practically nothing, it was important we learned how to care for each other. Our family seemed to fulfill that responsibility well, especially the caring for each other.

Research has repeatedly concluded that love is such an indispensable nutrient, infants can die without it. The condition is called *Marasmus*. No wonder we survived. During that nascent period in my life, there was a sad lack of food on the table, but a happy surplus of affection in our family. Looking back, June and I were nourished more by the security of mother's love than by our skimpy meals.

When I was about three and June seven, we had never seen a movie or tasted the cold smooth sweetness of ice cream. Nevertheless, we had an icebox that offered us the fun of sucking on occasional splinters of ice. Just about everything we wore was second or third-hand relief offerings and the only time we ever heard radio music was when someone played theirs too loudly.

We were very poor, yet secure, and even content in our poverty. We knew Mom would never abandon us, that we'd be hugged until our eyes bulged, that our shelter was always warm and cozy, and that, as she used to promise, "We'll never go hungry."

It's ironic that I've forgotten most of the early childhood I would like to remember. Yet, I too clearly remember much of the adolescence I would like to forget. Those early years, with my sister and mother, are disappointingly blurred out of focus. I only know that those hazy feelings rising from the past are all warm, tender and caring.

There is, however, one early family memory still indelibly catalogued in my musty, aging attic of fading memories. The set and setting are always the same, which hopefully punctuates its accuracy. As my thoughts recreate the fleeting scenes, I reliably smile first—then cry.

It was an unusually warm San Francisco Sunday. Many apartment windows were opened to harvest the slight breeze. Mom was busily washing clothes, the way of the times. She washed by hand with washboard, sink and wringer, all in the basement. She kept the basement door open to watch us play. It was comforting to know she was close. We could even hear her hum along with the music wafting its way out of some open window.

June was sitting on the sidewalk, with legs crossed

and concealed under her flowery Sunday dress. A big book was opened on her lap. With one hand she held the pages while, with the other, she guided her reading with her pointed index finger. I laid on the sidewalk next to her, sprawled like a seal on my belly, hands cupping my chin, with elbows resting on the cement sidewalk.

I listened indifferently, dreamily as my eyes wandered along the huge apartment buildings that lined both sides of Jackson Street. My eyes absently drifted into windows where I could imagine all sorts of intriguing activities. Those windows offered endless glimpses of silhouetted movements. At my age, I couldn't read; and although June was only seven, she was always reading—aloud and haltingly. She occasionally paused in painstaking deliberation. Then slowly, with a deep sigh, she would mispronounce some new word.

We seemed content with practically nothing because our little family had grown quite accustomed to nothing. At that time, we probably didn't think of movies, ice cream, new toys or richly abundant meals. We were mercifully spared missing what we never had. Sundays were a time of pleasant relaxation for us, even Mom. June had no school and aside from helping Mother hang clothes on the backyard clothesline, she would have no special chores that day. She also didn't have to be as vigilant in watching me, because Mother was more available on Sundays.

I probably felt more relaxed and content as well. During the week, there was the busy schedule of piece-work commitments for Mom, homework and school activities for June and my unsettled feelings that I was a hindrance to the whole hectic process. But, this was Sunday and all was well and comfortable. As June kept trying to read, there was still the background music,

Mom's humming and muffled traffic noises coming from North Beach.

Then my wandering eyes noticed a green piece of paper, sliding, rotating and drifting along the sidewalk toward me. Meandering helplessly with the wind, it was different from other discarded pieces of paper. It seemed important, maybe because I remembered Mom treating similar paper with grave respect. One more puff of wind and the little paper glided between my elbows. I lazily dropped one hand from my chin and picked up the greenish piece of paper. I just knew Mom might want it. June, struggling with the big book of words, was still reading aloud, oblivious to my discovery or the loss of her little audience.

Mom was shaking out a smashed shirt. She had just turned it through the wringer that squeezes clothes from dripping wet, to just wet. Smiling down at me, she noticed my outstretched arm, "Whatcha got, Honey?" she asked as she scooped me up to eye level.

Before I could answer, she gave me that universal mother's hug and playful raspberry kiss on the neck. By that time, the paper, still clutched in my hand, was practically resting on her shoulder.

In an instant, Mother's relaxed smile shifted to rigid, stunned silence. It was scary and I must have thought I did something wrong. As she grabbed the paper and gently put me back on the floor, she still seemed stunned, but no longer silent.

"Oh my God, where did you get this money?" It was a twenty-dollar bill.

Once I convinced her I hadn't the slightest idea where it came from, Mom gave me another universal mother's response to a happy situation. She began to cry as she hugged me again.

Then she ran to the open basement door, "June,

June," she shouted, with a hint of urgency.

While running to Mom, June dog-eared the page she was reading and closed the book. "Has anyone been talking to you or Larry, did anyone drop something near you?"

Mom knew that our Jackson Street area was liberally sprinkled with rich neighbors, who could have carelessly dropped the twenty-dollar bill blocks away. She was also convinced it came to us fairly and innocently. Besides we *really* needed it.

Perhaps it's also vivid in my mind because it was the best Christmas I ever had, and it wasn't even Christmas. It was the day my mother couldn't stop joking and smiling and tickling us. It was the unforgettable day when June and I had our first ice cream soda, and saw our first movie at the "talkies" motion picture show on Columbus Avenue. There were brand new shoes for June and me, some new clothes and toys—lots of toys.

Mom said the rent was paid in advance, and the little apartment was stacked with groceries. There were no new clothes for Mom, but, as a family, we were her gifts, which was all the reward she seemed to need or want. I'll never forget how happily she cried when I found that twenty-dollar bill.

📖   📖   📖

During my elementary school years, our family situation changed considerably. After eight years of caring for us alone, my mother had remarried a good provider. He was a kind, generous man, yet never quite able to develop a close fatherly relationship with June or me. Mother had waited until we were both of school age before accepting the added role of wife. I guess she figured we could pretty much take care of ourselves by then, especially with the added financial security and a safe middle class neighborhood.

She was right about June, neither needing nor wanting close parental supervision. But I was just the opposite. Shy, scrawny and frail-looking, I could use all the parental help I could get.

Those marked differences in my sister and I crafted an unusually close symbiotic relationship. Strangely, neither of us had any solid peer relationships at the time, perhaps because June was too strong and I was too weak. At twelve, June was four years older and twenty years tougher than I. She was exceptionally popular at school, yet her competitive spirit, self-sufficiency and pushiness tended to keep other kids at a distance, despite their respect for her.

Those were the very qualities I longed to have and deeply admired in her. School easily intimidated me in those days, and June was always there to support me or occasionally rescue me from a schoolyard bully. She could outstare the most formidable bullies. "Get outta here and leave my brother alone," she would shout, and the bully would leave.

Whenever I was away from home, June became my mother surrogate. Sometimes, however, her maternal role clashed with Mom's efforts to discipline me at home.

"Leave him alone, Mom," she would plead. "He didn't wet the bed on purpose." or "He didn't break the lamp. I accidentally hit his arm while we were playing."

June also taught me how to wrap food I couldn't eat in toilet paper and flush it down the toilet when Mom wasn't looking. I think Mom tolerated June's interference, mainly because she took such good care of me.

June's physical appearance and athletic ability were also venerable. Her hair was a lively golden blond with springy curls that bounced in rhythm with her energetic stride. The Shirley Temple similarly continued where the curls adorned deeply dimpled cheeks, with sparkling blue eyes that danced flirtatiously with each new vision. She also had creamy smooth skin, full well-contoured lips and a small straight nose that turned slightly upward at the tip. Her body was athletically solid and slender, with not a trace of fat. It was an exceptionally feminine body, as trim as a modern day gymnast.

Although academically she wasn't the greatest student, her energy and many talents were well-known at Gratten Grammar School. She organized kiddy variety shows, played baseball with the boys, danced solo at school rallies and frequently argued with teachers who admonished her for being too much of a "Tomboy."

Standing in her shadow, I cringed and beamed at the same time when she would defy a schoolyard teacher's order.

"June, you're supposed to be playing volleyball with the girls, not baseball with the boys, now get over there!"

"Why should I?" she'd argue, "No one seems to mind but you. I like baseball and I'm the best pitcher they have."

Not too far beneath her dogged self-determination and defiant independence, however, were qualities only a few were privileged to witness, sometimes in amazement. Aside from caring for me, she was warmly sensitive to practically anyone in need. She would unhesitatingly defend against an injustice, attempt to protect the underdog or just try to help anyone who seemed distressed—even on Saturday.

📖 📖 📖

Going to the Saturday matinee with its double feature, two serials and three cartoons was always the high point of our week. There was no television around to dull the imagination or dilute our eager fantasies. Movies were still a thrilling adventure. It was an exciting way to spend Saturday afternoon, shouting, screaming, laughing and jeering. The epidemic of blasé kids, gorged on TV, was gratefully absent.

June and I would walk the seven blocks to the Haight Theater early enough to get good front row seats for that three and a half hours of unbridled fantasy that seemed like wizardry.

The Haight was one of many magnificent theaters that succumbed to our new era of electronic technology and entertainment efficiency. Today we know their replacements well. The Multiplex theaters with twenty simultaneous movies in what look like "viewer rooms." There, jammed together, you're enveloped in ear-splitting Dolby sounds, apparently intended to compensate for the weak plot. Today it seems, louder is better.

The Haight was sadly trashed by the hippie invasion. They renovated much of the neighborhood into what is now known as "The Haight-Ashbury District." Before then, the Haight Theater offered comfort and elegance instead of "viewer room" stark efficiency. It was truly magnificent enough to entertain royalty and, during my youth, we were the royalty. We just didn't know it. Even then, we had the often bad habit of taking things for granted.

What seemed like a 10,000 square foot velvet curtain, cloaking the enormous screen, was embossed with intricate arabesque patterns, and before the movie screen was unveiled, just scanning the entire theater was a rare creative experience.

During the evening hours, a white-gloved usher led you down a thick presidential-looking carpet, tightly woven and colorfully patterned. The deeply cushioned seats of rich velvets were attached to carved hardwood backrests by rivets of brass. Two kids could easily accommodate those large, sofa-like chairs, as many parents scornfully discovered.

Any connoisseur of the classic arts or even history could applaud the Haight Theater's artistic details and superb craftsmanship. Gigantic chandeliers hung beneath frescoed ceilings while the thousands of lights refracting through the crystals showered the entire theater with a rainbow display of glistening colors.

There was the posh rear balcony with brocade curtains draping each entranceway, rows of high-backed, velvety cushioned rocking chairs and shiny brass guardrails above the balcony's gilded facade of golden leaves and flowers. There were even side balconies that forever seemed to be awaiting nobility, and all of that before the lights dimmed to show the movies.

It was our show of promised magical adventures. That wonderful theater was near the corner of Haight and Ashbury Streets, and admission was only twenty-five cents for adults and ten cents for kids. What a deal, and you could stay just about as long as you wanted.

June and I were finally greeted by another Saturday. It seemed to take forever to arrive, with a tendency to leave in an instant. Following a huge good-bye hug from Mom, we were off with twenty cents apiece clutched in our hands and blazing grins on our faces. We had show and candy money and we didn't have to be home until after the second cartoon showing at about 2:00 o'clock.

As we strolled along at a good clip, it was time to begin speculating about last week's serial. Would Flash

Gordon escape the cowardly ambush by the Mud People? We couldn't wait to find out. The big Haight marquee was finally in sight. Nearing our destination, we couldn't contain ourselves any longer. June grabbed my free hand and we eagerly broke into a run to the finish line.

Along that last block, however, we saw Mrs. Brimskill. She was a shriveled, hunch-backed lady who I used to think was the oldest person in the entire world. Just as we reached her, at a full gallop, Mrs. Brimskill dropped one of the three bags of groceries she was trying desperately to hold.

June skidded to a stop, nearly dislocating my arm. "Don't move Mrs. Brimskill," she said, "or you'll..." Then, as the two remaining bags dropped from her arms, "...or you'll lose the other bags," June whispered.

We, June mainly, spent the next five minutes chasing cans of vegetables, rolls of toilet paper, peaches, oranges and apples. Mrs. Brimskill, with wide eyes and opened mouth, clutched her old purse and watched helplessly. I was absently picking up an item or two, while more intently watching the line grow at the Haight Theater. The bags had spilled over a steep driveway. That made retrieval more hectic since everything in Mrs. Brimskill's bags was round and moving. The only things that had lain motionless on impact were the once round, smashed eggs.

Poor Mrs. Brimskill was nearly hysterical, half blaming everybody, including herself. "My grandson was supposed to drive me to the store... Oh, I shouldn't have carried so much... Look out, don't step on my tomatoes."

June kept nodding as she listened patiently. "I'm sorry, Mrs. Brimskill, I know you must feel awful." June's eyes and manner radiated a rare softness, and I knew that she genuinely felt sorry for that decrepit old lady.

After all the bags were restuffed, I was still whimsically hoping we might make the serial, when June announced, "Now don't you worry anymore, Mrs. Brimskill, we'll help you home with the bags."

Then, without a chance to protest, I was following along behind June and Mrs. Brimskill with two big cans tucked under my arms. Trudging sideways, I kept looking back longingly at that beckoning theater marquee slowly sinking beneath Ashbury Street rooftops.

We missed the movie that Saturday; and as a reward, Mrs. Brimskill let us eat some of her home-baked coconut cookies, which we both hated.

"Oh, thank you Mrs. Brimskill," June mumbled as she tried to neutralize the taste with large gulps of milk. "They're so good, aren't they, Larry?"

The Reunion

Those good years seemed to rocket by until one day I was no longer that scrawny protected child. I had grown bigger. June—with longer golden hair, a more angelic face and Mother's willowy body—had grown prettier and our little family had grown in separate directions.

June quit high school, launched into a dancing career and eventually married. I thought of her often through high school and college, and although I no longer needed her protection, I missed her presence. Occasionally she wrote, telling me about her successful career and wonderful marriage. As I read her letters, I would beam with pride and nostalgia.

"You're still my little brother," she'd often write, "and I'm so proud of you."

Several years of military service in Korea, followed

by graduate school, moved me even further from June's life. I had lost all contact with her, yet June was always a consoling memory. Whenever I was troubled over life's frequent stresses, thoughts of our childhood together were a pleasant retreat.

Early in 1960, after almost ten years of thinning memories, June finally called me. It was a brief call and I had no idea how she found me. It didn't matter, I was thrilled.

"Hello, little brother."

"June?" Suddenly my voice was higher and louder than ever. "I can't believe it. Where are you?"

Unmistakably June, she shelved my question with another comment. "I heard you graduated from college and have a good job. I'm still so proud of you. A lot's happened to me since I last saw you."

Again I asked, "Where are you?"

"Well," said June after a short pause, "I'm down on Ellis Street, can you come and see me? I know it's a little late."

Ellis Street revived a rush of early Tenderloin memories. Looking back, I had a lot to learn and there I had learned plenty about life, the streets and humility. Those were Tenderloin lessons I'll never forget.

June gave me the address of the old Mentone Hotel on Ellis and Jones, so reminiscent of my first apartment building in the Tenderloin.

"I'll be down in less than an hour. Is that okay?"

"That's fine, Larry," she said. "See ya then."

Within a half hour I was parking my car on Jones Street. That area was once jammed with bars, brothels, clubs and ribald shows, in its wilder days. Now it looked old and tired. As I walked past the Chez Paree, a bored-looking doorman mustered a strained show of enthusiasm. He acknowledged my disinterest with a shrug of his shoulders and another bored look. The old club, like so many others in the Tenderloin, was struggling to survive with raunchy jokes, striptease and a musty smelling bar that had lost its naughty glamour and "uptown customers."

I thought of my many past walks down Turk, Jones, Eddy, Larkin and so many other Tenderloin streets, when this was my brief home. I remembered how those initially uneasy short walks became long delightful strolls—as I learned about the people of the Tenderloin.

I was still comfortable there, yet saddened by its rundown condition. The bright, colorful array of neon signs were broken and dimming, along with its tawdry reputation. There seemed to be sluggishness, a loss of vitality in the Tenderloin accompanying the gradual deterioration of its buildings. I just hoped its rich history could withstand an emerging new era of social change in the 60's San Francisco.

Entering the lobby of that once lively, bustling Tenderloin hotel, I suddenly felt I should tiptoe through its oppressive, musty heaviness, before being noticed. It didn't matter; the dark, dingy lobby appeared as if it had been empty for centuries. It seemed to have lost interest in itself or any new guests. As I crept toward the antique elevator, a huge, breathy voice stopped me in the middle of a step.

"Hey, where ya goin'?" the voice cracked like a whip, jolting me out of my more pleasant reveries.

"Room 420," I shouted, somewhat startled and annoyed by the unseen voice.

"No one's allowed after 10. Don't ya see the sign?" the voice boomed back.

A closer scan of the old lobby led me to a counter with a backdrop of mail slots, hanging keys and the top of a barely visible head. Hunched over a magazine, his jutting goateed jaw exaggerated the length of his narrow, cylindrical head. His deep set, squinty eyes, thin crusty, droopy lips and pinched nostrils gave him an angry look, probably even when he slept.

There wasn't the slightest trace of softness in the man's face. It was also obvious that an anemic appeal to him would have been useless.

"June is my sister, in 420. She asked me to come over, so I'm going up."

Leaning back in his chair, the desk clerk looked up, and dropped his magazine. "Your sister? June's your sister?" he repeated.

"Why don't you call her?" My reply was more of a demand than a request.

Turning to the switchboard, the desk clerk seemed to surrender, with a testy, "OK, OK."

While I waited for June to answer his call, the clerk kept glancing in my direction with furtive leers. "There's a guy here, says he's your brother." After listening for a few moments, the desk clerk's voice faded to an inaudible whisper, then raspy chuckles and another leering glance at me. "You can go up to 420, she's waiting." After a quick shake of his head in disbelief and one more leer, the clerk resumed reading his magazine.

On my way up in the rickety old elevator, I again slipped into pleasant reveries of our family's earlier years, of Mother's love and devotion, our childhood innocence, older sister's loyalty and affection to me and, of course, Saturday matinees. Then, with a loud crunch, the elevator jolted to a swaying stop. My thoughts were jolted back to the hotel. After a few tugs, the old elevator door creaked open and I was walking down a dingy corridor, looking for 420, my sister's room.

The brass number plate on the door was hanging

sideways on one screw. As I readied my fist to knock, I was almost dizzy with mixed feelings of anticipation. She must have heard my footsteps because one light hesitant knock sent the door flying open.

I thought I'd knocked on the wrong door. A pudgy-faced, double-chinned, fat woman with straight short black hair and flowery robe was standing there grinning. "Oh, Larry, my little brother, give me a big hug."

The words were unmistakably June, but the face, body, hair, even her clothes were sadly not the sister I had known. Those weren't the kind of differences that understandably occur over time. Her appearance was regrettably offensive and alien to me.

Suddenly, June's fleshy dimpled arms were around me and I was lightly resting my hands on her shoulders. I felt smothered in sickening sweet-smelling perfume. As she pressed me tighter against her lumpy body, I was trying to decide whether to hug back or apologize for knocking on the wrong door.

Then, still holding me, June pulled back, stared at me with an affectionate smile and again whispered, "Little brother," so I hugged back.

"God, I'm so proud of you!" she proclaimed, leading me into her room. "You're a grown man now and so handsome. Tell me about your work."

June sat close, holding my hands and asking a steady stream of questions that I kept trying to answer. Despite her smiles, it seemed more like an interrogation than a friendly exchange. There was no doubt that June still held deep affectionate feelings for me. It was equally obvious that I remained the "little brother" she could easily control. Each time I tried to ask her a question, she would smoothly interrupt with another question. It finally dawned on me that my sister was avoiding self-disclosures by focusing solely on my life.

Eventually, we sidestepped each new pause with a "remember when we" nudge that spiraled us back to our childhood. That sort of compromise enabled us to safely reminisce, exchange memories and smile and laugh a lot.

Feeling a bit more at ease, I began to absently scan her barren room, containing two chairs, a bed, a night-stand and a sink. Missing were homey little items such as pictures on the walls, a radio or even a magazine.

When June and I finally ran out of compliments and safe pleasantries, I felt comfortable enough to blurt out a question, I wouldn't have dared ask earlier. "Say, what are you doing here anyway?"

June stopped smiling and all traces of softness and affection vanished. "For Christ's sake, Larry, grow up. I'm a whore!"

That was the last time I saw my sister. Several years later, I learned that she never reached her thirtieth birthday. She was reportedly killed somewhere in the Tenderloin. I also learned that our mother barely reached her fiftieth birthday. She reportedly died alone somewhere in California, ironically during the year of my sister's death. I don't know where they're buried.

※　　※　　※

Despite some inquiries before completing this second edition, the burial locations of my mother and sister remain mysteries.

I guess I really don't want to know. Those indelible memories of a proud sister, protecting her timid brother and a beautiful mother selflessly caring for us, may be memory enough.

23

SEAN

Heavenly Angels

Throughout San Francisco's stormy history, the Tenderloin has survived as both a public disgrace and a public sanctuary. It has been a haven for predator and prey, givers and takers, misfits and unfits, all shunned by many of San Francisco's moral conservatives. Yet despite the dangers of living together with such differences, it's been a place where their similarities strangely belong. For lots of reasons, many of those exiles believe they're stuck in the only place in San Francisco that accepts them. So, having nowhere else to go, they tend to look after each other.

Human beings have many common bonds, especially related to their basic needs. Tenderloin people are no different—just a bit more frantic. They need companionship, affection, sustenance and encouragement; and when all else seems to fail, they need an occasional miracle.

That's when Heavenly Angels appear. Not as some apparition, but as an advocate who offers the hopeless another chance.

Skeptics will argue that no one, at least those sane and sober residents, has ever noticed a Heavenly Angel gliding, floating or fluttering down Eddy Street. That, however, is no valid argument against their existence. It should be apparent to anyone who has survived into the third millennium, that Heavenly Angels aren't seen, they're experienced!

Just about anyone who believes in miracles acknowledges Heavenly Angels. But even the most zealous believers might question Angels patrolling the Tenderloin, of all places. The answer should be obvious to anyone who's ever lived in the Tenderloin. Angels are totally oblivious to geographic location, socioeconomic status, appearance or hygiene. They operate best where they're needed most. That gives the Tenderloin a high priority in San Francisco. Eligibility for Heavenly Angel assistance has everything to do with need. Preferential consideration is given to those who can show innocence, fear, compassion, desperation and determination.

📖 📖 📖

Sean had all the prerequisites—at least he did over forty years ago when he finally arrived in California. Tall, lanky, and impishly Irish, Sean's ruggedly handsome face says it all, long before he opens his mouth. Whether he's happy, sad, mad or bored, his face describes in glowing detail his instant feelings.

Fortunately, Sean has a warm, compassionate heart and a generous sense of humor that contributes to his likable personality and many friends, including me. Otherwise his short-fused temper might be a problem.

Besides, his face telegraphs his short fuse long before he erupts, and even without the warning, Sean's anger dissipates rapidly.

On The Road

In the summer of '62, when the hippies were preparing the Haight Ashbury for their flower children, Sean was preparing to leave his hometown of Holyoke, Massachusetts for the West Coast, toward an adventure teeming with goose bumps, heartaches and an Angel or two.

Glorious youth is that period of life when some of us believe we are immortal and invincible. That's the time when youth know everything, as long as it has a happy ending. There are no risks of failure, just the cautions of well-meaning parents. Everything that constitutes youth is burgeoning—hormones, expectations, confidence, self-esteem, arrogance and more hormones.

When Sean backed from his parents Massachusetts driveway, he was one of those youth. Yet, as the first born of ten children, Sean couldn't help feeling older, tougher, more responsible and better prepared to care for his family. After all, against great odds, he had put himself through Notre Dame, though his mother constantly said, "Only God knows how."

He had everything he needed to make it to California. A 1953, $115 Plymouth station wagon that could go anywhere. A bright, pretty and devoted pregnant wife who would support his plans to anywhere, a ten-month-old son slurping away on a bottle, a backseat loaded with diapers and $160. Tons of money, or so he thought.

He'd worked for months on construction prior to the trip and when he told his wife how much he had, she gasped, "That's incredible!" Marian, too, came from a family where cash was an endangered species.

If his $160 in cash somehow ran out—hardly possible Sean thought—he knew he could easily get jobs along the way. After all, Sean was a fine writer with a solid resume. He had been a reporter in the dying mill town of Holyoke, Massachusetts and a copy editor for the *Wall Street Journal.* He expected to be in demand wherever they went.

The plan was simple enough. Hug good-bye to friends and family, hang a right toward Canada, then across the border into Quebec, turn left, camping along the two thousand mile stretch of the Trans-Canadian Highway. Hang another left back across the border down to Seattle, Washington, work a few months at the World's Fair before finishing the journey to San Francisco. What a wonderful journey...what an exciting dream...what blissful innocence.

It didn't take long for Sean to learn what he wasn't prepared to know. Unexpected expenses destroy budgets. Their first day on the road had been uneventful. They took a wrong turn near Toronto and backtracked a hundred miles. That done, they stopped at a farm that provided camping space.

It was early June and the farmer's picnic tables were freshly painted—until Sean set one of them on fire. The cause was an inability to work a Coleman stove. Sean, clever but incredibly unhandy, fiddled with levers and gadgets on the stove, lit a match, held it to the stove, and watched in horror as the stove and picnic table lit the darkening sky.

Resisting the urge to throw himself on the flames, he found a hose and doused the burning pyre. The stove was no worse the wear, though the family did go hungry that night. The table was a charred mess, so early the next morning, the three rose early and sheepishly stole away before the farmer awoke.

Two days later, they spent a pleasant evening in an Ontario park, and when they prepared to leave the next morning, everybody was enthusiastic and healthy— except their station wagon. A local mechanic offered the sad diagnosis, the generator had given up. Even sadder, it was a four-day wait until another generator arrived from across the border in Detroit. Trying to preserve their collapsing savings once the generator was repaired, Sean decided to chase their lost time with twelve to fourteen hour-a-day drives. Food stops were rare. Several arduous days later, that proverbial "disaster waiting to happen" did, somewhere in central Canada.

While briefly stopped at a gas station, Marian passed out on her way to the restroom. Sean quickly picked her up and helped her to the station wagon, where she immediately began convulsing. Sean ran around to the passenger side and pulled Marian out of the car. As she slumped on the grass, the convulsions stopped, but Sean's concern and feelings of guilt didn't. He realized that the constant travel and skimpy food had exhausted her. His top priority was caring for his family before they continued their journey. Thankfully, baby Sean was fine, despite his incessant need for diapers, and Marian would recover with rest and encouragement. Doctors later said she had suffered a concussion in the fall.

After a thirty-five-mile drive to another park, Sean bought ten pounds of liver at a local store. They spent the next four days eating liver and resting. When Marian had recovered sufficiently to travel, they agreed to drive only six to eight hours a day.

So, after weeks of driving through Canada, they were still driving through Canada. They had been living in a tent and out of the station wagon for nearly a month, with gas stations, rest stops and campsites as their neighborhood and bathrooms.

Trying to keep both his family and the old station wagon well-nourished was monopolizing the little money they had left. Their meals had been reduced to bologna and peanut butter and jelly sandwiches.

A week later, with a few feeble cheers, Sean and his worn-out family crossed back into the United States. They ended up later that day in Pocatello, Idaho. After a short rest and some peanut butter and jelly, they felt they were really on their way to work in Washington. Rumbling along Interstate 84 toward Seattle, Sean smiled at Marian, "We're almost there."

Marian smiled back as she changed baby Sean's diapers. "You mean to tell me there really is a state of Washington?" She laughed.

Then, within seventy miles of Seattle, everything shut down at once. The wagon cried uncle and stopped halfway up a slight grade. That was too much for Marian, who just cried for a real bed, a real meal, a healthy car and some more diapers.

The baby actually stopped crying, perhaps bewildered by mother's tears; Sean simply gritted his teeth and eased the station wagon into the curb near a park. He knew that he had to find work or call their parents for money before they all started begging for mercy.

That was their first preview of a dusting by Angels. Some kind campers helped push the station wagon about an eighth of a mile into a small campsite. After two hungry, worrisome days, Sean took a big gulp of his pride, choked away a little more innocence and called his parents for money.

Dan, his younger brother by three years, accepted the collect call intended for Dad.

"Dan, could you ask Dad to wire $7 to us at Western

Union?"

"Heck," Dan replied, "I'll kick in a buck and we'll make it 8."

Within a few hours, another kind camper drove Sean to a Western Union office, where $50 was already waiting for him. Clutching those five $10 bills, he sniffed back a tear of gratitude, reminded that Dad, Dan and the rest of his family were always there for him.

Then another camper pushed him to a garage in the small town of Monroe, Washington, where he met a real angel, Al Mann. Al repaired the wagon's broken timing chain for the cost of parts only. He told Sean he could pay the labor charge—the money Al would get to keep—when he got a job. With a deep sense of indebtedness, Sean agonized over that bill until he could afford to pay it months later.

The night before that charitable repair on the station wagon, Sean rewarded himself and Marian for their pioneer toughness with some of the money from home. The only rooms they had known since their good-bye hugs in Massachusetts were public bathrooms, with their characteristic stench and lack of privacy.

That was a fragrant night, when they got long hot showers, a white-sheeted bed, a room with walls, ceiling, a carpeted floor and even a private toilet. All of this for $15 at the Ritz Hotel, a name that didn't match its appearance, except to Sean and Marian. For them it was "The Ritz." They also had a feast of fast foods and the baby got some more diapers.

Their renewed exuberance only lasted the seventy mile drive to Seattle. Once they arrived, Sean and Marian were pelted with disappointments. It was late June, schools were out and Sean was too late to obtain any kind of World's Fair job.

The anticipated free state and national parks were

filled to capacity. Camporama, near the Seattle-Tacoma Airport, had the only available spaces, which amounted to about ten square feet for a whopping $3 per night.

They had traveled back to the stench of public toilets, squashed between a quagmire of endless tents, flapping clotheslines, trucks and cars. There were hordes of people, belching a constant mix of talk, screams, shouts and laughter that tormented silence until the early morning hours. It was the saddest of Steinbeck.

While Marian endured the maelstrom, Sean looked for a job. That was as far as they could go without money. Empowered by his mighty resume, Sean drove to Seattle daily, expecting to find a newspaper job. Each night he returned to the tent city squalor with bruised ego, less money and no job.

The wagon was also sick again with some sort of respiratory problem. It wheezed, choked and coughed a blinding trail of thick white smoke at a maximum speed of 35 miles per hour. It created a regular traffic jam as drivers crawled by in search of clearer visibility. A blown head gasket he learned and no money for repairs.

Following a week of tent city torture and agonizingly slow, smoke clogged drives to Seattle, there was no money for anything. With 23¢ left, no job and pangs of hunger, that was the humiliating end of the line. The only sensible solution was to abandon the last traces of pride, call home, euthanize the wagon and fly back to Massachusetts.

Before that lonely walk to the phone, he took one last look through the want ads of yesterday's discarded newspaper. What Sean saw offered an anemic tinge of hope. *Reporter needed on small Aberdeen daily, experience required.* Quickly scanning their old tattered map, Sean located Aberdeen near the coast, 100 miles away. *This is it*, he thought, *it's now or never, there's nothing to lose that isn't already lost.*

Like some mortally wounded warrior, charging for the last time up the well-fortified hill, Sean called the Aberdeen Daily "collect." He knew no one was about to hire a reporter who couldn't afford the price of a call. At that point, he really didn't care.

Thankfully, he was totally wrong. Suddenly, Sean experienced another fleeting glimpse of a gentle fluttering brilliance, a wisp of sweet scented purity, a dream of a soft caressing smile. He smiled back, knowing his family was rescued for a while longer.

📖 📖 📖

Ade Frederikson, managing editor of the *Aberdeen Daily World*, did accept his call, and after a long phone conversation, he agreed to an interview.

"Well," Sean gulped, "I don't have money for gas. Is it possible to get mileage?" He knew he was pushing his luck, he also knew he had no choice.

"Sure," Frederikson said quickly, "come down and we'll pay you for the trouble."

Sean went to the nearest gas station, filled the car with gas and asked the owner, "Do you take checks?"

Of course, the owner didn't take checks from a hippy-looking guy in a wagon from a state thousands of miles away, but the gas was already in the car.

"Sure," he said, and without complaint he accepted a check for $8 on a checking account that was completely empty. Later Sean made another painful call to his family, who took care of the check.

The car bucked and wheezed to Aberdeen. They made it and Sean looked around, searching for that angel lurking somewhere. With 18¢ in their pockets, they purchased a copy of the *Aberdeen Daily World.* That left them with 8¢ and they were very hungry.

Then, there was the sweet aura of another angel as they read that Aunt Jemima would be at the local supermarket the next day, serving free pancakes and orange juice. "Come one, come all." First, second and third in line the next morning, were Sean, Marian and the baby. Sean stationed the family next to his now-favorite aunt and ate…and ate.

Later that morning, Sean went to his interview. When Frederikson extended an offer, to be the paper's police and court reporter for $85 a week, Sean strangely hesitated, saying, "Let me talk to my wife. I'll be right back." As he began to debate the job decision with Marian, she wasn't moved by his youthful confidence or temporary insanity.

"If you don't take it, I will," she said.

Sean smiled. "I'll take it."

Sean extended that survival pause in the little tired town of Aberdeen to October 1963. They also extended their family. Meghan, their second, was born in January 1963. As they waved good-bye to Aberdeen and their new friends, Marian was six months pregnant with her third. Revitalized and secure with a $200 savings, they were loaded with diapers and a more subdued optimism. Remarkably, the station wagon seemed well enough to travel. Once again, the Sullivan's were off to San Francisco.

Their trip was a cheerful, downward slide along the coast. Laughing, singing and telling jokes, they were again beginning to naively feel invincible.

In The Tenderloin

On Halloween day, 1963, the station wagon, seeming a

bit tired, carried the Sullivan's from Marin County, across the Golden Gate Bridge, into the heart of San Francisco. Their odyssey had taken one and a half years. Teeming with open mouth and wide-eyed enthusiasm, they were ready for anything and it was about to happen.

An off-ramp from the highway led them through the downtown section, across Market Street, into an area of seedy looking hotels, bars and restaurants. That's when they realized their loyal wagon was terminally ill. The engine seized on Ellis Street, near the corner of Jones. Sean pushed the deceased old station wagon to the curb next to an apartment building called the St. George.

The name was apt. The myth has St. George slaying a dragon. In this case, the station wagon was slain, then towed to the junkyard, where it was unceremoniously sold for parts. The money barely paid the towing fee. For the Sullivan's, San Francisco had become Ellis and Jones, off Market Street, and the St. George Apartments became their home. They didn't have much choice. With two children and a station wagon full of belongings, the apartment beckoned convincingly.

Situated above the Jonell Bar, the St. George required a $50 security deposit and $95 rent in advance for their one bedroom, furnished, third floor home. In less than two hours, the bewildered Sullivan's had lost their station wagon and all but $50 of their savings. At least the location was convenient. It was centrally located and near most streetcar lines. Not bad, they thought, unaware that their new home was in the "notorious" Tenderloin.

The lobby was a bit worn and barren, yet clean. It had a rickety old elevator that persuaded boarders to take the stairs. Their apartment, billed as a furnished one bedroom, was basically one room with a bed and a kitchen. It also had one of those ancient gas stoves with scrawny, but shapely white legs, big levers, like white enameled fingers to turn on the gas and a half-century's blackened grease encrusted on the old burners.

The Sullivan's first stop in San Francisco became a location for ordeals and Angels

The bathroom was a putrid shade of green with a rust stained sink and huge bathtub, perched on its four claws. The Sullivan's had the luxury of a private toilet in a tiny room. Unfortunately, over six feet tall Sean couldn't sit on the toilet seat with the door closed, without crushing both of his knees.

An old brown four-drawer dresser, a faded maroon couch, a small lamp on the dresser with burn marks on the paper shade and a cracking linoleum floor legitimized the word "furnished." There was also a window, overlooking another window across the huge skylight that barely offered light. At least, the small closet was large enough to sleep the two babies. It was

Spartan, but it was home during their short stay. Sean would be working soon.

Lessons that first few days were fast and furious. Without trying, they learned that the neighborhood was very friendly, outgoing and service oriented.

Sean was propositioned to buy sex about ten times by the second day. Marian, on the other hand, was propositioned to sell sex about twelve times the first day. They were offered assorted watches, clothing and gaming bets, including bookie services.

Drugs weren't a prominent item in those days, and despite their discovery that the Tenderloin wasn't your typical residential neighborhood, it had its redeeming features. Practically everyone tried to sell you something, but no one leaned on you. Curiously, for them those hustles weren't the least bit intimidating.

Back in the 60's, both Sean and Marian felt safe in the Tenderloin, partly because they didn't know its reputation. They also had nothing to buy, sell or entice a thief. They were virtually broke, Sean was unemployed and their only transportation was of the public variety. It was day three in the Tenderloin, and the only things they had left were a month's apartment rent, the promise of getting back their security deposit, good health, about $45, a few groceries and of course, diapers.

Sean wasted no time rushing to find a job before the money ran out. While still in Aberdeen, he was offered some solid San Francisco job contacts as a writer. He was assured all he needed was personal interviews. Now that he was in San Francisco, all of those good job prospects turned out to be empty gestures.

Undaunted, Sean got a paper, the phone book and a map of the city to plan his job hunting day. His first applications were at the *Examiner*, the *Chronicle*, and the *Call Bulletin*. He also managed interviews with

Harper Collins Publishers, *Newsweek*, BBD & O, TWA and Pan Am.

By the end of the first Tenderloin week, Sean had canvassed just about every major business associated with writing or advertising. As the babies happily gummed Gerber's, he and Marian munched candy bars, their remaining luxury. That first Saturday night in San Francisco, however, would be their last candy bar night in the Tenderloin.

Everywhere he went for a job, he was listened to with warm, friendly encouragement. That didn't put food on the table, however. No jobs developed.

"The holidays are coming up," he was often told. "No one is hiring now, wait 'til January."

He realized, by January, he and the family would be history.

"We'll call you," others said with probable sincerity.

A phone, however, was a luxury the family couldn't afford. *Phone or food*, he thought. The food won. The family was broke…not virtually broke, not almost broke or down to spare change. They had nothing left except a few diapers and basic clothing. They could hardly afford a local phone call that cost a dime.

Sean remembered one of his first applications had been at Macy's, when he was still choking on his pride instead of swallowing it. He had hesitantly applied for a temporary Christmas sales job. That turned out to be a stock boy job in the "Trim a Tree" department, which opened a few months before Christmas.

The personnel department had advised him that he was over-qualified and, quietly relieved, he left with a "thank you." Sean still felt he could do a little better than Macy's.

During the next two days, however, he was learning that a sense of pride was no match for feelings of desperation. Sean was too old for some unskilled, menial jobs, too young for others, too over-qualified, and even too unqualified for some. He was learning that the most menial job had fierce competition from other desperate, menial people.

📖　📖　📖

Wandering frantically through the Tenderloin, it finally dawned on Sean that working at Macy's wasn't demeaning after all. He couldn't run there fast enough. This time he was relieved that Macy's was still hiring temporaries. The over-qualified label was no longer a compliment, and when he asked to see the personnel manager, he explained with calm resolve, "Look at me. Do I look over-qualified?" With hands out-stretched, he added, "I have a pregnant wife and two kids living in the Tenderloin about five blocks from here. I'm broke, they're hungry and I need a job."

The personnel manager seemed to listen thoughtfully; and Sean was working as a temporary Christmas helper for Macy's the next morning.

It's amazing how values and priorities change when no longer faced with homelessness and hunger. Working afternoons and evenings at Macy's, Sean spent most days applying for special career jobs. Then, about two weeks later, he was called for a second interview for one of those special jobs. With mounting confidence, Sean was so convinced he would be hired; he quit his job at Macy's.

Ironically, Sean was learning more from failures than successes. Such terms as practically, almost or nearly don't count. Elation is only guaranteed when you win. Sean lost. He came in second for that special job. At least this time, he was neither naive nor bewildered.

He blew it; no one else, and all he could do was keep trying.

He ran back to Macy's hoping to regain his menial job. However, a genuinely menial worker was happily trimming trees and stacking boxes. He realized that such unskilled work was the only way that other man could ever earn a living. He momentarily envied that cheerful, man with the menial job.

For seven days, Sean must have seriously challenged all job-hunting records. He was more determined than ever to get a special job that would utilize his writing skills. He expanded his search to the Peninsula, Marin County and the East Bay. His furthest contact was in San Jose, where he was able to submit a resume to IBM. Sean managed 25 special job interviews in those seven days. *Not bad*, he thought, *for an ex-grunt without a car.*

A week had gone by since Sean's record-breaking interviews; and once again like a horrible deja vu, they were really broke. There was no money for tomorrow's rent, no money to replace shrinking food supplies, no carfare and those indispensable diapers were on the critical list.

This time, Sean set out to contact each previous agency in person with a polite inquiry. Those next few days were brutal. Some bluntly said he wasn't what they were looking for, while not explaining just what they were looking for. A few were downright rude with a "don't call us, we'll call you" reply. The cruelest was the agency that told him they had no positions available, after he had returned three times at their request. That time Sean almost lost it, as he cursed and raved his way out the door. No one got in his way.

While Sean was hunting jobs, Marian was doing her own hunting. She was becoming a real street savvy survivor. She even managed to talk the corner store owner into a charge account. Then one afternoon, Marian once again felt that ominous cold as the foreboding grays swept over the Tenderloin, leaving an eerie omen of black shadows and howling winds.

Marian tucked her two babies into bed for a nap, and shivered a bit as she turned on the oven to cook another shepherd's pie, of mashed potatoes and 19¢ hamburgers; a favorite Irish dish. The shepherd's pie at home alternated with trips to a local "all-you-can-eat for 99¢" restaurant. That's the place where Marian and the kids would share a dinner for one, with milk, while Sean ate all the free bread he could get.

📖 📖 📖

Although the gas was on as Marian prepared the meal, the pilot light was out; and as she lit a match, an explosion of searing flame and power threw her halfway across the room. The full force struck her face and hands, yet mercifully, the babies didn't feel the blast, and there was no lingering fire. However, she needed medical attention.

Several hours later Sean returned after a long walk and another disappointing day. In his hallway were more people than usual, all of whom were sympathetically or curiously looking at him. The manager told him about the blast, Marian's burns, her ambulance trip to General Hospital, and that little Sean and Meghan were staying with their friend Betty, the prostitute with a big heart, down the hall.

With a loan from the manager and trust in Betty, Sean hugged his babies and ran for a cab to the hospital. Heavily sedated, Marian was in bed, with bandaged hands, greasy, tail-light red face and singed remnants of hair. She had second-degree facial burns, some deeper, third degree hand burns and enough pain and shock to keep her in the hospital ward overnight. Fortunately there were no serious injuries. He kissed her gently on an unburned area of her neck; then for a long time he sat on the edge of the bed motionless, watching her sleep and searching through their hardships.

When Sean finally returned to the apartment late that night, he was physically exhausted with agonizing concerns that would keep him awake until early morning.

Betty had taken good care of the babies who were sleeping peacefully with her two children. As Sean carried his children back to their apartment, he thought about the kind Tenderloin people he met. He worried about the money he owed people he hardly knew, and how he was going to pay for tomorrow's cab fare.

In the morning, a kind Mr. O'Keefe gave him $5, knowing Sean was broke. That was enough to return to the hospital to get Marian.

Marian's face had swollen during the night and her mumbles were barely audible through taut, crusted lips. It was another cold, gloomy day for both of them, as they silently returned to the apartment in a cab.

As soon as they arrived in their room, Betty returned the babies again and Marian became tearful when she saw her children. Before leaving, Betty even offered Sean a few dollars that he gratefully took. Now he was taking money from a kind, caring prostitute. He was still learning.

On the third day since Marian's return from the hospital, Sean left the apartment long enough to charge a few groceries. He actually dreaded going out. This was the first time in his life he owed money to virtual strangers. He was also filled with rejection, disappointment and, worst of all, fear that Marian and the kids were in danger. But then, once again, Sean was blessed with another of the fluttering wing experiences.

📖 📖 📖

John Sullivan was no relative, yet every bit like family. Head of Public Relations for Standard Oil, John was so impressed by Sean's struggle, he went beyond offering the usual job contacts, including gifts for Sean's family, Christmas dinner, money for a phone installation and one of Sean's resumes to a friend at IBM. Sean was deeply grateful, despite waning optimism.

As a few more dreary weeks dragged by, the Sullivans were indebted to just about everyone. They were dangerously close to their January rent payment and Marian was due to have another baby in six weeks. Prospects were grim.

Then one cloudy day as he was returning from the store where he was refused further credit, a strange feeling came over him. He looked up just as those cold, steel gray skies were opening in splashes of radiance and bright velvety hues. He felt the warmth caressing his body, and inexplicably he started running toward the St. George. He ran through the lobby, up the staircase, and onto the third floor where the phone was ringing.

As if he had known that the call was for him, he dove for the phone before Marian had a chance to answer it.

"Hello" he said, panting. The call was from IBM in San Jose.

"Do you have a position yet?" the voice asked.

All of his early confidence and panache had disappeared. "No sir," he replied clearly.

"Can you stop by tomorrow to discuss a job?"

The voice was strong, yet benign and supportive, like Santa Claus or the Lord, Sean thought; and at that moment in his life, it could have been either.

After agreeing to the 10 a.m. appointment, he started doubting the call ever happened. *Maybe I misunderstood or I wanted a job so badly I day-dreamed the call,* he thought. *My God, of course it happened,* he argued with himself. Sean ran down the stairs to the Tenderloin street and felt the brilliance of the glowing sun through the vanishing clouds. He knew the call had really happened.

An hour later, a glance in his mirror was a grim awakening that if first impressions were everything, he was nothing. He looked more like a derelict than a businessman. His hair was long—he hadn't had a haircut in two months. His trench coat was worn and creased. His cash assets amounted to 65¢.

Borrowing small change from several neighbors, he managed a Tenderloin barber college haircut, while Marian washed his only dress shirt and ironed his tie and wrinkled suit. His old trench coat would just have to do without dry cleaning.

Nervously Sean felt ready, provided he could get to San Jose, a fifty-five-mile trip, by 10 a.m. the following day, December 28th. One big swallow of his few remaining crumbs of stale pride and he was able to borrow a car from a friend and fellow "trim-a-treer" at Macy's.

Leaving nothing to chance, Sean arrived at 8:00 the next morning, with huge butterflies that tormented his stomach for the next two hours. Clutching his well-folded trench coat, Sean met dapper Bill Smith of IBM's personnel department, yesterday's phone voice. After an hour interview, he was hired immediately by well-dressed plant manager, Gav Cullen, who mentioned the head of personnel, Bud Hurst, his friend John Sullivan and their unqualified recommendations.

"Would you like to come to work for IBM?"

"Yes, sir!" Sean replied, thinking, *my God, it's divine winged intervention.*

Happily expecting a possible $6,000 a year, Sean was offered $8,400.

"Is that OK?" asked Cullen.

Sean had less than a dollar in his pocket. "Yes, quite," he softly replied. Inside he was shouting with joy, laughing and hugging the man who just gave him the entire universe. There was one final embarrassing obstacle. He had to admit his family was broke.

With a wry smile, Cullen gave Sean a $100 advance.

Sean was speechless. A motel! Food! Spending money!

Cullen broke the silence, asking, "Now, what moving van line would you like to move your household furnishings?"

"Moving van?"

"Yes, moving van."

"Ah, would it be alright if we just rented a station wagon and drive our stuff here ourselves? We don't have much."

"Sure, that would be fine," he said, realizing that Sean wasn't your typical IBM recruit.

After calling Marian and parking in the Tenderloin, Sean chose to walk the rest of the way back to his apartment. He felt weightless and knew what a moon-walk was like as he bounded along the San Francisco streets smiling at everyone and everything.

When he reached Ellis Street, near his apartment, the sun seemed especially warm and comforting, and with a deep sigh, he realized this was his sacred place that would forever be special. A place of trials, failures, desperation, determination and the soothing presence of Heavenly Angels.

Two days later, on December 31st, the Sullivan family piled their tired belongings and diapers into their brand new rented station wagon. They circled the block twice, slowly traveling west on Ellis, north on Leavenworth, east on O'Farrell and south on Jones past Jonell's, beneath the St. George Apartments in the heart of the Tenderloin. One last look up toward their third floor apartment, one last glimpse at where they experienced their angels, a wave good-bye and they were gone.

📖   📖   📖

Now, over forty years later, Sean is a millionaire. He started a company and sold it, then made additional money in other investments. He has never forgotten the Tenderloin and his earlier poverty struggle to survive. He still remembers the kindness of strangers who didn't have much themselves.

During our lasting friendship, he has often mentioned those days of desperation and angels, and how his profound gratitude has enriched his life. He left IBM for five years to take on the hardships of a Peace Corps volunteer for two years, after serving as a Peace Corps Director in Southern Africa for three years. That's where we met.

Sean has also generously provided for all members of his large family and their families. He finally understands that tenacity is more important than talent; that hard work is more important than luck, that kindness is better than blood sport, that nothing's more important than family, that angels prowl the Tenderloin.

Whenever Sean visits San Francisco, he returns to the Tenderloin and his early memories. Standing across the street from Jonell's Bar, he pensively pauses to look up at the third floor window of the St. George Apartments wondering who lives there now. He hopes their stories turn out as well as his did—even better.

St. George Apartment Building

St. Francis Hotel

Then he heads for his favorite hotel in the entire world, the Westin St. Francis on Powell Street, just a short stroll from the Tenderloin. He used to walk by it in the old poverty days with his wife and children. Ragged and worried, they would watch with envy and excitement, all of those well-dressed people being greeted by the uniformed doorman. He vowed that one day he would be a greeted guest. Since then, he has, many times. Yet Sean reflectively admits he might never have appreciated what the St. Francis and prosperity truly mean, without the Tenderloin, the St. George and his Angels.

Since first writing this chapter, now seven years later, Sean has richly retired into an active life of travel throughout the world in search of old memories, new experiences and maybe a few more angels.

24

BRAD

Lights, Camera, Action

I've often wondered why, as a species, our conspicuous human similarities are virtually obscured by our individual differences. The second we begin to move, by opening our mouth, smiling, shaking someone's hand or scratching our head, we become a unique person, not just a snapshot of a human. Even our laughs are superficially identical, yet so uniquely individual.

It no doubt has something to do with those genomes from our ancestral legacy. It also has plenty to do with our responses to an environment that endlessly challenges our behaviors from birth to death. It's what we call *feedback* and it's at least as important as our biology in shaping who we are as individuals.

Feedback can be unnoticeably subtle or ear splittingly obvious. Parents, teachers, friends, co-workers, even strangers constantly give us unsolicited feedback that somehow alters our behavior, and too often we're unaware of how feedback affects our lives.

At a social gathering you tell a joke to a group of friendly strangers who don't laugh or even grin. That's when you slink away to another group who later wondered why you were so shy and quiet. If, on the other hand, that first group had roared with laughter at your joke, you would have probably been the life of the party that evening. Two different feedbacks; two different responses.

It seems straight forward enough, until you intentionally try to change someone's behavior with positive or negative feedback. Parents and teachers may be the most prolific of feedbackers, yet there are all sorts of reasons why feedback affects are rarely textbook apparent.

All I still know with reasonable certainty is that feedback does have some sort of indelible affect on all of us, that each of us tend to respond to the same feedback differently and that our most affective feedback may come from the least expected of all persons—ourselves.

$$\square \quad \square \quad \square$$

This true story occurred during the days of BetaMax vs. VHS video cassettes. I made a technologically astute, terrible choice in buying the now defunct BetaMax, including camera, tripod, cassette recorder and battery pack for an unaffordable fortune. My initial purpose was to rent Beta videos and record sailing along the California coast.

Then I attended some psychology conference, which marketed all kinds of therapeutic gimmicks, and learned about video recording group therapy sessions.

I immediately flashed on a more profitable use of my expensive toy. I could use the Beta to record some of my clients and write off the Beta equipment costs. I knew there was something worthwhile about psychology conferences.

In my Tenderloin practice there were many wary clients who put up with me only because the courts said they had to. So, I was always trying to figure out ways to keep the most resistant ones coming back, especially the superficially compliant, "passive aggressive" ones. Clients who had openly rebelled against court mandated therapy weren't my major problem. Their negative attitudes at least provoked a relevant, honest clinical dialogue which is part of what therapy is all about.

My quandary was with those comfortably recalcitrant clients who either simply shut down any communication with me or consistently said *yes* when they really meant *no*. Their responses were typically a bunch of contrived words they thought I wanted to hear. Of course I still got my MediCal sticker—along with a gnawing sense of discomfort that I was permitting a con-game which was neither fun nor worthwhile.

Through experience, therapists know that communication through dialogue is also available non-verbally via body language, facial expressions, eye contact or what a client doesn't say.

So letting those passive aggressive clients actually view video sessions of their oppositional ploys was worth a try and a write-off. I really had nothing to lose except a client I probably couldn't help anyway.

Darrell, my first video candidate, was a pot-bellied, 24-year-old, court-referred wife-beater who may have sensed by my own body language and facial cues, that I didn't like guys who beat their women. At the outset, he performed in a politely obedient, yet too cavalier manner, with obviously selectively innocuous replies that annoyed me.

When he returned for a second session, the camera was ready. During our first take, however, he grinningly declined having his "privacy" violated with a video performance. He even added some jailhouse "lawyer" talk about my liability if the film was somehow seen by others without his permission. That was "strike one" for me. I decided I was no match for his righteous strategy, which prompted a referral of him to another clinician.

My second attempt was a 30-something, female drug substance abusing prostitute who, after three sessions, had pleasantly avoided even a pretense of dialogue. After her fourth session and first video performance, she dropped me as her therapist. "Strike two."

📖   📖   📖

Shortly after those video fiascos, I received another court referral who, following two sessions, became my third and most memorable video attempt. Brad was a real charmer, who any respectable parent would proudly trust dating their virtuous daughter. He was handsome, muscular and exceptionally articulate, with a great gift of gab and a good sense of humor. On the surface, he fit the profile of either a successful business-man, prominent attorney, outgoing likeable neighbor or parolee who, at 29, had spent most of his adult life effectively conning anyone willing to listen to his persuasive small talk. Brad's background clearly fit the latter option.

He was the prototypical "ex-con" who had easily risen to the top of the Tenderloin pecking-order. He reminded me of those 1960's California Rehabilitation Center (CRC) inmates who had managed to totally undermine a new rehab program. University graduate student social workers were placed at CRC to complete their internship by helping inmates with narcotic records develop clinically-sound prerelease plans. The program quickly backfired when many of the female social work students began sneaking in drugs and other contraband, and sexually surrendering to their captives. Their tragic excuse was they were "in love."

After reading Brad's correctional counselor reports, previous psychological evaluations and prior criminal record, I wasn't at all surprised by his well-choreo-graphed first appointment. He was just a little early (not too early) with waiting room time to read a few pages of Steinbeck's *East of Eden* after announcing his presence with a clear, yet unobtrusive knock on my door. Brad made sure I'd remember the book. As he entered my office I couldn't miss the eye-level book cover and his comment.

"I don't mind waiting if you're not ready, this John Steinbeck book is an absorbing read."

Throughout that first session, he offered a smooth blend of moderate cheerfulness, compliance and humil-ity, along with an appropriate amount of spontaneity and a sprinkling of roguish grins. There wasn't a hint of resistance or arrogance. He was merely a nice, easy-going guy chatting with a superior—not too superior. Actually, had I not read his record, I would have probably believed his seemingly effortless, natural performance. There was nothing obnoxious about Brad, as long as you didn't get to know him too well.

Those first two sessions suggested he was ready to meet my Beta tax write-off. Beneath his convincing charm, was a well-documented history of heroin use and sales, chronic thefts to supplement supporting a huge habit, and the admiration of his "peers," both in and out of prison. He was apparently a leader, not a follower.

When confronted with his arrests and convictions, however, he adamantly denied, in his typically calm persuasive manner, ever stealing.

"No, Dr. Wonderling, I openly admit selling drugs to support my own habit which provided all the money I needed. These were victimless crimes since I only sold to other hard-core users. We were all victims. Drugs are like a Faust novel. They pleasure you first and control you later."

The Faust analogy was a distorted inaccurate stretch, but his message was clear. He wasn't a bad guy; he was just a harmless addict. Further confrontations underscored his sociopathic resolve.

"What about all these burglary and shop lifting convictions? They're three pages long."

"You're right, Dr. Wonderling. It sure looks incriminating. But if you carefully read all the arrest reports you'll find that I was never alone. I never committed those crimes; I hung out with a lot of professional thieves who I thought were my friends. I was with them at the wrong times."

Yeah sure, I thought.

Near the end of our second appointment, Brad agreed to the video sessions without a tinge of hesitation.

Arriving a "trifle" early, Brad was unusually well-groomed and neatly dressed in casual open shirt and slacks. He sat in a laid-back, relaxed fashion like some celebrity performer, and I never saw him even glance at the camera. In fact, he maintained riveting eye contact with me, as I thought; *60 Minutes would welcome an interview with this guy.*

One question by me and it was "lights, camera, action" by him.

"What have you been up to the last few weeks?"

"I attend several Narcotic Anonymous meetings a week... I'm in the process of enrolling in some community college courses... I take my urine tests and methadone at the clinic... I help serve lunches at St Anthony's..." No clumsy mannerisms or groping pauses. He was a real performer.

My strategy was to provide him with video feedback during the next session. Yet as I replayed the video, I couldn't help a smile, thinking *once he views his performance, he'll probably go into real acting.* Then, what I saw next was unbelievable.

Since I started a practice I'd grown accustomed to placing my wrist watch in an inconspicuous spot on my desk to keep track of the fifty-minute hour. That way I could avoid trying to sneak those all-too-obvious glances at the watch on my wrist. True, I had a wall clock, but clients also had an uncanny sensitivity to my eye movement toward the wall. I figured that might represent another dead giveaway I was bored or impatient. Anyway, the camera recorded Brad's "five-second caper."

As I had leaned over to the pot of coffee on a nearby table, Brad's fingers galloped along my desk, plucking up my wrist watch, and in a flash, the watch retreated into his coat pocket. I marveled at his speed and dexterity, while his eyes remained focused on my movements toward the coffee pot.

Yet the finale to Brad's steely, tactical brilliance was his casual, unflinching look at my wall clock with the comment, "I'd better leave a little early. I have a job interview in a half hour."

"That's fine," I said as I wrote out the slip for his next appointment. "See you in a couple of weeks,"

Even as we stood up, Brad remained masterfully composed. He appeared comfortably relaxed, in no hurry and exuded a warm friendly smile and a firm, prolonged hand shake. "Thanks again for everything."

The "for everything" made a lot of sense after watching the video. *Oh well*, I thought. *It was only a cheap Timex.*

I guess I wasn't too surprised when Brad didn't show for his next appointment. Disappointed maybe, but not really surprised. And no, I didn't contact his parole officer. Weirdly, I considered the theft confidential. Then, about a month later, another unbelievable thing happened. Brad called me.

"A few days after I left your office I realized what I did was video-taped. You hadn't turned the camera off yet. I want to thank you for not telling my parole agent. I'm mailing you your watch because I'm embarrassed to see you again. Dr. Wonderling, you're the first person I've ever told that I'm a thief as well as a drug dealer. I guess I'm not very good at either."

📖 📖 📖

I got my Timex back, and never again heard from Brad. During my last Tenderloin visit in October 2006, street rumors were that he was back in prison. Probably, yet thanks to his feedback from the BetaMax video, rather than me, he actually made a critical therapeutic self-disclosure—to both of us.

I still wonder if Brad may some day realize he would have made a much better legitimate actor than a practicing thief. What a waste of talent.

My video feedback strategy abruptly ended after Brad, and the BetaMax equipment remains buried somewhere in my store room with other useless stuff.

25

SARAH

The Wish

One of human nature's anomalies is wanting what we haven't got and taking for granted what we have. Another is to longingly imagine being somewhere else, while never really appreciating where we are. So, it may be a puzzling irony of humans that having good health is not really enviable until it's lost, or living in fantasy can sometimes be more gratifyingly real than living in the best of reality.

This chapter is especially unique in telling a Tenderloin story of someone who was never in the Tenderloin. It's a true story borrowed from *Seductive Illusions,* my first book, because of its relevance to both editions of this book. It's about innocence, frailty and compassion, which may be the essence of our humanity. It's simply a story worth retelling.

Many years ago, one of my first jobs as a therapist was at a convalescent home overlooking downtown San Francisco and its Tenderloin. In one of the wards, I met a deeply beautiful woman in her early twenties. Her name was Sarah. She had bright blue eyes, a baby soft clear complexion, full rosy red lips and smooth cheeks that dimpled when she smiled. Completing this lovely portrait was shoulder length, silky brown hair that framed her pretty face.

Below this beauty was her twisted, gnarled tiny body, like some fleshy pretzel, with legs bent around her torso and arms crossed and intertwined with her legs. Her body movements were mainly twitches and jerks, and her voice was a barely audible whisper, with heavy sighs and exhausting efforts to breathe between gasps for another word.

A nurse's aide had told me that Sarah spent hours perched in her little crib, gazing in wonderment through a small window that unveiled a treasure of sights and sounds. Before the nurse's aide thoughtfully moved her crib to the window, Sarah had spent hours gazing plaintively at a pale green wall.

Like a Cinamax screen, the new view gave Sarah: Market Street, the Tenderloin, neon lights and all kinds of people. Through her rich imagination, she strolled the Tenderloin, talked with neighbors and shopkeepers, ate in the best of their restaurants and even attended theaters on Market Street. Although she was aware the experience was enchanting fantasy, she knew there was no other way to get there. At least, Sarah was content with her vivid reveries—or so I thought.

As I noticed her for the first time, she was peering through her window. She apparently sensed my presence; and when Sarah turned her head toward me, her unblinking eyes seemed to plead with me to stay for a while. So I sat by her crib and introduced myself.

That was before I began to even slightly grasp the severity of her condition. Her eyes reminded me of a little puppy whose wide-eyed innocence holds you in its intense stare of affection and curiosity. As I sat almost transfixed by her staring, she seemed to be trying to speak. I leaned over her crib with my ear at her mouth as she said something in sighs and whispers that I couldn't understand. Her eyes followed me closely as I left her side.

Later that same day I learned from records about her abandonment by parents, her progressively severe Cerebral Palsy and a bright intellect with clear thinking, despite an increasing inability to communicate. She had never walked.

When I left the convalescent home that afternoon, Sarah was still wandering through my mind's eye. I kept seeing her angelic face staring at me with a strangely enchanting melancholy. I couldn't forget her entangled little body, propped against the side of the crib as she carefully scanned her Tenderloin view. Then there were her faint panting whispers that I couldn't understand. What she was trying to say, was the nagging question dominating most of my dinner thoughts that evening.

Returning to Sarah's ward the next day, I wasn't surprised to find her gazing wistfully out her window toward Market Street and the Tenderloin. Again, she seemed to know I was near before I said anything. Again, I strained to listen with no idea what Sarah was trying to say. Learning how to understand Sarah became my major preoccupation, yet I soon discovered that no one else could grasp her speech. Although discouraged, I learned that the convalescent home was seriously understaffed. Everyone was just too busy to listen to her—everyone except me.

So every week I spent hours listening to her breathy whispers, sighs and gasps that were trying to tell me something. After a month, her dimpled smiles and wide-eyed stare assured me she enjoyed my company, even though I still didn't know what she was trying to say. It was a sad reminder that no one but I and the overworked nurse's aide had paid any attention to Sarah in years.

At that point, I thought whatever she was trying to say, didn't matter. Maybe her smiles were saying all that needed to be understood. I had to admit, I really didn't believe such a possibility. Sarah wanted to tell me something and I had to learn her language. I would keep trying while, in the meantime; this lonely woman was offered some comfort through her window and my efforts to understand her. I was also hoping we were learning something from each other about friendship.

During our second month, her whispers were growing louder, with greater urgency. That was even more frustrating to me. I knew the words were there, but I still couldn't decipher the message. However, there was always that other, much clearer message, the one without words. She kept holding me with her eyes and dimpled smiles that replied so emphatically to whatever I had to say. She could show laughter, sadness, excitement and even gratitude with her eyes.

Her eyes, I thought, *say almost everything I need to know about her.* Once a week, I'd take her for a spin around the wards in a small buggy, and her eyes would tell me that she loved every minute of it. I also told her stories about the Tenderloin that might help embrace her windowed fantasies in some meaningful way. She always seemed to cling to every word.

As I learned how to read her unflinching eyes, however, I began to worry even more, without knowing why. All I knew for sure was that my concern had something to do with her increasingly less expressive eyes, along with the fading of her once dimpled smile. I was beginning to feel helpless and mocked by my failure to hear the words buried somewhere within her urgent whispers.

Whenever she tried to talk, her eyes would moisten with sadness, and I used to jokingly tell her that she would always be my favorite because she never talked back.

Then she would offer a feeble laugh with her eyes, and I'd mask my own concerns with a strained smile. The sad paradox was that Sarah had nothing to laugh about. She was cruelly gifted with a clear thinking mind within a tragically useless body.

It happened during the fourth month of my many visits. After her usual uncanny sense of my presence, she shifted her window gaze to me.

When I sat beside her, she began her slow, painstaking whisper, and as I had done so many times before, I leaned into her crib, put my ear to her mouth and listened.

Her barely audible words shrieked in my ear, "I want to die… I want to die…I want to die!" She knew I heard, and together we cried, long and hard.

Mercifully, she died in her sleep at another convalescent home about a year later. There's no happy ending to this story, no postscript of some miraculous therapeutic intervention that guided her gleefully into her death, and there's no inspiring epitaph. She reportedly had no funeral.

At least it's comforting to know that Sarah really didn't die alone. Her wish was finally understood. This beautiful little woman, with the tiny twisted body, must have known in death that her dying was deeply mourned and her need to die was, at last, understood by someone.

She may have also sensed that wisp of immortality that comes with being openly remembered.

Re-reading the first edition, I realized there are so many Sarah's in the world who are too soon forgotten—as if they never existed. After several decades, Sarah is still not one of the forgotten ones and she may never be. She's part of this book, as well as my first book, and a legacy of extraordinary people who will be remembered as long as their chapters survive.

26

HENRIETTA

The Party Surprise

It seemed fitting to conclude this Second Edition with a collage of memories. It's kind of a group portrait of all those other Tenderloin residents I knew so well. Each had a special true story that may have influenced my life in some incalculable way. It doesn't take much of a reminder for me to smile or tear up over a nearly forgotten Tenderloin client or friend. All it takes is someone from my past to ask "what ever happened to what's his name?"

After my retirement, that necessary ritual of shredding clients' records provided another reflective glimpse at some troubled face within a story. Even music of the 80's and 90's can put me back in the Tenderloin reliving failures, a few triumphs and a sense of helplessness when a fallen client wouldn't get up. But it's a virtual album of fading pictures that really pulls me back—sometimes with too much clarity when the stories are sad. This last story, however, needed to have a happy face.

☐   ☐   ☐

Even though retired, I look forward to holidays—especially Thanksgiving and Christmas. They still mean heartfelt family gatherings and that deep contentment of belonging.

Just watching others during Christmas reveals its timeless essence as a genuine family affair. Kids love Christmas, so do relatives. It binds us together with a coveted sense of being somebody after all!

For my Tenderloin clients, however, most of their families had been lost long ago. Not belonging can be painfully lonely, especially when they've even forgotten how to belong. So holidays for too many of my clients were taunting reminders of loss and being less than somebody.

I was also one of those deprived of my birth family's joys and pains. Then, as a therapist, I later discovered that the gnawing feeling of something missing wasn't necessary. I learned that those we later meet and care for are the only family we really need. Maybe that's why I chose psychology, and my practice became so much more than one-on-one psychotherapy. It was also on-going group counseling, occasional bus trips with clients to nearby scenic spots and parties during major holidays that gradually created a family of somebodies.

Christmas was the grandest get together, probably because that's when the group needed our family bond the most. For ten years those Christmas parties were held at the Mariposa Hunters Point Yacht Club in China Basin, which was an easy public transportation ride from the Tenderloin.

During our last Christmas party in 1996, the yacht club's main dining room was mobbed with clients, some of their friends, some of my friends and all kinds of food and desserts donated from San Francisco restaurants and bakeries. Entrees included several lasagnas, roasts of beef, T-bone steaks, barbequed ribs galore, meatloaves, plenty of veggies, breads, pies and cakes.

As usual, many of my clients and friends also brought food. After all it was their family too. They weren't just invited guests—they belonged.

About eight of the clients, whose stories are already in this book, were alive and well at our 1996 "family" gathering. There were also several dozen other clients at the party with untold stories of their own.

📖 📖 📖

Richard Carroll, one of my original Tenderloin clients, was one of them. When we met in 1976, he was sleeping on a dirty mat with five howling, barking dogs literally under a decrepit house in the Western Edition. It was owned by an equally decrepit black man who cared for any neighborhood strays, including Richard.

How could I have ever forgotten my first meeting with him? Leaning against the rickety old house, it was hard to tell Richard from the stinky, scraggy, itching dogs lying around him. His long matted hair and beard were out of a Bella Logosi werewolf movie with smelly realism. Those smells were an overpowering combination of dog and human feces, infected flesh covering his arms, the movement of tiny vermin over his body and a searing stench of decay. His inaudible mumblings told me he was alive, while my knee-jerk, clinical response to that first interview was to call an ambulance.

At our Christmas party, twenty years later, Richard was the clean-shaven, neatly dressed, nice smelling president of his housing project tenant association. How he overcame the insurmountable is a story of his show of gratitude, dogged persistence and resilience in discovering there were people who cared for him after all. He rose from a lonely, hopeless wretch to a well-liked advocate of the less fortunate. Richard died in 2000 with over fifty friends at his funeral, including me.

📖   📖   📖

Also at the party were Marge, June, Ron, Barbara, Bill, James and Harold. Those are the true first names of some of my earliest clients not mentioned in previous chapters. I've lost contact with all of them but Marge. She's a prolific writer, and we still correspond regularly.

Although there were no uninvited quests, since anyone was welcomed, some of the acquaintances and friends of clients' offered me a polite greeting and a knot in my stomach. They were an assortment of Tenderloin parolees, junkies, high violence potential crazies and pimps. I hoped they were only looking for a free meal with a party of peers, nothing more.

Typical of Tenderloin people, their stunning differences were their signature similarities, which gave them a sense of social comfort and belonging. There was scarlet red hair, green hair and orange hair. There was also the no hair guy with Medusa-like tattoos of snakes crawling from a hatched egg—his bald head.

There was black, traditional red and blue lipstick framing gleaming white teeth, brown, black and green teeth, and of course, no teeth. There seemed to be earring-like jewelry dangling from or embedded in every orifice or skin surface, especially the women's.

Eye brows, ear lobes, nostrils, lips, tongues, and probably nipples, seemed their favorite spots. The men
there were a bit more conservative. They favored their
ears. On one guy whom I didn't know, I counted eight
ear studs on one of his ears. *Wow*, I thought. Even the
clothes were Tenderloin style, comfortably outrageous
and a seamless blend of differences.

Marge, a devout Catholic, wore a white, lacy holy
communion-type dress; which contrasted indifferently
with her dear friend Barbara's twelve inch long, black
skirt, with a matching eight to ten inch, sleeveless
blouse exposing plenty of cleavage and more than a hint
of nipples.

Kenny, with Macy's heavy fragrance, wore his best
"convention" suit and tie, while the friend he brought
was probably the most disheveled and menacing newcomer, with a dirty tank top, plenty of muscles and
tattoos, dirty jeans, and a Bowie-type, sheathed knife in
his back pocket. I forget his name but I remember his
huge knife and that, despite the cold, he never shivered.
When Kenny introduced him, I offered a big, warm
smile and a proactive, tightly gripped handshake to prevent him from squeezing my fingers. He didn't try and I
was relieved.

"I have an extra coat in my car if you're cold, and
would you mind checking your knife? Promise I'll
return it when you're ready to leave."

"No problem, I forgot I brought it here. And no
thanks, I'm never cold."

📖 📖 📖

One of the late arrivals was Bonnie, a tough old hustler
who became a Tenderloin legend a few years ago when
she punched out a 200 pound street thug that grabbed

her purse. Her self-defense seemed even more amazing when I first met this dimpled, 5'1", frail-looking little lady who couldn't have weighed over 100 lbs. Her age? I wondered, about 40 to 80 I figured.

Also noted for her fierce independence and uncanny street savvy, Bonnie could have been a Tenderloin reporter. She seemed aware of events before they happened, and although she was neither my client nor a personal friend of any party guests, Bonnie had appeared three years in a row. This time she brought her old companion Henrietta which was a little surprising, even for her. Yet, Bonnie truly knew how to graciously crash a party. With a warm, easy smile, she walked straight to me from her front door entrance.

"Hello Dr Wonderling, I want to thank you for having another of your wonderful Christmas parties. This is Henrietta…"

"I'm glad you could come, and Henrietta, I've heard about you and you're sure welcome."

Henrietta was the strangest looking of all the guests. She strutted around like she owned the place while seemingly ignoring everyone even though no one could possibly ignore her.

Oh well, I thought, *after all, she's just a chicken.* Henrietta, however, was more than that. She was an unusually big, fat healthy-looking hen that Bonnie had apparently kept in her little Tenderloin two-room apartment for several years.

Each year, those parties added another friend or colleague who brought their own offerings of food, small gifts, and a willingness to help prepare the accumulation of food stacked by the hug stoves in a kitchen that would rival any restaurant's. As coffee, soft drinks and juices flowed from the adjoining bar, there was a steady stream of cheerful chit chat, laughter and friendly exchanges between the young and old, my clients and friends, even those rough-looking strangers all of whom seemed to know Bonnie. Such a compatible mix of explosive difference was gratifying I thought, despite my awaiting that proverbial "other shoe to drop."

Carrying Henrietta in her arms, Bonnie again approached me with an even more surprising offer.

"Oh, I almost forgot, my new apartment owner will evict me unless I get rid of Henrietta, so I'm donating her to your party. About time she earned her keep. I see you got those big ovens, and after somebody here prepares her, I'll help roast her; she'll be good eatin'."

"Prepare her? What do you mean prepare her?"

"Come on, Dr Wonderling, you know. Shit, we can't eat her alive."

I was beginning to get a knot in my stomach. "Why don't you do it; she's your chicken."

"I can't, Henrietta's been my friend too long. Hey, there's plenty of guys here that wouldn't mind doin' it. Hell, I know some of these street guys. They're bad, I mean *bad.* They'd do it for kicks."

I wasn't at all interested in gory resumés of party guests, nor was I willing to let some sadistic street thug eagerly strangle Henrietta.

"That's all right. I'll see if one of my friends doing the cooking will 'put her down' so to speak. If that's what you really want."

Bonnie quickly agreed.

By that time, Henrietta was strutting and clucking all over the place with occasional interruptions when someone would pick her up and pet her.

"Bonnie just gave us the hen for our big feast, so would one of you get her ready for the oven?"

The replies from the kitchen help of colleagues and friends were a swift and silent heading shaking. Then came the indignant comments.

"You want one of us to kill and disembowel one of the guests? No way."

"That's not a hen. It's Henrietta for Christ sake."

"I wouldn't know how. That's what supermarkets are for."

"Why don't you do it?"

They all had valid points. I personally had a problem offing a "daddy long legs" in my living room which I felt disqualified me as a chicken assassin.

Bonnie had heard all the objections, and before I could muffle her mouth, she returned to the main room with the announcement that someone needed to kill and dress Henrietta for the oven.

I was astonished when the whole room went from raucous banter to utter silence. I could feel that knot nudging my stomach again when Bonnie turned to the table with the "bad" guys I didn't know, including the Bowie knife guy. The pause was unnerving, and the reply from the meanest looking guy with the convict neck tattoos couldn't have been more unexpected and welcomed.

"Come on, Bonnie, there's plenty of food here. Leave her alone, she ain't fuckin with nobody."

For me, it was our last and best Christmas party. If people are judged by what they do, there weren't any bad guys there—just lots of laughter, loud music, raunchy jokes and plenty of great food. There was also a genuine sense of belonging as Henrietta strutted on just about all the tables, pecking away at the scraps and crumbs she graciously accepted from the other guests.

Last I heard, Bonnie took Henrietta to an animal shelter for adoption—I sure do miss those parties.

Epilogue

Learning may be the essence of human life and our memories its treasures. It required two years of writing and a lifetime of preparation to complete this book of memories and priceless lessons.

Memories provide meaning to our observations. Otherwise, we would wander through life looking, but never really seeing. For me, San Francisco is infinitely more than those sturdy little cable cars trundling up steep hills, the awesome Golden Gate Bridge swaying with the winds or Lombard's serpentine curves like some huge labyrinth. It's a city of precious experiences, that vital ingredient of memories.

It's Grattan Grammar School, where innocents romped near the Haight Ashbury; Polytechnic High School, where boys became gladiators across the street at Kezar Stadium and it is Golden Gate Park, a peaceful place of beautiful lush green over sand dunes. They all have special meaning to me that beckon my return for another walk through the past.

There are treasures everywhere that effortlessly bond me and so many others to San Francisco. Although we may all see the same place differently, it is special to all of us.

Perhaps it's strange to others that, in San Francisco, one of my most precious strolls is through the Tenderloin. To those who only look, the Tenderloin is run down, worn out; yet, like the "Roman Coliseum," its ruins are steeped in rich history.

St. Anthony's Dining Room on Ellis Street and the Glide Memorial Church, beneath the monolithic Hilton are still there, feeding the poor, the disabled and even the hustlers. The lines are much longer now, but Father Boeddeker's message of the 50's is the same, "If you're hungry, come to St. Anthony's and we will feed you. If you're not hungry, please donate to St. Anthony's, so we can feed others."

The Aloha Club has gone, vanished, but I know it was on the south side of Turk, near Hyde Street. That's where my short career as a bouncer ended when someone knocked me cold with a bottle as I left work one night. It was 1949.

Strolling along Ellis toward Jones awakens more of the past. Sean's St. George Apartments loom memorably on the corner and I furtively search for Angels.

Half way down the north side of Turk Street is the Coral Sea, a bar where many of my clients sat sadly, happily or tragically for years. Most people passing by won't see the Coral Sea. The new sign says "Cafe Asia," but its history is the Coral Sea, to those who remember.

Even though Polo's is gone from O'Farrell Street, I have fond memories of their fine Italian food, George Moscone, Jim Ginella and other old friends. Continuing my walk along O'Farrell to Mason Street, there's Original Joe's, as good as ever for food and memories.

There's also the Marlton Manor, just down the street on Taylor. So many clients lived there, so many died there. So many memories.

Threading my way through the virtual mob of street people, like vagrants, hanging around the corner of Jones and Post, I look up and mourn the memory of Sandy, falling through space to a merciful death and peace. The building is no longer there—just the space.

If all memories were pleasant, life would be reduced

to a shallow illusion. There would be no tears; no deep-felt compassion, not much to learn—just fixed smiles. I grieve for the Sandys I have known in the Tenderloin, while feeling stronger and more human with the lessons I have learned from their memories.

A couple of young blacks smile at me as I stroll along Larkin Street.

"Looking for something light or heavy?" they ask.

I smile back, "No thanks," and as usual, they then turn away and ignore me. That's when I notice the Mentone Hotel, on the corner of Jones and Larkin. It looks different now, as weary and run-down as during my last visit, but colder and less hospitable, with its barricaded front door and warning signs.

Oddly, the Mentone still draws a torrent of associations about the love and security of our poor struggling family. A loyal mother, always strong in caring for her children yet so fragile in caring for herself; and June, my sister, whom I saw for the last time at the Mentone Hotel in the Tenderloin. I even remember walking by the Chez Paree that evening, 45 years ago.

In the final analysis, all of those memories are richly human. So perhaps the Tenderloin is too dynamic to ever deserve its static reputation.

After all, the Tenderloin is not just a place; it is people and a sanctuary for those who have nowhere else to go.

It still is and hopefully it always will be!

One of the Tenderloin's prominent landmarks for over 60 years was unceremoniously warehoused in 2003.

Bibliography

Readings and Interviews

AMERICAN PSYCHIATRIC ASSOCIATION, *Diagnostic and Statistical Manual of Mental Disorders,* Third Edition Revised. (DSM III) Washington, DC, 1980

ASHBURY, HERBERT, *The Gangs of New York - An Informal History of the Underworld,* New York and London, Alfred A. Knopf, 1978

ATHERTON, GERTRUDE, *My San Francisco,* San Francisco History Center, San Francisco Public Library

BACON, DAN, *Good Life and Hard Times - San Francisco in the 20's,* San Francisco History Center, San Francisco Public Library

BRADY, MATTHEW, *The Old Town, Real Life in Early San Francisco,* Independent Books, San Francisco, 1992

CITY LIGHTS ANTHOLOGY, *Reclaiming San Francisco - History, Politics, Culture,* 1998, City Lights Books, San Francisco

DEMPSEY, JAMES and MITCHELL, GEORGE, *The Ace in the Hole,* Jerry Vogel Music Company, Inc., 58 West 45th Street, New York, NY 10036

DURANT, WILL, *The Story of Philosophy,* Washington Square Press, New York 1966

FITZER, BOB, Sergeant, San Francisco Police Department Personal Interview

FLACH, F., *Psychobiology and Psychopharmacology,* W. W. Norton & Company, New York, 1988

FLAMM, JERRY, *Good Life and Hard Times - San Francisco in the 20's,* Phat Willie and Dave Scottwall Associates, San Francisco, 1996

FREER, JOHN L., Ph.D., J.D., *The Myth of Risk Management,* Bulletin of Division 42 of the American Psychological Association, *The Independent Practitioner,* Spring, 1999, Vol. 19

FROMMER, *Irreverent Guide to San Francisco,* 2nd Edition

GODFREY, B.J., *Inner City Neighborhoods in Transition: The Morphogenesis of San Francisco Ethnic and Nonconformist Communities,* Dissertation for Ph.D., 1984

JEFFREY, KURT, *Madams of San Francisco,* San Francisco

History Center, San Francisco Public Library

KIMBALL, NELL, *Unpublished Memoirs of San Francisco Brothel Keeping,* San Francisco History Center, San Francisco Public Library

KLOPER, B. and DAVIDSON, H.H., *The Rorschach Technique, An Introductory Manual,* Harcourt, Brae & World, Inc, 1962

LAING, R.D., *The Politics of Experience,* Ballantine Books, New York, 1967

LONGSTREET, STEPHEN, *The Wilder Shore - A History of the Gala Days,* Doubleday & Company, 1968

MARTIN, DON and BETTY, *Inside San Francisco,* Pine Cone Press, 1991

MEW, CHARLIE, Tenderloin Resident, Personal Interview

MONGO, RAY, *San Francisco Confidential,* Carol Publishing Group, 1995

MULLEN, KEVIN J. Deputy Chief of San Francisco Police Department, Personal Interview, E-mail: KM870@aol.com

NUNIS, DOYCE B., JR., *The San Francisco Vigilance Committee of 1856,* The Los Angeles Westerners Publishing, 1971

O'BRIEN, ROBERT, *This is San Francisco,* Chronicle Books,

PDR - *Physicians Desk Reference,* Published by Medical Economics Company, yearly

RANDALL, H., JOHNSON, P.C., REINHARDT, R.W., *San Francisco As It Is, As It Was,* Doubleday & Co., Inc., New York

REID, W.H., *Treatment of the DSM III - Psychiatric Disorders,* Brunner Mazel, Inc., New York, NY, 1983

ROBERTS, LARENDA LYLES, *San Francisco Uncovered* Wordware Publishing, Inc., 1996

ROTH, JOHN K., *The Philosophy of Josiah Royce* Thomas Crowell Corporation, Inc. New York, 1971

ROYCE, JOSIAH, *California in 1948 - A Study of American Character,* Alfred A. Knopf, New York

SAN FRANCISCO PLANNING AND RESEARCH, *History of the San Francisco Police Department,* 1972, San Francisco History Center, San Francisco Public Library

SHEPHARD, SUSAN, *In the Neighborhood,* 1981, Chronicle Books, San Francisco

STANFORD, SALLY, *Lady in the House,* G. P. Putnam & Sons, New York, 1966

WONDERLING, LAWRENCE V., Ph.D., *Seductive Illusions* Cape Foundation Publications, San Francisco, 1997

INDEX

ABOUT THE AUTHOR

 Dr. Larry Wonderling is well-qualified to write a book about the San Francisco Tenderloin and its people. As a native San Franciscan, some of his earliest personal experiences were in the Tenderloin, where he was first exposed to gentle winos and tough bars in the late 1940's.

A clinical and forensic psychologist with over forty years of professional experience, he is well-respected in the San Francisco community. Dedicated to helping the disadvantaged, his clinical practice was almost exclusively with Tenderloin clients for over twenty years.

The Second Edition of this critically acclaimed book was inspired as new true stories emerged during the author's more recent visits to the Tenderloin. Also, the first, second and third printings of the original *SAN FRANCISCO TENDERLOIN* were completely sold out.

The Editor